LINUX SERVER HACKS

Rob Flickenger

O'REILLY®

Beijing · Cambridge · Farnham · Köln · Paris · Sebastopol · Taipei · Tokyo

Linux Server Hacks
by Rob Flickenger

Copyright © 2003 O'Reilly & Associates, Inc. All rights reserved.
Printed in the United States of America.

Published by O'Reilly & Associates, Inc., 1005 Gravenstein Highway North,
Sebastopol, CA 95472.

O'Reilly & Associates books may be purchased for educational, business, or sales pro-
motional use. Online editions are also available for most titles (*safari.oreilly.com*). For
more information, contact our corporate/institutional sales department: (800) 998-9938
or *corporate@oreilly.com*.

Editor:	Dale Dougherty
Production Editor:	Sarah Sherman
Cover Designer:	Edie Freedman
Interior Designer:	David Futato

Printing History:

January 2003:	First Edition.

ISBN: 0-596-00461-3
[C]   [3/03*]

Contents

Credits

About the Author

Rob Flickenger authored the majority of hacks in this book. Rob has worked with Linux since Slackware 3.5. He was previously the system administrator of the O'Reilly Network (an all-Linux shop, naturally) and is the author of *Building Wireless Community Networks*, also by O'Reilly.

Contributors

The following people contributed their hacks, writing, and inspiration to this book:

- Rael Dornfest ("Apache Toolbox" **[Hack #75]**) is a maven at the O'Reilly & Associates focusing on technologies just beyond the pale. He assesses, experiments, programs, and writes for the O'Reilly network and O'Reilly publications.

- Schuyler Erle (contributed code for httptop, mysql-table-restore, balance-push, find-whois, and vtundgen) is, by day, a mild-mannered Internet systems developer for O'Reilly & Associates. By night, he crusades for justice and freedom as a free software hacker and community networking activist.

- Kevin Hemenway ("Quick Configuration Changes with IfDefine" **[Hack #75]**, "Simplistic Ad Referral Tracking" **[Hack #75]**, "Mimicking FTP Servers with Apache" **[Hack #75]**), better known as Morbus Iff, is the creator of disobey.com, which bills itself as "content for the discontented." Publisher and developer of more home cooking than you could ever imagine, he'd love to give you a Fry Pan of Intellect upside the head. Politely, of course. And with love.

- Seann Herdejurgen ("iptables Tips & Tricks" **[Hack #44]**, "Disk Age Analysis" **[Hack #53]**) has been working with Unix since 1987 and now architects high availability solutions as a senior systems engineer with D-Tech corporation in Dallas, Texas. He holds a master's degree in computer science from Texas A&M University. He may be reached at: *http://seann.herdejurgen.com/*.

- Dru Lavigne ("Archiving with Pax" **[Hack #36]**) is an instructor at a private technical college in Kingston, ON where she teaches the fundamentals of TCP/IP networking, routing, and security. Her current hobbies include matching every TCP and UDP port number to its associated application(s) and reading her way through all of the RFCs.

- Cricket Liu ("Views in BIND 9" **[Hack #75]**) matriculated at the University of California's Berkeley campus, that great bastion of free speech, unencumbered Unix, and cheap pizza. He worked for a year as Director of DNS Product Management for VeriSign Global Registry Services, and is a co-author of *DNS and BIND*, also published by O'Reilly & Associates.

- Mike Rubel ("Automated Snapshot-Style Incremental Backups with rsync" **[Hack #36]**, *http://www.mikerubel.org*) studied mechanical engineering at Rutgers University (B.S. 1998) and aeronautics at Caltech (M.S. 1999), where he is now a graduate student. He has enjoyed using Linux and GNU software for several years in the course of his numerical methods research.

- Jennifer Vesperman (all of the CVS pieces except "CVS: Anonymous Repositories" **[Hack #22]** were adapted from her online CVS pieces for O'ReillyNet) contributes to open source as a user, writer, and occasional programmer. Her coding experience ranges from the hardware interface to an HDLC card to the human interface of Java GUIs. Jenn is the current coordinator and co-sysadmin for Linuxchix.org.

Acknowledgments

I would like to thank my family and friends for their support and encouragement. Thanks especially to my dad for showing me "proper troubleshooting technique" at such an early age and inevitably setting me on the path of the Hacker before I had even seen a computer.

Of course, this book would be nothing without the excellent contributions of all the phenomenally talented hackers contained herein. But of course, our hacks are built by hacking the shoulders of giants (to horribly mix a metaphor), and it is my sincere hope that you will in turn take what you learn here and go one better, and most importantly, tell everyone just how you did it.

How to Become a Hacker

The Jargon File contains a bunch of definitions of the term "hacker," most having to do with technical adeptness and a delight in solving problems and overcoming limits. If you want to know how to *become* a hacker, though, only two are really relevant.

There is a community, a shared culture, of expert programmers and networking wizards that traces its history back through decades to the first time-sharing minicomputers and the earliest ARPAnet experiments. The members of this culture originated the term "hacker." Hackers built the Internet. Hackers made the Unix operating system what it is today. Hackers run Usenet. Hackers make the Web work. If you are part of this culture, if you have contributed to it and other people in it know who you are and call you a hacker, you're a hacker.

The hacker mind-set is not confined to this software-hacker culture. There are people who apply the hacker attitude to other things, like electronics or music—actually, you can find it at the highest levels of any science or art. Software hackers recognize these kindred spirits elsewhere and may call them "hackers" too—and some claim that the hacker nature is really independent of the particular medium the hacker works in. But in the rest of this document, we will focus on the skills and attitudes of software hackers, and the traditions of the shared culture that originated the term "hacker."

There is another group of people who loudly call themselves hackers, but aren't. These are people (mainly adolescent males) who get a kick out of breaking into computers and breaking the phone system. Real hackers call these people "crackers" and want nothing to do with them. Real hackers mostly think crackers are lazy, irresponsible, and not very bright—being able to break security doesn't make you a hacker any more than being able to hotwire cars makes you an automotive engineer. Unfortunately, many journalists and writers have been fooled into using the word "hacker" to describe crackers; this irritates real hackers no end.

The basic difference is this: hackers build things, crackers break them.

If you want to be a hacker, keep reading. If you want to be a cracker, go read the alt.2600 newsgroup and get ready to do five to ten in the slammer after finding out you aren't as smart as you think you are. And that's all I'm going to say about crackers.

The Hacker Attitude

Hackers solve problems and build things, and they believe in freedom and voluntary mutual help. To be accepted as a hacker, you have to behave as though you have this kind of attitude yourself. And to behave as though you have the attitude, you have to really believe the attitude.

But if you think of cultivating hacker attitudes as just a way to gain acceptance in the culture, you'll miss the point. Becoming the kind of person who believes these things is important for *you*—for helping you learn and keeping you motivated. As with all creative arts, the most effective way to become a master is to imitate the mind-set of masters—not just intellectually but emotionally as well.

Or, as the following modern Zen poem has it:

> To follow the path:
> look to the master,
> follow the master,
> walk with the master,
> see through the master,
> become the master.

So if you want to be a hacker, repeat the following things until you believe them.

1. The world is full of fascinating problems waiting to be solved.

Being a hacker is a lot of fun, but it's a kind of fun that takes a lot of effort. The effort takes motivation. Successful athletes get their motivation from a kind of physical delight in making their bodies perform, pushing themselves past their own physical limits. Similarly, to be a hacker you have to get a basic thrill from solving problems, sharpening your skills, and exercising your intelligence.

If you aren't the kind of person that feels this way naturally, you'll need to become one in order to make it as a hacker. Otherwise you'll find your hacking energy is zapped by distractions like sex, money, and social approval.

Checkout Receipt

Valparaiso Public Library
103 E. Jefferson St, Valparaiso, IN
(219) 462-0524
Renew items online www.pcpls.lib.in.us
Renew items by phone (219) 531-9054

05/23/05 06:09PM
****

Barcode: 23410000042709

Professional Java, JDK /
33410008015549   06/06/05

Linux server hacks : 100 industrial-stre
33410007219449   06/06/05

TOTAL: 2

****

(You also have to develop a kind of faith in your own learning capacity—a belief that even though you may not know all of what you need to solve a problem, if you tackle just a piece of it and learn from that, you'll learn enough to solve the next piece—and so on, until you're done.)

2. No problem should ever have to be solved twice.

Creative brains are a valuable, limited resource. They shouldn't be wasted on re-inventing the wheel when there are so many fascinating new problems waiting out there.

To behave like a hacker, you have to believe that the thinking time of other hackers is precious—so much so that it's almost a moral duty for you to share information, solve problems, and then give the solutions away just so other hackers can solve *new* problems instead of having to perpetually re-address old ones.

(You don't have to believe that you're obligated to give *all* your creative product away, though the hackers that do are the ones that get most respect from other hackers. It's consistent with hacker values to sell enough of it to keep you in food and rent and computers. It's fine to use your hacking skills to support a family or even get rich, as long as you don't forget your loyalty to your art and your fellow hackers while doing it.)

3. Boredom and drudgery are evil.

Hackers (and creative people in general) should never be bored or have to drudge at stupid repetitive work, because when this happens it means they aren't doing what only they can do—solve new problems. This wastefulness hurts everybody. Therefore boredom and drudgery are not just unpleasant but actually evil.

To behave like a hacker, you have to believe this enough to want to auto-mate away the boring bits as much as possible, not just for yourself but for everybody else (especially other hackers).

(There is one apparent exception to this. Hackers will sometimes do things that may seem repetitive or boring to an observer as a mind-clearing exer-cise, or in order to acquire a skill or have some particular kind of experience you can't have otherwise. But this is by choice—nobody who can think should ever be forced into a situation that bores them.)

4. Freedom is good.

Hackers are naturally anti-authoritarian. Anyone who can give you orders can stop you from solving whatever problem you're being fascinated by—and, given the way authoritarian minds work, will generally find some appallingly stupid reason to do so. So the authoritarian attitude has to be fought wherever you find it, lest it smother you and other hackers.

(This isn't the same as fighting all authority. Children need to be guided and criminals restrained. A hacker may agree to accept some kinds of authority in order to get something he wants more than the time he spends following orders. But that's a limited, conscious bargain; the kind of personal surrender authoritarians want is not on offer.)

Authoritarians thrive on censorship and secrecy. And they distrust voluntary cooperation and information-sharing—they only like "cooperation" that they control. So to behave like a hacker, you have to develop an instinctive hostility to censorship, secrecy, and the use of force or deception to compel responsible adults. And you have to be willing to act on that belief.

5. Attitude is no substitute for competence.

To be a hacker, you have to develop some of these attitudes. But copping an attitude alone won't make you a hacker, any more than it will make you a champion athlete or a rock star. Becoming a hacker will take intelligence, practice, dedication, and hard work.

Therefore, you have to learn to distrust attitude and respect competence of every kind. Hackers won't let posers waste their time, but they worship competence—especially competence at hacking, but competence at anything is good. Competence at demanding skills that few can master is especially good, and competence at demanding skills that involve mental acuteness, craft, and concentration is best.

If you revere competence, you'll enjoy developing it in yourself—the hard work and dedication will become a kind of intense play rather than drudgery. That attitude is vital to becoming a hacker.

The complete essay can be found online at *http://www.tuxedo.org/~esr/faqs/hacker-howto.html* and in an appendix to the "The Cathedral and the Bazaar" book (O'Reilly.)

—Eric S. Raymond

Eric S. Raymond is the author of the New Hacker's Dictionary, based on the Jargon File, and the famous "Cathedral and the Bazaar" essay that served as a catalyst for the Open Source movement. The text in this Foreword is an excerpt from his 1996 essay, "What is a hacker?" Raymond argues that hackers are ingenious at solving interesting problems, an idea that is the cornerstone of O'Reilly's Hacks series.

Preface

A hacker does for love what others
would not do for money.
—/usr/games/fortune

The word *hack* has many connotations. A "good hack" makes the best of the situation of the moment, using whatever resources are at hand. An "ugly hack" approaches the situation in the most obscure and least understandable way, although many "good hacks" may also appear unintelligible to the uninitiated.

The effectiveness of a hack is generally measured by its ability to solve a particular technical problem, inversely proportional to the amount of human effort involved in getting the hack running. Some hacks are scalable and some are even sustainable. The longest running and most generally accepted hacks become standards and cause many more hacks to be invented. A good hack lasts until a better hack comes along.

A hack reveals the interface between the abstract and wonderfully complex mind of the designer, and the indisputable and vulgar experience of human needs. Sometimes, hacks may be ugly and only exist because someone had an itch that needed scratching. To the engineer, a hack is the ultimate expression of the Do-It-Yourself sentiment: no one understands how a hack came to be better than the person who felt compelled to solve the problem in the first place. If a person with a bent for problem solving thinks a given hack is ugly, then they are almost always irresistibly motivated to go one better—and hack the hack, something that we encourage the readers of this book to do.

In the end, even the most capable server, with the most RAM and running the fastest (and most free) operating system on the planet, is still just a fancy back-scratcher fixing the itch of the moment, until a better, faster and cheaper back-scratcher is required.

Where does all of this pseudo-philosophical rambling get you? Hopefully, this background will give you some idea of the mindset that prompted the compiling of this collection of solutions that we call Linux Server Hacks. Some are short and simple, while some are quite complex. All of these hacks are designed to solve a particular technical problem that the designer simply couldn't let go without "scratching." I hope that some of them will be directly applicable to an "itch" or two that you may have felt yourself as a new or experienced administrator of Linux servers.

How This Book Is Organized

A competent sysadmin must be a jack-of-all-trades. To be truly effective, you'll need to be able to handle every problem the system throws at you, from power on to halt. To assist you in the time in between, I present this collection of time-saving and novel approaches to daily administrative tasks.

- *Chapter 11Server Basics* begins by looking at some of the most common sorts of tasks that admins encounter: manipulating the boot process, effectively working with the command line, automating common tasks, watching (and regulating) how system resources are used, and tuning various pieces of the Linux kernel to make everything run more efficiently. This isn't an introduction to system administration but a look at some very effective and non-obvious techniques that even seasoned sysadmins may have overlooked.

- *Revision Control* gives a crash-course in using two fundamental revision control systems, RCS and CVS. Being able to recall arbitrary previous revisions of configuration files, source code, and documentation is a critical ability that can save your job. Too many professional admins are lacking in revision control basics (preferring instead to make the inevitable, but unsupportable *.old* or *.orig* backup). This section will get you up and running quickly, giving you commands and instructions that are succinct and to the point.

- The next section, *Backups*, looks at quick and easy methods for keeping spare copies of your data. I pay particular attention to network backups, *rsync*, and working with ISOs. I'll demonstrate some of the enormous flexibility of standard system backup tools and even present one way of implementing regular "snapshot" revisions of a filesystem (without requiring huge amounts of storage).

- *Networking* is my favorite section of this entire book. The focus isn't on basic functionality and routing, but instead looks at some obscure but insanely useful techniques for making networks behave in unexpected ways. I'll set up various kinds of IP tunnels (both encrypted and otherwise), work with NAT, and show some advanced features that allow for interesting behavior based on all kinds of parameters. Did you ever want to decide what to do with a packet based on its data contents? Take a look at this section.

- *Monitoring* is an eclectic mix of tips and tools for finding out exactly what your server is up to. It looks at some standard (and some absolutely required "optional") packages that will tell you volumes about who is using what, when, and how on your network. It also looks at a couple of ways to mitigate inevitable service failures and even help detect when naughty people attempt to do not-so-nice things to your network.

- Truly a font of hackery unto itself, the *SSH* section describes all sorts of nifty uses for *ssh*, the cryptographically strong (and wonderfully flexible) networking tool. There are a couple of versions of *ssh* available for Linux, and while many of the examples will work in all versions, they are all tested and known to work with OpenSSH v3.4p1.

- *Scripting* provides a short digression by looking at a couple of odds and ends that simply couldn't fit on a single command line. These hacks will save you time and will hopefully serve as examples of how to do some nifty things in shell and Perl.

- *Information Services* presents three major applications for Linux: *BIND 9*, *MySQL*, and *Apache*. This section assumes that you're well beyond basic installation of these packages, and are looking for ways to make them deliver their services faster and more efficiently, without having to do a lot of work yourself. You will see methods for getting your server running quickly, helping it scale to very large installations and behave in all sorts of slick ways that save a lot of configuration and maintenance time.

How to Use This Book

You may find it useful to read this book from cover to cover, as the hacks do build on each other a bit from beginning to end. However, each hack is designed to stand on its own as a particular example of one way to accomplish a particular task. To that end, I have grouped together hacks that fit a particular theme into sections, but I do cross-reference quite a bit between hacks from different sections (and also to more definitive resources on the subject). Don't consider a given section as a cut-and-dried chapter with rigidly defined subject boundaries but more as a convenient way of collecting similar (and yet independent) hacks. You may want to read this book much like the way most people browse web pages online: follow whatever interests you, and if you get lost, follow the links within the piece to find more information.

Conventions Used in This Book

The following is a list of the typographical conventions used in this book:

Italic

> Used to indicate new terms, URLs, filenames, file extensions, directories, commands and options, and program names.

`Constant Width`

> Used to show code examples, the contents of files, or the output from commands.

`Constant Width Bold`

> Used in examples and tables to show commands or other text that should be typed literally.

`Constant Width Italic`

> Used in examples and tables to show text that should be replaced with user-supplied values.

The thermometer icons, found next to each hack, indicate the relative complexity of the hack:

 beginner   moderate   expert

How to Contact Us

We have tested and verified the information in this book to the best of our ability, but you may find that features have changed (or even that we have made mistakes!). Please let us know about any errors, inaccuracies, bugs, misleading or confusing statements, and typos that you find in this book.

You can write to us at:

> O'Reilly & Associates, Inc.
> 1005 Gravenstein Hwy N.
> Sebastopol, CA 95472
> (800) 998-9938 (in the U.S. or Canada)
> (707) 829-0515 (international/local)
> (707) 829-0104 (fax)

To ask technical questions or to comment on the book, send email to:

> *bookquestions@oreilly.com*

Visit the web page for *Linux Server Hacks* to find additional support information, including examples and errata. You can find this page at:

> *http://www.oreilly.com/catalog/linuxsvrhack*

For more information about this book and others, see the O'Reilly web site:

http://www.oreilly.com

Gotta Hack?

Got a good hack you'd like to share with others? Go to the O'Reilly Hacks web site at:

http://hacks.oreilly.com

You'll find book-related resources, sample hacks and new hacks contributed by users. You'll find information about additional books in the Hacks series.

Server Basics
Hacks #1–22

A running Linux system is a complex interaction of hardware and software where invisible daemons do the user's bidding, carrying out arcane tasks to the beat of the drum of the uncompromising task master called the Linux kernel.

A Linux system can be configured to perform many different kinds of tasks. When running as a desktop machine, the visible portion of Linux spends much of its time controlling a graphical display, painting windows on the screen, and responding to the user's every gesture and command. It must generally be a very flexible (and entertaining) system, where good responsiveness and interactivity are the critical goals.

On the other hand, a Linux server generally is designed to perform a couple of tasks, nearly always involving the squeezing of information down a network connection as quickly as possible. While pretty screen savers and GUI features may be critical to a successful desktop system, the successful Linux server is a high performance appliance that provides access to information as quickly and efficiently as possible. It pulls that information from some sort of storage (like the filesystem, a database, or somewhere else on the network) and delivers that information over the network to whomever requested it, be it a human being connected to a web server, a user sitting in a shell, or over a port to another server entirely.

It is under these circumstances that a system administrator finds their responsibilities lying somewhere between deity and janitor. Ultimately, the sysadmin's job is to provide access to system resources as quickly (and equitably) as possible. This job involves both the ability to design new systems (that may or may not be rooted in solutions that already exist) and the talent (and the stomach) for cleaning up after people who use that system without any concept of what "resource management" really means.

The most successful sysadmins remove themselves from the path of access to system resources and let the machines do all of the work. As a user, you know that your sysadmin is effective when you have the tools that you need to get the job done and you never need to ask your sysadmin for anything. To pull off (that is, to hack) this impossible sounding task requires that the sysadmin anticipate what the users' needs will be and make efficient use of the resources that are available.

To begin with, I'll present ways to optimize Linux to perform only the work that is required to get the job done and not waste cycles doing work that you're not interested in doing. You'll see some examples of how to get the system to do more of the work of maintaining itself and how to make use of some of the more obscure features of the system to make your job easier. Parts of this section (particularly Command Line and Resource Management) include techniques that you may find yourself using every day to help build a picture of how people are using your system and ways that you might improve it.

These hacks assume that you are already familiar with Linux. In particular, you should already have root on a running Linux system available with which to experiment and should be comfortable with working on the system from the command line. You should also have a good working knowledge of networks and standard network services. While I hope that you will find these hacks informative, they are certainly not a good introduction to Linux system administration. For in-depth discussion on good administrative techniques, I highly recommend the *Linux Network Administrator's Guide* and *Essential System Administration*, both by O'Reilly and Associates.

The hacks in this chapter are grouped together into the following five categories: Boot Time, Command Line, Automation, Resource Management, and Kernel Tuning.

Boot Time
1. Fine tune your server to provide only the services you really want to serve
2. Forgoing the Console Login
3. Common Boot Parameters
4. Creating a Persistent Daemon with init

Command Line
5. n>&m: Swap Standard Output and Standard Error
6. Building Complex Command Lines
7. Working with Tricky Files in xargs

HACK #1 Removing Unnecessary Services

Fine tune your server to provide only the services you really want to serve

When you build a server, you are creating a system that should perform its intended function as quickly and efficiently as possible. Just as a paint mixer has no real business being included as an espresso machine attachment, extraneous services can take up resources and, in some cases, cause a real mess that is completely unrelated to what you wanted the server to do in the first place. This is not to say that Linux is incapable of serving as both a top-notch paint mixer and making a good cup of coffee simultaneously—just be sure that this is exactly what you intend before turning your server loose on the world (or rather, turning the world loose on your server).

When building a server, you should continually ask yourself: what do I really need this machine to do? Do I really need FTP services on my web server? Should NFS be running on my DNS server, even if no shares are exported? Do I need the automounter to run if I mount all of my volumes statically?

To get an idea of what your server is up to, simply run a *ps ax*. If nobody is logged in, this will generally tell you what your server is currently running. You should also see what programs for which your *inetd* is accepting connections, with either a grep -v ^# /etc/inetd.conf or (more to the point) netstat -lp. The first command will show all uncommented lines in your *inetd.conf*, while the second (when run as root) will show all of the sockets that are in the LISTEN state, and the programs that are listening on each port. Ideally, you should be able to reduce the output of a *ps ax* to a page of information or less (barring preforking servers like *httpd*, of course).

Here are some notorious (and typically unnecessary) services that are enabled by default in many distributions:

portmap, rpc.mountd, rpc.nfsd
> These are all part of the NFS subsystem. Are you running an NFS server? Do you need to mount remote NFS shares? Unless you answered *yes* to either of these questions, you don't need these daemons running. Reclaim the resources that they're taking up and eliminate the potential security risk.

smbd and nmbd
> These are the Samba daemons. Do you need to export SMB shares to Windows boxes (or other machines)? If not, then these processes can be safely killed.

automount
> The automounter can be handy to bring up network (or local) filesystems on demand, eliminating the need for root privileges when accessing them. This is especially handy on client desktop machines, where a user needs to use removable media (such as CDs or floppies) or to access network resources. But on a dedicated server, the automounter is probably unnecessary. Unless your machine is providing console access or remote network shares, you can *kill* the automounter (and set up all of your mounts statically, in */etc/fstab*).

named
> Are you running a name server? You don't need *named* running if you only need to resolve network names; that's what */etc/resolv.conf* and the bind libraries are for. Unless you're running name services for other machines, or are running a caching DNS server (see "Setting Up Caching DNS with Authority for Local Domains" [Hack #78]), then *named* isn't needed.

lpd

Do you ever print to this machine? Chances are, if it's serving Internet resources, it shouldn't be accepting print requests anyway. Remove the printer daemon if you aren't planning on using it.

inetd

Do you really need to run any services from *inetd*? If you have *ssh* running in standalone mode, and are only running standalone daemons (such as Apache, BIND, MySQL, or ProFTPD) then *inetd* may be superfluous. In the very least, review which services are being accepted with the *grep* command grep -v ^# /etc/inetd.conf. If you find that every service can be safely commented out, then why run the daemon? Remove it from the boot process (either by removing it from the system rc's or with a simple chmod -x /usr/sbin/inetd).

telnet, rlogin, rexec, ftp

The remote login, execution, and file transfer functionality of these venerable daemons has largely been supplanted by *ssh* and *scp*, their cryptographically secure and tremendously flexible counterparts. Unless you have a *really* good reason to keep them around, it's a good idea to eliminate support for these on your system. If you really need to support *ftp* connections, you might try the *mod_sql* plugin for *proftpd* (see "Using proftpd with a mysql Authentication Source" **[Hack #85]**).

finger, comsat, chargen, echo, identd

The *finger* and *comsat* services made sense in the days of an open Internet, where users were curious but generally well-intentioned. In these days of stealth portscans and remote buffer overflow exploits, running extraneous services that give away information about your server is generally considered a *bad* idea. The *chargen* and *echo* ports were once good for testing network connectivity, but are now too inviting for a random miscreant to fiddle with (and perhaps connect to each other to drive up server load quickly and inexpensively).

Finally, the *identd* service was once a meaningful and important source of information, providing remote servers with an idea of which users were connecting to their machines. Unfortunately, in these days of local root exploits and desktop Linux machines, installing an *identd* that (perish the thought!) actually *lies* about who is connected has become so common that most sites ignore the author information anyway. Since *identd* is a notoriously shaky source of information, why leave it enabled at all?

To eliminate unnecessary services, first shut them down (either by running service stop in */etc/rc.d/init.d/*, removing them from */etc/inetd.conf*, or by killing them manually). Then to be sure that they don't start again the next time the machine reboots, remove their entry from */etc/rc.d/**. Once you have your system trimmed down to only the services you intend to serve, reboot the machine and check the process table again.

If you absolutely need to run insecure services on your machine, then you should use tcp wrappers or local firewalling to limit access to only the machines that absolutely need it.

See also:

- "Creating a Firewall from the Command Line of any Server" **[Hack #45]**
- "Setting Up Caching DNS with Authority for Local Domains" **[Hack #78]**
- "Using proftpd with a mysql Authentication Source" **[Hack #85]**

HACK #2 Forgoing the Console Login
All of the access, none of the passwords

It will happen to you one day. You'll need to work on a machine for a friend or client who has "misplaced" the root password on which you don't have an account.

If you have console access and don't mind rebooting, traditional wisdom beckons you to boot up in single user mode. Naturally, after hitting Control-Alt-Delete, you simply wait for it to POST and then pass the parameter single to the booting kernel. For example, from the LILO prompt:

```
LILO: linux single
```

On many systems, this will happily present you with a root shell. But on some systems (notably RedHat), you'll run into the dreaded emergency prompt:

```
Give root password for maintenance
(or type Control-D for normal startup)
```

If you knew the root password, you wouldn't be here! If you're lucky, the *init* script will actually let you hit ^C at this stage and will drop you to a root prompt. But most *init* processes are "smarter" than that, and trap ^C. What to do? Of course, you could always boot from a rescue disk and reset the password, but suppose you don't have one handy (or that the machine doesn't have a CD-ROM drive).

All is not lost! Rather than risk running into the above mess, let's modify the system with extreme prejudice, right from the start. Again, from the LILO prompt:

```
LILO: linux init=/bin/bash
```

What does this do? Rather than start */sbin/init* and proceed with the usual */etc/ rc.d/** procedure, we're telling the kernel to simply give us a shell. No passwords, no filesystem checks (and for that matter, not much of a starting environment!) but a very quick, shiny new root prompt.

Unfortunately, that's not quite enough to be able to repair your system. The root filesystem will be mounted read-only (since it never got a chance to be checked and remounted read/write). Also, networking will be down, and none of the usual system daemons will be running. You don't want to do anything more complicated than resetting a password (or tweaking a file or two) at a prompt like this. Above all: don't hit ^D or type Exit! Your little shell (plus the kernel) constitutes the entire running Linux system at the moment. So, how can you manipulate the filesystem in this situation, if it is mounted read-only? Try this:

```
# mount -o remount,rw /
```

That will force the root filesystem to be remounted read-write. You can now type passwd to change the root password (and if the original admin lost the password, consider the ramifications of giving them access to the new one. If you were the original admin, consider writing it in invisible ink on a post-it note and sticking it to your screen, or stitching it into your underwear, or maybe even taking up another hobby).

Once the password is reset, DO NOT REBOOT. Since there is no *init* running, there is no process in place for safely taking the system down. The quickest way to shutdown safely is to remount root again:

```
# mount -o remount,ro /
```

With the root partition readonly, you can confidently hit the Reset button, bring it up in single-user mode, and begin your actual work.

HACK #3 Common Boot Parameters

Manipulate kernel parameters at boot time

As we saw in "Forgoing the Console Login" [Hack #2], it is possible to pass parameters to the kernel at the LILO prompt allowing you to change the program that is first called when the system boots. Changing init (with the init=/bin/bash line) is just one of many useful options that can be set at boot time. Here are more common boot parameters:

single
> Boots up in single user mode.

root=
> Changes the device that is mounted as /. For example:
> ```
> root=/dev/sdc4
> ```

will boot from the fourth partition on the third scsi disk (instead of whatever your boot loader has defined as the default).

hdX=

Adjusts IDE drive geometry. This is useful if your BIOS reports incorrect information:

```
hda=3649,255,63 hdd=cdrom
```

This defines the master/primary IDE drive as a 30GB hard drive in LBA mode, and the slave/secondary IDE drive as a CD-ROM.

console=

Defines a serial port console on kernels with serial console support. For example:

```
console=ttyS0,19200n81
```

Here we're directing the kernel to log boot messages to ttyS0 (the first serial port), at 19200 baud, no parity, 8 data bits, 1 stop bit. Note that to get an actual serial console (that you can log in on), you'll need to add a line to */etc/inittab* that looks something like this:

```
s1:12345:respawn:/sbin/agetty 19200 ttyS0 vt100
```

nosmp

Disables SMP on a kernel so enabled. This can help if you suspect kernel trouble on a multiprocessor system.

mem=

Defines the total amount of available system memory. See "Using Large Amounts of RAM" **[Hack #21]**.

ro

Mounts the / partition read-only (this is typically the default, and is remounted read-write after *fsck* runs).

rw

Mounts the / partition read-write. This is generally a bad idea, unless you're also running the *init* hack. Pass your *init* line along with *rw*, like this:

```
init=/bin/bash rw
```

to eliminate the need for all of that silly mount -o remount,rw / stuff in "Forgoing the Console Login" **[Hack #2]**. Congratulations, now you've hacked a hack.

You can also pass parameters for SCSI controllers, IDE devices, sound cards, and just about any other device driver. Every driver is different, and typically allows for setting IRQs, base addresses, parity, speeds, options for auto-probing, and more. Consult your online documentation for the excruciating details.

See also:

- man bootparam
- /usr/src/linux/Documentation/*

Creating a Persistent Daemon with init
Make sure that your process stays up, no matter what

There are a number of scripts that will automatically restart a process if it exits unexpectedly. Perhaps the simplest is something like:

```
$ while : ; do echo "Run some code here..."; sleep 1; done
```

If you run a foreground process in place of that *echo* line, then the process is always guaranteed to be running (or, at least, it will *try* to run). The : simply makes the *while* always execute (and is more efficient than running /bin/ true, as it doesn't have to spawn an external command on each iteration). Definitely do *not* run a background process in place of the *echo*, unless you enjoy filling up your process table (as the *while* will then spawn your command as many times as it can, one every second). But as far as cool hacks go, the *while* approach is fairly lacking in functionality.

What happens if your command runs into an abnormal condition? If it exits immediately, then it will retry every second, without giving any indication that there is a problem (unless the process has its own logging system or uses syslog). It might make sense to have something watch the process, and stop trying to respawn it if it returns too quickly after a few tries.

There is a utility already present on every Linux system that will do this automatically for you: *init*. The same program that brings up the system and sets up your terminals is perfectly suited for making sure that programs are always running. In fact, that is its primary job.

You can add arbitrary lines to /etc/inittab specifying programs you'd like *init* to watch for you:

```
zz:12345:respawn:/usr/local/sbin/my_daemon
```

The *inittab* line consists of an arbitrary (but unique) two character identification string (in this case, zz), followed by the runlevels that this program should be run in, then the respawn keyword, and finally the full path to the command. In the above example, as long as my_daemon is configured to run in the foreground, *init* will respawn another copy whenever it exits. After making changes to *inittab*, be sure to send a HUP to *init* so it will reload its configuration. One quick way to do this is:

```
# kill -HUP 1
```

If the command respawns too quickly, then *init* will postpone execution for a while, to keep it from tying up too many resources. For example:

```
zz:12345:respawn:/bin/touch /tmp/timestamp
```

This will cause the file */tmp/timestamp* to be *touch*ed several times a second, until *init* decides that enough is enough. You should see this message in */var/log/messages* almost immediately:

```
Sep 8 11:28:23 catlin init: Id "zz" respawning too fast: disabled for 5
minutes
```

In five minutes, *init* will try to run the command again, and if it is still respawning too quickly, it will disable it again.

Obviously, this method is fine for commands that need to run as root, but what if you want your auto-respawning process to run as some other user? That's no problem: use *sudo*:

```
zz:12345:respawn:/usr/bin/sudo -u rob /bin/touch /tmp/timestamp
```

Now that *touch* will run as rob, not as root. If you're trying these commands as you read this, be sure to remove the existing */tmp/timestamp* before trying this *sudo* line. After sending a HUP to *init*, take a look at the *timestamp* file:

```
rob@catlin:~# ls -al /tmp/timestamp
-rw-r--r-- 1 rob users 0 Sep 8 11:28 /tmp/timestamp
```

The two drawbacks to using *init* to run arbitrary daemons are that you need to comment out the line in *inittab* if you need to bring the daemon down (since it will just respawn if you *kill* it) and that only root can add entries to *inittab*. But for keeping a process running that simply must stay up no matter what, *init* does a great job.

See also:

- "Make sudo Work Harder" [Hack #12]

HACK #5 n>&m: Swap Standard Output and Standard Error

Direct standard out and standard error to wherever you need them to go

By default, a command's standard error goes to your terminal. The standard output goes to the terminal or is redirected somewhere (to a file, down a pipe, into backquotes).

Sometimes you want the opposite. For instance, you may need to send a command's standard output to the screen and grab the error messages (standard error) with backquotes. Or, you might want to send a command's standard output to a file and the standard error down a pipe to an error-processing command. Here's how to do that in the Bourne shell. (The C shell can't do this.)

File descriptors 0, 1, and 2 are the standard input, standard output, and standard error, respectively. Without redirectrion, they're all associated with the terminal file */dev/tty*. It's easy to redirect any descriptor to any file—if you know the filename. For instance, to redirect file descriptor to *errfile*, type:

```
$ command 2> errfile
```

You know that a pipe and backquotes also redirect the standard output:

```
$ command | ...\
$ var=`command`
```

But there's no filename associated with the pipe or backquotes, so you can't use the 2> redirection. You need to rearrange the file descriptors without knowing the file (or whatever) that they're associated with. Here's how.

Let's start slowly. By sending both standard output and standard error to the pipe or backquotes. The Bourne shell operator *n>&m* rearranges the files and file descriptors. It says "make file descriptor *n* point to the same file as file descriptor *m*." Let's use that operator on the previous example. We'll send standard error to the same place standard output is going:

```
$ command 2>&1 | ...
$ var=`command 2>&1`
```

In both those examples, 2>&1 means "send standard error (file descriptor 2) to the same place standard output (file descriptor 1) is going." Simple, eh?

You can use more than one of those *n>&m* operators. The shell reads them left-to-right before it executes the command.

"Oh!" you might say, "To swap standard output and standard error—make *stderr* go down a pipe and *stdout* go to the screen—I could do this!"

```
$ command 2>&1 1>&2 | ... (wrong...)
```

Sorry, Charlie. When the shell sees 2>&1 1>&2, the shell first does 2>&1. You've seen that before—it makes file descriptor 2 (*stderr*) go the same place as file descriptor 1 (*stdout*). Then, the shell does 1>&2. It makes *stdout* (1) go the same place as *stderr* (2), but *stderr* is already going the same place as *stdout*, down the pipe.

This is one place that the other file descriptors, 3 through 9, come in handy. They normally aren't used. You can use one of them as a "holding place" to remember where another file descriptor "pointed." For example, one way to read the operator 3>&2 is "make 3 point the same place as 2". After you use

3>&2 to grab the location of 2, you can make 2 point somewhere else. Then, make 1 point to where 2 used to (where 3 points now).

The command line you want is one of these:

```
$ command 3>&2 2>&1 1>&3 | ...
$ var=`command 3>&2 2>&1 1>&3`
```

Open files are automatically closed when a process exits. But it's safer to close the files yourself as soon as you're done with them. That way, if you forget and use the same descriptor later for something else (for instance, use F.D. 3 to redirect some other command, or a subprocess uses F.D. 3), you won't run into conflicts. Use *m<&-* to close input file descriptor *m* and *m>&-* to close output file descriptor *m*. If you need to close standard input, use *<&- ; >&-* will close standard output.

HACK #6 Building Complex Command Lines

Build simple commands into full-fledged paragraphs for complex (but meaningful) reports

Studying Linux (or indeed any Unix) is much like studying a foreign language. At some magical point in the course of one's studies, halting monosyllabic mutterings begin to meld together into coherent, often used phrases. Eventually, one finds himself pouring out entire sentences and paragraphs of the Unix Mother Tongue, with one's mind entirely on the problem at hand (and not on the syntax of any particular command). But just as high school foreign language students spend much of their time asking for directions to the toilet and figuring out just what the dative case really is, the path to Linux command-line fluency must begin with the first timidly spoken magic words.

Your shell is very forgiving, and will patiently (and repeatedly) listen to your every utterance, until you get it just right. Any command can serve as the input for any other, making for some very interesting Unix "sentences." When armed with the handy (and probably over-used) up arrow, it is possible to chain together commands with slight tweaks over many tries to achieve some very complex behavior.

For example, suppose that you're given the task of finding out why a web server is throwing a bunch of errors over time. If you type less error_log, you see that there are many "soft errors" relating to missing (or badly linked) graphics:

```
[Tue Aug 27 00:22:38 2002] [error] [client 17.136.12.171] File does not
exist: /htdocs/images/spacer.gif
[Tue Aug 27 00:31:14 2002] [error] [client 95.168.19.34] File does not
exist: /htdocs/image/trans.gif
```

```
[Tue Aug 27 00:36:57 2002] [error] [client 2.188.2.75] File does not exist:
/htdocs/images/linux/arrows-linux-back.gif
[Tue Aug 27 00:40:37 2002] [error] [client 2.188.2.75] File does not exist:
/htdocs/images/linux/arrows-linux-back.gif
[Tue Aug 27 00:41:43 2002] [error] [client 6.93.4.85] File does not exist: /
htdocs/images/linux/hub-linux.jpg
[Tue Aug 27 00:41:44 2002] [error] [client 6.93.4.85] File does not exist: /
htdocs/images/xml/hub-xml.jpg
[Tue Aug 27 00:42:13 2002] [error] [client 6.93.4.85] File does not exist: /
htdocs/images/linux/hub-linux.jpg
[Tue Aug 27 00:42:13 2002] [error] [client 6.93.4.85] File does not exist: /
htdocs/images/xml/hub-xml.jpg
```

and so on. Running a logging package (like *analog*) reports exactly how
many errors you have seen in a day but few other details (which is how you
were probably alerted to the problem in the first place). Looking at the logfile directly gives you every excruciating detail but is entirely too much information to process effectively.

Let's start simple. Are there *any* errors other than missing files? First we'll
need to know how many errors we've had today:

```
$ wc -l error_log
1265 error_log
```

And how many were due to File does not exist errors?

```
$ grep "File does not exist:" error_log | wc -l
1265 error_log
```

That's a good start. At least we know that we're not seeing permission problems or errors in anything that generates dynamic content (like *cgi* scripts.) If
every error is due to missing files (or typos in our html that point to the
wrong file) then it's probably not a big problem. Let's generate a list of the
filenames of all bad requests. Hit the up arrow and delete that wc -l:

```
$ grep "File does not exist:" error_log | awk '{print $13}' | less
```

That's the sort of thing that we want (the 13th field, just the filename), but
hang on a second. The same couple of files are repeated many, many times.
Sure, we could email this to the web team (all whopping 1265 lines of it),
but I'm sure they wouldn't appreciate the extraneous spam. Printing each
file exactly once is easy:

```
$ grep "File does not exist:" error_log | awk '{print $13}' | sort | uniq |
less
```

This is much more reasonable (substitute a wc -l for that less to see just
how many unique files have been listed as missing). But that still doesn't
really solve the problem. Maybe one of those files was requested once, but
another was requested several hundred times. Naturally, if there is a link
somewhere with a typo in it, we would see many requests for the same

"missing" file. But the previous line doesn't give any indication of which files are requested most. This isn't a problem for *bash*; let's try out a command line *for* loop.

```
$ for x in `grep "File does not exist" error_log | awk '{print $13}' | sort
| uniq`; do \
echo -n "$x : "; grep $x error_log | wc -l; done
```

We need those backticks (`) to actually execute our entire command from the previous example and feed the output of it to a *for* loop. On each iteration through the loop, the $x variable is set to the next line of output of our original command (that is, the next unique filename reported as missing). We then *grep* for that filename in the *error_log*, and count how many times we see it. The *echo* at the end just prints it in a somewhat nice report format.

I call it a somewhat nice report because not only is it full of single hit errors (which we probably don't care about), the output is very jagged, and it isn't even sorted! Let's sort it numerically, with the biggest hits at the top, numbers on the left, and only show the top 20 most requested "missing" files:

```
$ for x in `grep "File does not exist" error_log | awk '{print $13}' | sort
| uniq`; do \
grep $x error_log | wc -l | tr -d '\n'; echo " : $x"; done | sort +2 -rn |
head -20
```

That's *much* better and not even much more typing than the last try. We need the tr to eliminate the trailing newline at the end of wc's output (why it doesn't have a switch to do this, I'll never know). Your output should look something like this:

```
595 : /htdocs/images/pixel-onlamp.gif.gif
156 : /htdocs/image/trans.gif
139 : /htdocs/images/linux/arrows-linux-back.gif
 68 : /htdocs/pub/a/onjava/javacook/images/spacer.gif
 50 : /htdocs/javascript/2001/03/23/examples/target.gif
```

From this report, it's very simple to see that almost half of our errors are due to a typo on a popular web page somewhere (note the repeated .gif.gif in the first line). The second is probably also a typo (should be images/, not image/). The rest are for the web team to figure out:

```
$ ( echo "Here's a report of the top 20 'missing' files in the error_log.";
echo; \
for x in `grep "File does not exist" error_log | awk '{print $13}' | sort |
uniq`; do \
grep $x error_log | wc -l | tr -d '\n'; echo " : $x"; done | sort +2 -rn |
head -20 )\
| mail -s "Missing file report" webmaster@oreillynet.com
```

and maybe one hardcopy for the weekly development meeting:

```
$ for x in `grep "File does not exist" error_log | awk '{print $13}' | sort
| uniq`; do \
grep $x error_log | wc -l | tr -d '\n'; echo " : $x"; done | sort +2 -rn |
head -20 \
| enscript
```

Hacking the Hack

Once you get used to chunking groups of commands together, you can
chain their outputs together indefinitely, creating any sort of report you like
out of a live data stream. Naturally, if you find yourself doing a particular
task regularly, you might want to consider turning it into a shell script of its
own (or even reimplementing it in Perl or Python for efficiency's sake, as
every | in a command means that you've spawned yet another program). On
a modern (and unloaded) machine, you'll hardly notice the difference, but
it's considered good form to clean up the solution once you've hacked it out.
And on the command line, there's plenty of room to hack.

HACK #7   Working with Tricky Files in xargs
Deal with many files containing spaces or other strange characters

When you have a number of files containing spaces, parentheses, and other
"forbidden" characters, dealing with them can be daunting. This is a problem that seems to come up frequently, with the recent explosive popularity
of digital music. Luckily, tab completion in *bash* makes it simple to handle
one file at a time. For example:

```
rob@catlin:~/Music$ ls
Hallucinogen - The Lone Deranger
Misc - Pure Disco
rob@catlin:~/Music$ rm -rf Misc[TAB]
rob@catlin:~/Music$ rm -rf Misc\ -\ Pure\ Disco/
```

Hitting the Tab key for [TAB] above replaces the command line with the line
below it, properly escaping any special characters contained in the file.
That's fine for one file at a time, but what if we want to do a massive trans-
formation (say, renaming a bunch of mp3s to include an album name)? Take
a look at this:

```
rob@catlin:~/Music$ cd Hall[TAB]
rob@catlin:~/Music$ cd Hallucinogen\ -\ The\ Lone\ Deranger/
rob@catlin:~/Music/Hallucinogen - The Lone Deranger$ ls
Hallucinogen - 01 - Demention.mp3
Hallucinogen - 02 - Snakey Shaker.mp3
Hallucinogen - 03 - Trancespotter.mp3
Hallucinogen - 04 - Horrorgram.mp3
Hallucinogen - 05 - Snarling (Remix).mp3
Hallucinogen - 06 - Gamma Goblins Pt. 2.mp3
Hallucinogen - 07 - Deranger.mp3
```

```
Hallucinogen - 08 - Jiggle of the Sphinx.mp3
rob@catlin:~/Music/Hallucinogen - The Lone Deranger$
```

When attempting to manipulate many files at once, things get tricky. Many system utilities break on whitespace (yielding many more chunks than you intended) and will completely fall apart if you throw a) or a { at them. What we need is a delimiter that is guaranteed never to show up in a filename, and break on that instead.

Fortunately, the *xargs* utility will break on NULL characters, if you ask it to nicely. Take a look at this script:

Listing: albumize

```
#!/bin/sh

if [ -z "$ALBUM" ]; then
echo 'You must set the ALBUM name first (eg. export ALBUM="Greatest Hits")'
exit 1
fi

for x in *; do
echo -n $x; echo -ne '\000'
echo -n `echo $x|cut -f 1 -d '-'`
echo -n " - $ALBUM - "
echo -n `echo $x|cut -f 2- -d '-'`; echo -ne '\000'
done | xargs -0 -n2 mv
```

We're actually doing two tricky things here. First, we're building a list consisting of the original filename followed by the name to which we'd like to *mv* it, separated by NULL characters, for all files in the current directory. We then feed that entire list to an *xargs* with two switches: *-0* tells it to break on NULLs (instead of newlines or whitespace), and *-n2* tells it to take two arguments at a time on each pass, and feed them to our command (*mv*).

Save the script as *~/bin/albumize*. Before you run it, set the $ALBUM environment variable to the name that you'd like injected into the filename just after the first -. Here's a trial run:

```
rob@catlin:~/Music/Hallucinogen - The Lone Deranger$ export ALBUM="The Lone
Deranger"
rob@catlin:~/Music/Hallucinogen - The Lone Deranger$ albumize
rob@catlin:~/Music/Hallucinogen - The Lone Deranger$ ls
Hallucinogen - The Lone Deranger - 01 - Demention.mp3
Hallucinogen - The Lone Deranger - 02 - Snakey Shaker.mp3
Hallucinogen - The Lone Deranger - 03 - Trancespotter.mp3
Hallucinogen - The Lone Deranger - 04 - Horrorgram.mp3
Hallucinogen - The Lone Deranger - 05 - Snarling (Remix).mp3
Hallucinogen - The Lone Deranger - 06 - Gamma Goblins Pt. 2.mp3
Hallucinogen - The Lone Deranger - 07 - Deranger.mp3
Hallucinogen - The Lone Deranger - 08 - Jiggle of the Sphinx.mp3
rob@catlin:~/Music/Hallucinogen - The Lone Deranger$
```

What if you would like to remove the album name again? Try this one, and call it ~/*bin/dealbumize*:

```
#!/bin/sh

for x in *; do
echo -n $x; echo -ne '\000'
echo -n `echo $x|cut -f 1 -d '-'`; echo -n ' - '
echo -n `echo $x|cut -f 3- -d '-'`; echo -ne '\000'
done | xargs -0 -n2 mv
```

and simply run it (no $ALBUM required):

```
rob@catlin:~/Music/Hallucinogen - The Lone Deranger$ dealbumize
rob@catlin:~/Music/Hallucinogen - The Lone Deranger$ ls
Hallucinogen - 01 - Demention.mp3
Hallucinogen - 02 - Snakey Shaker.mp3
Hallucinogen - 03 - Trancespotter.mp3
Hallucinogen - 04 - Horrorgram.mp3
Hallucinogen - 05 - Snarling (Remix).mp3
Hallucinogen - 06 - Gamma Goblins Pt. 2.mp3
Hallucinogen - 07 - Deranger.mp3
Hallucinogen - 08 - Jiggle of the Sphinx.mp3
rob@catlin:~/Music/Hallucinogen - The Lone Deranger$
```

The *-0* switch is also popular to team up with the *-print0* option of find (which, naturally, prints matching filenames separated by NULLs instead of newlines). With *find* and *xargs* on a pipeline, you can do anything you like to any number of files, without ever running into the dreaded Argument list too long error:

```
rob@catlin:~/Pit of too many files$ ls
bash: /bin/ls: Argument list too long
```

A *find/xargs* combo makes quick work of these files, no matter what they're called:

```
rob@catlin:/Pit of too many files$ find -type f -print0 | xargs -0 ls
```

To delete them, just replace that trailing *ls* with an *rm*, and away you go.

Immutable Files in ext2/ext3
Create files that even root can't manipulate

Here's a puzzle. Suppose we're cleaning up /*tmp*, and run into some trouble:

```
root@catlin:/tmp# rm -rf junk/
rm: cannot unlink `junk/stubborn.txt': Operation not permitted
rm: cannot remove directory `junk': Directory not empty
root@catlin:/tmp# cd junk/
root@catlin:/tmp/junk# ls -al
total 40
drwxr-xr-x 2 root root 4096 Sep 4 14:45 ./
drwxrwxrwt 13 root root 4096 Sep 4 14:45 ../
```

```
-rw-r--r-- 1 root root 29798 Sep 4 14:43 stubborn.txt
root@catlin:/tmp/junk# rm ./stubborn.txt
rm: remove write-protected file `./stubborn.txt'? y
rm: cannot unlink `./stubborn.txt': Operation not permitted
```

What's going on? Are we root or aren't we? Let's try emptying the file instead of deleting it:

```
root@catlin:/tmp/junk# cp /dev/null stubborn.txt
cp: cannot create regular file `stubborn.txt': Permission denied
root@catlin:/tmp/junk# > stubborn.txt
bash: stubborn.txt: Permission denied
```

Well, /tmp certainly isn't mounted read-only. What is going on?

In the ext2 and ext3 filesystems, there are a number of additional file attributes that are available beyond the standard bits accessible through chmod. If you haven't seen it already, take a look at the manpages for chattr and its companion, lsattr.

One of the very useful new attributes is -i, the immutable flag. With this bit set, attempts to unlink, rename, overwrite, or append to the file are forbidden. Even making a hard link is denied (so you can't make a hard link, then edit the link). And having root privileges makes no difference when immutable is in effect:

```
root@catlin:/tmp/junk# ln stubborn.txt another.txt
ln: creating hard link `another.txt' to `stubborn.txt': Operation not
permitted
```

To view the supplementary ext flags that are in force on a file, use lsattr:

```
root@catlin:/tmp/junk# lsattr
---i--------- ./stubborn.txt
```

and to set flags a la chmod, use chattr:

```
root@catlin:/tmp/junk# chattr -i stubborn.txt
root@catlin:/tmp/junk# rm stubborn.txt
root@catlin:/tmp/junk#
```

This could be terribly useful for adding an extra security step on files you know you'll never want to change (say, /etc/rc.d/* or various configuration files.) While little will help you on a box that has been r00ted, immutable files probably aren't vulnerable to simple overwrite attacks from other processes, even if they are owned by root.

There are hooks for adding compression, security deletes, undeletability, synchronous writes, and a couple of other useful attributes. As of this writing, many of the additional attributes aren't implemented yet, but keep watching for new developments on the ext filesystem.

Speeding Up Compiles
Make sure you're keeping all processors busy with parallel builds

If you're running a multiprocessor system (SMP) with a moderate amount of RAM, you can usually see significant benefits by performing a parallel make when building code. Compared to doing serial builds when running make (as is the default), a parallel build is a vast improvement.

To tell make to allow more than one child at a time while building, use the *-j* switch:

```
rob@mouse:~/linux$ make -j4; make -j4 modules
```

Some projects aren't designed to handle parallel builds and can get confused if parts of the project are built before their parent dependencies have completed. If you run into build errors, it is safest to just start from scratch this time without the *-j* switch.

By way of comparison, here are some sample timings. They were performed on an otherwise unloaded dual PIII/600 with 1GB RAM. Each time I built a bzImage for Linux 2.4.19 (redirecting STDOUT to */dev/null*), and removed the source tree before starting the next test.

```
time make bzImage:

real 7m1.640s
user 6m44.710s
sys  0m25.260s

time make -j2 bzImage:

real 3m43.126s
user 6m48.080s
sys  0m26.420s

time make -j4 bzImage:

real 3m37.687s
user 6m44.980s
sys  0m26.350s

time make -j10 bzImage:

real 3m46.060s
user 6m53.970s
sys  0m27.240s
```

As you can see, there is a significant improvement just by adding the *-j2* switch. We dropped from 7 minutes to 3 minutes and 43 seconds of actual time. Increasing to *-j4* saved us about five more seconds, but jumping all the way to *-j10* actually hurt performance by a few seconds. Notice how user and system seconds are virtually the same across all four runs. In the end, you need to shovel the same sized pile of bits, but -*j* on a multi-processor machine simply lets you spread it around to more people with shovels.

Of course, bits all eventually end up in the bit bucket anyway. But hey, if nothing else, performance timings are a great way to keep your cage warm.

At Home in Your Shell Environment

HACK
#10   Make bash more comfortable through environment variables

Consulting a manpage for *bash* can be a daunting read, especially if you're not precisely sure what you're looking for. But when you have the time to devote to it, the manpage for *bash* is well worth the read. This is a shell just oozing with all sorts of arcane (but wonderfully useful) features, most of which are simply disabled by default.

Let's start by looking at some useful environment variables, and some useful values to which to set them:

```
export PS1=`echo -ne "\033[0;34m\u@\h:\033[0;36m\w\033[0;34m\$\033[0;37m "`
```

As you probably know, the PS1 variable sets the default system prompt, and automatically interprets escape sequences such as \u (for username) and \w (for the current working directory.) As you may not know, it is possible to encode ANSI escape sequences in your shell prompt, to give your prompt a colorized appearance. We wrap the whole string in backticks (`) in order to get *echo* to generate the magic ASCII escape character. This is executed once, and the result is stored in PS1. Let's look at that line again, with bold-face around everything that isn't an ANSI code:

```
export PS1=`echo -ne "\033[0;34m\u@\h:\033[0;36m\w\033[0;34m\$\033[0;37m "`
```

You should recognize the familiar \u@\h:\w\$ prompt that we've all grown to know and love. By changing the numbers just after each semicolon, you can set the colors of each part of the prompt to your heart's content.

Along the same lines, here's a handy command that is run just before *bash* gives you a prompt:

```
export PROMPT_COMMAND='echo -ne "\033]0;${USER}@${HOSTNAME}: ${PWD}\007"'
```

(We don't need backticks for this one, as *bash* is expecting it to contain an actual command, not a string.) This time, the escape sequence is the magic string that manipulates the titlebar on most terminal windows (such as xterm, rxvt, eterm, gnometerm, etc.). Anything after the semicolon and before the \007 gets printed to your titlebar every time you get a new prompt. In this case, we're displaying your username, the host you're logged into, and the current working directory. This is quite handy for being able to tell at a glance (or even while within *vim*) to which machine you're logged in, and to what directory you're about to save your file. See "Constant Load Average Display in the Titlebar" [Hack #59] if you'd like to update your titlebar in real time instead of at every new *bash* prompt.

Have you ever accidentally hit ^D too many times in a row, only to find yourself logged out? You can tell *bash* to ignore as many consecutive ^D hits as you like:

```
export IGNOREEOF=2
```

This makes *bash* follow the Snark rule ("What I tell you three times is true") and only log you out if you hit ^D three times in a row. If that's too few for you, feel free to set it to 101 and *bash* will obligingly keep count for you.

Having a directory just off of your home that lies in your path can be extremely useful (for keeping scripts, symlinks, and other random pieces of code.) A traditional place to keep this directory is in *bin* underneath your home directory. If you use the ~ expansion facility in *bash*, like this:

```
export PATH=$PATH:~/bin
```

then the path will always be set properly, even if your home directory ever gets moved (or if you decide you want to use this same line on multiple machines with potentially different home directories—as in *movein.sh*). See "Get Settled in Quickly with movein.sh" [Hack #72].

Did you know that just as commands are searched for in the PATH variable (and manpages are searched for in the MANPATH variable), directories are likewise searched for in the CDPATH variable every time you issue a *cd*? By default, it is only set to ".", but can be set to anything you like:

```
export CDPATH=.:~
```

This will make *cd* search not only the current directory, but also your home directory for the directory you try to change to. For example:

```
rob@caligula:~$ ls
bin/ devel/ incoming/ mail/ test/ stuff.txt
rob@caligula:~$ cd /usr/local/bin
rob@caligula:/usr/local/bin$ cd mail
bash: cd: mail: No such file or directory
rob@caligula:/usr/local/bin$ export CDPATH=.:~
rob@caligula:/usr/local/bin$ cd mail
/home/rob/mail
rob@caligula:~/mail$
```

You can put as many paths as you like to search for in CDPATH, separating each with a : (just as with the PATH and MANPATH variables.)

We all know about the up arrow and the *history* command. But what happens if you accidentally type something sensitive on the command line? Suppose you slip while typing and accidentally type a password where you meant to type a command. This accident will faithfully get recorded to your *~/.bash_history* file when you logout, where another unscrupulous user might happen to find it. Editing your *.bash_history* manually won't fix the problem, as the file gets rewritten each time you log out.

To clear out your history quickly, try this from the command line:

```
export HISTSIZE=0
```

This completely clears out the current bash history and will write an empty *.bash_history* on logout. When you log back in, your history will start over from scratch but will otherwise work just as before. From now on, try to be more careful!

Do you have a problem with people logging into a machine, then disconnecting their laptop and going home without logging back out again? If you've ever run a w and seen a bunch of idle users who have been logged in for several days, try setting this in their environment:

```
export TMOUT=600
```

The TMOUT variable specifies the number of seconds that *bash* will wait for input on a command line before logging the user out automatically. This won't help if your users are sitting in a *vi* window but will alleviate the problem of users just sitting at an idle shell. Ten minutes might be a little short for some users, but kindly remind them that if they don't like the system default, they are free to reset the variable themselves.

This brings up an interesting point: exactly where do you go to make any of these environment changes permanent? There are several files that *bash* consults when starting up, depending on whether the shell was called at login or from within another shell.

From bash(1), on login shells:

> ...it first reads and executes commands from the file */etc/profile*, if that file exists. After reading that file, it looks for *~/.bash_profile*, *~/.bash_login*, and *~/.profile*, in that order, and reads and executes commands from the first one that exists and is readable.... When a login shell exits, *bash* reads and executes commands from the file *~/.bash_logout*, if it exists.

For all other shells:

> *bash* reads and executes commands from *~/.bashrc*, if that file exists.

For the full definition of what constitutes a login shell (and for a whole bunch of information about the environment you work in every day), consult bash(1).

Finding and Eliminating setuid/setgid
Binaries

Eliminate potential root exploits before they have a chance to happen

While running Linux as a server, one guiding principle that has served me well is to continually ask, "what am I trying to achieve?" Does it make sense for a web server to have the printing subsystem installed? Should a system with no console have *gpm* installed? Usually, extra software packages just take up unnecessary disk space, but in the case of setuid or setgid binaries, the situation could be far worse.

While distribution maintainers work very hard to ensure that all known exploits for setuid and setgid binaries have been removed, it seems that a few new unexpected exploits come out every month or two. Especially if your server has more shell users than yourself, you should regularly audit the setuid and setgid binaries on your system. Chances are you'll be surprised at just how many you'll find.

Here's one command for finding all the files with a setuid or setgid bit set:

```
root@catlin:~# find / -perm +6000 -type f -exec ls -ld {} \; > setuid.txt &
```

This will create a file called *setuid.txt* that contains the details of all of the matching files present on your system. It is a very good idea to look through this list, and remove the s bits of any tools that you don't use.

Let's look through what we might find on a typical system:

```
-rws--x--x 1 root bin 35248 May 30 2001 /usr/bin/at
-rws--x--x 1 root bin 10592 May 30 2001 /usr/bin/crontab
```

Not much surprise here. *at* and *crontab* need root privileges in order to change to the user that requested the *at* job or *cron* job. If you're paranoid, and you don't use these facilities, then you could remove the setuid bits with:

```
# chmod a-s /usr/bin/{at,crontab}
```

Generally speaking, it's a bad idea to disable *cron* (as so many systems depend on timed job execution). But when was the last time you used *at*? Do your users even know what it's for? Personally, I find *at* a nice shortcut to setting up a full-blown *cron* job, and wouldn't like to part with it. But if there is no call for it on your particular system, you should consider defanging it. With the setuid bit removed, the commands will no longer be available to regular users but will still work fine as root.

```
-rws--x--x 1 root bin 11244 Apr 15 2001 /usr/bin/disable-paste
```

This is part of the *gpm* package (a mouse driver for the Linux console). Do you have a mouse attached to the console of this machine? Do you use it in text mode? If not, then why leave a setuid root binary in place that will never even be called?

```
-r-s--s--x 1 root lp 14632 Jun 18 2001 /usr/bin/lpq
-r-s--s--x 1 root lp 15788 Jun 18 2001 /usr/bin/lpr
-r-s--s--x 1 root lp 15456 Jun 18 2001 /usr/bin/lprm
-r-xr-s--x 1 root lp 23772 Jun 18 2001 /usr/sbin/lpc
```

These are all part of the printing subsystem. Does this machine actually use *lp* to print?

```
-rws--x--x 1 root bin 33760 Jun 18 2000 /usr/bin/chage
-rws--x--x 1 root bin 29572 Jun 18 2000 /usr/bin/chfn
-rws--x--x 1 root bin 27188 Jun 18 2000 /usr/bin/chsh
-rws--x--x 1 root bin 35620 Jun 18 2000 /usr/bin/passwd
```

These are all necessary for users to be able to set their passwords, shell, and finger information. Does your site use *finger* information at all? If, like most sites, you have a roster somewhere else (probably on the web) that isn't kept in sync with user's GECOS field, then this information is generally useless (except for the user's "real" name, which is still used in some email clients). Do you really need to allow users to change this information on their own, without admin intervention?

```
-r-xr-sr-x 1 root tty 9768 Jun 21 2001 /usr/bin/wall
-r-xr-sr-x 1 root tty 8504 Jun 21 2001 /usr/bin/write
```

Both wall and write need to be setgid *tty* to write to other user's terminals. This is generally a safe operation, but can be abused by miscreants who like to write bad data (or *lots* of bad data) to other user's terminals. If you don't need to provide this functionality to other users, why not disable the setgid bit? If you do, root will still be able to send walls and writes (for example, when a message is sent by shutdown when rebooting the system).

```
-rwsr-xr-x 1 root bin 14204 Jun 3 2001 /usr/bin/rcp
-rwsr-xr-x 1 root bin 10524 Jun 3 2001 /usr/bin/rlogin
-r-sr-xr-x 1 root bin 7956 Jun 3 2001 /usr/bin/rsh
```

The *r** commands are left from an age (perhaps not so long ago), before the days of *ssh*. Do you need to provide the *r* commands to your users? Is there anything that *ssh* and *scp* can't do that you absolutely need *rsh* and *rcp* for? More than likely, once you've worked with *ssh* for a while, you'll never miss the *r* commands, and can safely remove the potential ticking time bomb of a disused setuid *rsh* installation. If you're looking for interesting things to do with *ssh*, check out any of the *ssh* hacks elsewhere in this book.

```
-r-sr-xr-x 1 root bin 10200 Jun 3 2001 /usr/bin/traceroute
-r-sr-xr-x 1 root bin 15004 Jun 3 2001 /bin/ping
```

The *traceroute* and *ping* commands need the setuid root bit to be able to create ICMP packets. If you want your users to be able to run these network diagnostic tools, then they'll need to be setuid root. Otherwise, remove set-uid and then only root will be able to run *ping* and *traceroute*.

```
-r-sr-sr-- 1 uucp uucp 83344 Feb 10 2001 /usr/bin/uucp
-r-sr-sr-- 1 uucp uucp 36172 Feb 10 2001 /usr/bin/uuname
-r-sr-sr-- 1 uucp uucp 93532 Feb 10 2001 /usr/bin/uustat
-r-sr-sr-- 1 uucp uucp 85348 Feb 10 2001 /usr/bin/uux
-r-sr-sr-- 1 uucp uucp 65492 Feb 10 2001 /usr/lib/uucp/uuchk
-r-sr-sr-- 1 uucp uucp 213832 Feb 10 2001 /usr/lib/uucp/uucico
-r-sr-sr-- 1 uucp uucp 70748 Feb 10 2001 /usr/lib/uucp/uuconv
-r-sr-sr-- 1 uucp uucp 315 Nov 22 1995 /usr/lib/uucp/uusched
-r-sr-sr-- 1 uucp uucp 95420 Feb 10 2001 /usr/lib/uucp/uuxqt
```

When was the last time you connected to another machine with UUCP? Have you ever set up the UUCP system? I have been a network admin for ten years, and in that time, I have never come across a live UUCP installation. That's not to say that UUCP isn't useful, just that in these days of permanently connected TCP/IP networks, UUCP is becoming extremely uncommon. If you're not using UUCP, then leaving setuid and setgid binaries online to support it doesn't make much sense.

Do any of the binaries in the examples above have potential root (or other privilege elevation) exploits? I have no idea. But I do know that by removing unnecessary privileges, I minimize my exposure to the possibility that an exploit might be run on this system if one is discovered.

I have tried to present this hack as a process, not as a solution. This list is certainly by no means definitive. As you build a server, always keep in mind what the intended use is, and build the system accordingly. Whenever possible, remove privileges (or even entire packages) that provide functionality that you simply don't need. Consult the manpage if you ever wonder about what a particular binary is supposed to be doing, and why it is installed setuid (and when the manpage fails you, remember to use the source).

Make sudo Work Harder

HACK
#12

Use sudo to let other users do your evil bidding, without giving away the machine

The *sudo* utility can help you delegate some system responsibilities to other people, without giving away full root access. It is a setuid root binary that executes commands on an authorized user's behalf, after they have entered their current password.

As root, run */usr/sbin/visudo* to edit the list of users who can call *sudo*. The default *sudo* list looks something like this:

```
root ALL=(ALL) ALL
```

Unfortunately, many system admins tend to use this entry as a template and grant unrestricted root access to all other admins unilaterally:

```
root ALL=(ALL) ALL
rob ALL=(ALL) ALL
jim ALL=(ALL) ALL
david ALL=(ALL) ALL
```

While this may allow you to give out root access without giving away the root password, it is really only a useful method when all of the *sudo* users can be completely trusted. When properly configured, the *sudo* utility allows for tremendous flexibility for granting access to any number of commands, run as any arbitrary uid.

The syntax of the *sudo* line is:

user machine=(*effective user*) **command**

The first column specifies the *sudo* user. The next column defines the hosts in which this sudo entry is valid. This allows you to easily use a single *sudo* configuration across multiple machines.

For example, suppose you have a developer who needs root access on a development machine, but not on any other server:

```
peter beta.oreillynet.com=(ALL) ALL
```

The next column (in parentheses) specifies the effective user that may run the commands. This is very handy for allowing users to execute code as users other than root:

```
peter lists.oreillynet.com=(mailman) ALL
```

Finally, the last column specifies all the commands that this user may run:

```
david ns.oreillynet.com=(bind) /usr/sbin/rndc,/usr/sbin/named
```

If you find yourself specifying large lists of commands (or, for that matter, users or machines), then take advantage of *sudo*'s Alias syntax. An Alias can be used in place of its respective entry on any line of the *sudo* configuration:

```
User_Alias ADMINS=rob,jim,david
User_Alias WEBMASTERS=peter,nancy

Runas_Alias DAEMONS=bind,www,smmsp,ircd

Host_Alias WEBSERVERS=www.oreillynet.com,www.oreilly.com,www.perl.com

Cmnd_Alias PROCS=/bin/kill,/bin/killall,/usr/bin/skill,/usr/bin/top
Cmnd_Alias APACHE=/usr/local/apache/bin/apachectl

WEBMASTERS WEBSERVERS=(www) APACHE
ADMINS ALL=(DAEMONS) ALL
```

It is also possible to specify system groups in place of the user specification to allow any user who belongs to that group to execute commands. Just preface the group with a %, like this:

```
%wwwadmin WEBSERVERS=(www) APACHE
```

Now any user who is part of the wwwadmin group can execute *apachectl* as the www user on any of the web server machines.

One very useful feature is the NOPASSWD: flag. When present, the user won't have to enter his password before executing the command:

```
rob ALL=(ALL) NOPASSWD: PROCS
```

This will allow the user rob to execute *kill*, *killall*, *skill*, and *top* on any machine, as any user, without entering a password.

Finally, *sudo* can be a handy alternative to *su* for running commands at startup out of the system rc files:

```
(cd /usr/local/mysql; sudo -u mysql ./bin/safe_mysqld &)

sudo -u www /usr/local/apache/bin/apachectl start
```

For that to work at boot time, you'll need the default line root ALL=(ALL) ALL to be present.

Use *sudo* with the usual caveats that apply to setuid binaries. Particularly if you allow *sudo* to execute interactive commands (like editors) or any sort of compiler or interpreter, you should assume that it is possible that the *sudo* user will be able to execute arbitrary commands as the effective user. Still, under most circumstances this isn't a problem and is certainly preferable to giving away undue access to root privileges.

HACK #13 Using a Makefile to Automate Admin Tasks
Makefiles make everything (not just gcc) faster and easier

You probably know the *make* command from building projects (probably involving *gcc*) from source. But not many people also realize that since it keeps track of file modification times, it can be a handy tool for making all sorts of updates whenever arbitrary files are updated.

Here's a Makefile that is used to maintain sendmail configuration files.

Listing: Makefile.mail

```
M4= m4
CFDIR= /usr/src/sendmail-8.12.5/cf
CHMOD= chmod
ROMODE= 444
```

```
RM= rm -f

.SUFFIXES: .mc .cf

all: virtusers.db aliases.db access.db

access.db: access.txt
makemap -v hash access < access.txt

aliases.db: aliases
newaliases

virtusers.db: virtusers.txt
makemap -v hash virtusers < virtusers.txt

.mc.cf:
$(RM) $@
$(M4) ${CFDIR}/m4/cf.m4 $*.mc > $@ || ( $(RM) $@ && exit 1 )
$(CHMOD) $(ROMODE) $@
```

With this installed as *etc/mail/Makefile*, you'll never have to remember to run *newaliases* when editing your sendmail aliases file, or the syntax of that *makemap* command when you update virtual domain or access control settings. And best of all, when you update your master *mc* configuration file (you are using *mc* and not editing the *sendmail.cf* by hand, right?) then it will build your new *.cf* file for you—all by simply typing make. Since make keeps track of files that have been recently updated, it takes care of rebuilding only what needs to be rebuilt.

Here's another example, used to push Apache configuration files to another server (say, in *a round-robin Apache setup*, which you can learn more about in "Distributing Load with Apache RewriteMap" **[Hack #99]**. Just put this in your *usr/local/apache/conf* directory:

Listing: Makefile.push

```
#
# Makefile to push *.conf to the slave, as needed.
#
SLAVE= www2.oreillynet.com
APACHE= /usr/local/apache
RM= /bin/rm
TOUCH= /bin/touch
SSH= /usr/local/bin/ssh
SCP= /usr/local/bin/scp

.SUFFIXES: .conf .ts

all: test restart sites.ts globals.ts httpd.ts
```

```
configtest: test

test:
@echo -n "Testing Apache configuration: "
@$(APACHE)/bin/apachectl configtest

restart:
$(APACHE)/bin/apachectl restart

.conf.ts:
@$(RM) -f $@
@$(SCP) $*.conf $(SLAVE):$(APACHE)/conf
@$(SSH) $(SLAVE) $(APACHE)/bin/apachectl restart
@$(TOUCH) $@
```

This example is a little trickier because we're not actually building any new files, so it's difficult for *make* to tell if any of the configuration files have actually changed. We fake out *make* by creating empty *.ts* files (short for TimeStamp) that only serve to hold the time and date of the last update. If the real files (*httpd.conf*, *sites.conf*, or *globals.conf*) have changed, then we first run an *apachectl configtest* to verify that we have a good configuration. If all goes well, it will then restart the local Apache, copy the newly changed files over to the slave server, then restart Apache on the slave server. Finally, we touch the relevant *.ts* files so we won't process them again until the *.conf* files change.

This saves a lot of typing and is significantly quicker (and safer) than doing it all by hand on each update.

HACK #14 Brute Forcing Your New Domain Name

Find exactly the domain you'd like to register, whatever it turns out to be

There are many tools available online that will assist in performing whois queries for you to determine if your favorite domain name is still available, and if not, who has registered it. These tools are usually web based and allow you to submit a few queries at a time (and frequently suggest several inane alternatives if your first choice is taken).

If you're not so much interested in a particular name as in finding one that matches a pattern, why not let the command line do the work for you? Suppose you wanted to find a list of all words that end in the letters "st":

```
cat /usr/share/dict/words | grep 'st$' | sed 's/st$/.st/' | \
while read i; do \
(whois $i | grep -q '^No entries found') && echo $i; sleep 60; \
done | tee list_of_st_domains.txt
```

This will obligingly supply you with a visual running tab of all available words that haven't yet been registered to el Republica Democratica de Sào

Tomé e Príncipe (the domain registrar for the st TLD). This example searches the system dictionary and tries to find the whois record for each matching word, one at a time, every 60 seconds. It saves any nonexistent records to a file called *list_of_st_domains.txt*, and shows you its progress as it runs. Replace that st with any two letter TLD (like us or to) to brute force the namespace of any TLD you like.

Some feel that the domain name land grab is almost turning the Internet into a corporate ghetto, but I don't subscribe to that idea. I actually find the whole situation quite humorous.

HACK #15 Playing Hunt the Disk Hog

Browse your filesystem for heavy usage quickly with a handy alias

It always seems to happen late on a Saturday night. You're getting paged because a partition on one of the servers (probably the mail server) is dangerously close to full.

Obviously, running a *df* will show what's left:

```
rob@magic:~$ df
Filesystem 1k-blocks Used Available Use% Mounted on
/dev/sda1 7040696 1813680 4863600 27% /
/dev/sda2 17496684 13197760 3410132 79% /home
/dev/sdb1 8388608 8360723 27885 100% /var/spool/mail
```

But you already knew that the mail spool was full (hence, the page that took you away from an otherwise pleasant, non-mailserver related evening). How can you quickly find out who's hogging all of the space?

Here's a one-liner that's handy to have in your *.profile*:

```
alias ducks='du -cks * |sort -rn |head -11'
```

Once this alias is in place, running *ducks* in any directory will show you the total in use, followed by the top 10 disk hogs, in descending order. It recurses subdirectories, which is very handy (but can take a long time to run on a heavily loaded server, or in a directory with many subdirectories and files in it). Let's get to the bottom of this:

```
rob@magic:~$ cd /var/spool/mail
rob@magic:/var/spool/mail$ ducks
8388608 total
1537216 rob
55120 phil
48800 raw
43175 hagbard
36804 mal
30439 eris
```

```
30212 ferris
26042 nick
22464 rachael
22412 valis
```

Oops! It looks like my mail spool runneth over. Boy, I have orders of magnitude more mail than any other user. I'd better do something about that, such as appropriate new hardware and upgrade the */var/spool/mail* partition. ;)

As this command recurses subdirectories, it's also good for running a periodic report on home directory usage:

```
root@magic:/home# ducks
[ several seconds later ]
13197880 total
2266480 ferris
1877064 valis
1692660 hagbard
1338992 raw
1137024 nick
1001576 rob
925620 phil
870552 shared
607740 mal
564628 eris
```

For running simple spot checks while looking for disk hogs, *ducks* can save many keystrokes (although if we called it something like *ds*, it would save even more, but wouldn't be nearly as funny).

HACK #16   Fun with /proc

Directly view the kernel's running process table and system variables

The */proc* filesystem contains a representation of the kernel's live process table. By manipulating files and directories in */proc*, you can learn about (and fiddle with) all sorts of parameters in the running system. Be warned that poking around under */proc* as root can be extraordinarily dangerous, as root has the power to overwrite virtually anything in the process table. One slip of a redirector, and Linux will obligingly blow away your entire kernel memory, without so much as a "so long and thanks for all the kcore."

Here are some examples of interesting things to do with */proc*. In these examples, we'll assume that you're using a recent kernel (about 2.4.18 or so) and that you are logged in as root. Unless you're root, you will only be able to view and modify processes owned by your uid.

First, let's take a look at a lightly loaded machine:

```
root@catlin:/proc# ls
1/ 204/ 227/ 37/ bus/ hermes/ loadavg scsi/ version
1039/ 212/ 228/ 4/ cmdline ide/ locks self@
1064/ 217/ 229/ 5/ cpuinfo interrupts meminfo slabinfo
1078/ 220/ 230/ 6/ devices iomem misc stat
194/ 222/ 231/ 698/ dma ioports modules swaps
197/ 223/ 232/ 7/ driver/ irq/ mounts sys/
2/ 224/ 233/ 826/ execdomains kcore net/ sysvipc/
200/ 225/ 254/ 827/ filesystems kmsg partitions tty/
202/ 226/ 3/ apm fs/ ksyms pci uptime
```

The directories consisting of numbers contain information about every process running on the system. The number corresponds to the PID. The rest of the files and directories correspond to drivers, counters, and many other internals of the running kernel. The interface operates just as any other file or device in the system, by reading from and writing to each entry as if it were a file. Suppose you want to find out which kernel is currently booted:

```
root@catlin:/proc# cat version
Linux version 2.4.18 (root@catlin) (gcc version 2.95.3 20010315 (release))
#2 Sat Jun 22 19:01:17 PDT 2002
```

Naturally, you could find much of that out by simply running *uname -a*, but this way cuts out the middle man (and actually does what *uname* does internally).

Interested in how much RAM we have installed? Take a look at kcore:

```
root@catlin:/proc# ls -l kcore
-r-------- 1 root root 201330688 Aug 28 21:39 kcore
```

Looks like we have 192MB installed in this machine (201330688/1024/ 1024 == 192, more or less). Notice the restricted file permissions? That is the system's defense against anyone attempting to read the memory directly. Of course, you're root and can do whatever you like. There's nothing preventing you from running *grep* or *strings* on kcore and looking for interesting tidbits. This is the system memory, and things get cached in there until overwritten (making it possible to hunt down accidentally lost data or track down naughty people doing things they oughtn't). Grovelling over kcore is actually not much fun and is typically only a method used by the very desperate (or very bored).

Some other notable status files:

```
root@catlin:/proc# cat interrupts
CPU0
0: 34302408 XT-PIC timer
1: 2 XT-PIC keyboard
2: 0 XT-PIC cascade
3: 289891 XT-PIC orinoco_cs
```

```
8: 1 XT-PIC rtc
9: 13933886 XT-PIC eth0
10: 25581 XT-PIC BusLogic BT-958
14: 301982 XT-PIC ide0
NMI: 0
ERR: 0
```

These are the system counters for every interrupt that has ever been called, its number, and the driver that called it.

```
root@catlin:/proc# cat partitions
major minor #blocks name

8 0 8971292 sda
8 1 8707198 sda1
8 2 257040 sda2
3 64 29316672 hdb
3 65 29310561 hdb1
```

This is a list of all of the hard disk partitions (and devices) that were discovered at boot, along with their respective sizes. Here we have a 9GB SCSI disk, and a 30GB IDE disk. All available partitions are represented here, regardless of whether they are currently mounted (making it a handy reference to see if there are any unmounted disks on the system).

Let's leave the system parameters and take a look at the structure of an individual process.

```
root@catlin:/proc# cd 1
root@catlin:/proc/1# ls -l
total 0
-r--r--r-- 1 root root 0 Aug 28 22:05 cmdline
lrwxrwxrwx 1 root root 0 Aug 28 22:05 cwd -> //
-r-------- 1 root root 0 Aug 28 22:05 environ
lrwxrwxrwx 1 root root 0 Aug 28 22:05 exe -> /sbin/init*
dr-x------ 2 root root 0 Aug 28 22:05 fd/
-r--r--r-- 1 root root 0 Aug 28 22:05 maps
-rw------- 1 root root 0 Aug 28 22:05 mem
lrwxrwxrwx 1 root root 0 Aug 28 22:05 root -> //
-r--r--r-- 1 root root 0 Aug 28 22:05 stat
-r--r--r-- 1 root root 0 Aug 28 22:05 statm
-r--r--r-- 1 root root 0 Aug 28 22:05 status
```

There are three interesting symlinks in this directory. cwd points to the current working directory of this process (you can, for example, cd /proc/3852/cwd to land in the directory from which process ID 3852 was run.) The *exe* link points to full path to the binary that was called, and root points to the notion of the root directory that this process has. The root link will almost always be /, unless it has executed a *chroot*.

The *cmdline* and *environ* files contain the command line as it was originally called and the processes complete environment. These are separated by NULL characters, so to see them in a more human readable form, try this:

```
root@catlin:/proc/1# cat environ |tr '\0' '\n'
HOME=/
TERM=linux
BOOT_IMAGE=catlin
```

(or for a better example, try this on */proc/self/environ*, the environment of the currently running process):

```
root@catlin:/proc/1# cat /proc/self/environ |tr '\0' '\n'
PWD=/proc/1
HOSTNAME=catlin.nocat.net
MOZILLA_HOME=/usr/lib/netscape
ignoreeof=10
LS_OPTIONS= --color=auto -F -b -T 0
MANPATH=/usr/local/man:/usr/man:/usr/X11R6/man
LESSOPEN=|lesspipe.sh %s
PS1=\u@\h:\w\$
PS2=>
...
```

and so on. This can be tremendously handy for use in shell scripts (or other programs) where you need specific information about running processes. Just use it with care, and remember that unprivileged users can usually only access information about their own processes.

In closing, here's a practical example of one use for */proc*. By checking the output of *ps* against the running process table, you can see if the two agree:

```
# ls -d /proc/* |grep [0-9]|wc -1; ps ax |wc -1
```

This will give you a quick spot check of the number of running processes versus the number that *ps* actually reports. Many rootkits install a hacked *ps* that allows a miscreant to hide processes (by simply not displaying them when *ps* runs). You may hide from *ps*, but it's much more difficult to hide from */proc*. If the second number is considerably larger than the first (particularly if you run it several times in a row) then you might want to consider taking your box offline for further inspection. Quickly.

HACK #17 Manipulating Processes Symbolically with procps

Signal and renice processes by name, terminal, or username (instead of PID)

If you often find yourself running a `ps awux |grep something` just to find the PID of a job you'd like to kill, then you should take a look at some of the more modern process manipulation packages.

Probably the best known process tools package is *procps*, the same package that includes the Linux version of the ubiquitous *top* command. The *top* tool is so tremendously useful and flexible that it deserves its own discussion. Learn more about it in "Monitor System Resources with top" **[Hack #58]**.

Among the other nifty utilities included in *procps*: *skill* lets you send signals to processes by name, terminal, username, or PID, and *snice* does the same but *renices* processes instead of sending them signals.

For example, to freeze the user on terminal pts/2:

```
# skill -STOP pts/2
```

To release them from the grip of sleeping death, try this:

```
# skill -CONT pts/2
```

Or to renice all of *luser*'s processes to 5:

```
# snice +5 luser
```

pkill is similar to *skill*, but with more formal parameters. Rather than attempting to guess whether you are referring to a username, process name, or terminal, you specify them explicitly with switches. For example, these two commands do the same thing:

```
# skill -KILL rob bash
# pkill -KILL -u rob bash
```

pkill may take slightly more typing, but is guaranteed to be unambiguous (assuming that you happened to have a user and a process with the same name, for example).

pgrep works just like *pkill*, but instead of sending a signal to each process, it simply prints the matching PID(s) on STDOUT:

```
$ pgrep httpd
3211
3212
3213
3214
3215
3216
```

Finally, *vmstat* gives you a nice, easily parsed pinpoint measurement of virtual memory and cpu statistics:

```
$ vmstat
procs memory swap io system cpu
r b w swpd free buff cache si so bi bo in cs us sy id
0 0 0 5676 6716 35804 58940 0 0 9 9 7 9 0 0 29
```

If you'd like to watch how usage changes over time, give it a number on the command line. The number represents the number of seconds to pause before displaying the results of another measurement.

Learning how to use the lesser known *procps* utilities can save you lots of typing, not to mention wincing. Use *skill* or *pkill* to avoid accidentally mistyping a PID argument to *kill*, and suddenly bringing *sshd* (and the wrath of many angry users) down upon your unfortunate sysadmin head.

See also:

- *ftp://people.redhat.com/johnsonm/procps/*
- "Monitor System Resources with top" **[Hack #58]**
- manpages for *pkill*, *pgrep*, *skill*, *snice*, and *vmstat*

HACK #18 Managing System Resources per Process

Prevent user processes from running away with all system resources

Whether intentionally or accidentally, it is entirely possible for a single user to use up all system resources, leading to poor performance or outright system failure. One frequently overlooked way to deal with resource hogs is to use the *ulimit* functionality of *bash*.

To prevent a process (or any of its children) from creating enormous files, try specifying a *ulimit -f* (with the maximum file size specified in kilobytes).

```
rob@catlin:/tmp$ ulimit -f 100
rob@catlin:/tmp$ yes 'Spam spam spam spam SPAM!' > spam.txt
File size limit exceeded
rob@catlin:/tmp$ ls -l spam.txt
-rw-r--r-- 1 rob users 102400 Sep 4 17:05 spam.txt
rob@catlin:/tmp$
```

Users can decrease their own limits, but not increase them (as with *nice* and *renice*). This means that ulimits set in */etc/profile* cannot be increased later by users other than root:

```
rob@catlin:/tmp$ ulimit -f unlimited
bash: ulimit: cannot modify limit: Operation not permitted
```

Note that nothing is preventing a user from creating many files, all as big as their ulimit allows. Users with this particular temperament should be escorted to a back room and introduced to your favorite LART. Or alternately, you could look into introducing disk quotas (although this is usually less than fun to implement, if a simple stern talking to will fix the problem).

Likewise, *ulimit* can limit the maximum number of children that a single user can spawn:

```
rob@catlin:~$ cat > lots-o-procs
#!/bin/bash
export RUN=$((RUN + 1))
echo $RUN...
$0
^D
rob@catlin:~$ ulimit -u 10
rob@catlin:~$ ./lots-o-procs
1...
2...
```

```
3...
4...
5...
6...
7...
8...
9...
./lots-o-procs: fork: Resource temporarily unavailable
rob@catlin:~$
```

This limits the number of processes for a single user across all terminals (and back grounded processes). It has to be this way, because once a process is forked, it disassociates itself from the controlling terminal. (And how would you count it against a given subshell then?)

One other very useful *ulimit* option is *-v*, maximum virtual memory size. Once this ceiling is reached, processes will exit with Segmentation fault (which isn't ideal, but will keep the system from crashing as it runs out of RAM and swap). If you have a particularly badly behaving process that shows significant bloat (like Apache + mod_perl and poorly written CGI code, for example) you could set a ulimit to act as an "emergency brake" while debugging the real source of the trouble. Again, specify the limit in kilobytes.

To see all available ulimit settings, use *-a*:

```
rob@catlin:~$ ulimit -a
core file size (blocks) 0
data seg size (kbytes) unlimited
file size (blocks) unlimited
max locked memory (kbytes) unlimited
max memory size (kbytes) unlimited
open files 1024
pipe size (512 bytes) 8
stack size (kbytes) 8192
cpu time (seconds) unlimited
max user processes 1536
virtual memory (kbytes) unlimited
```

You can see that before setting system-wide hard limits, user processes can grow to be quite large. In *tcsh*, the analogous command you're after is *limit*:

```
rob@catlin:~> limit
cputime unlimited
filesize unlimited
datasize unlimited
stacksize 8192 kbytes
coredumpsize 0 kbytes
memoryuse unlimited
descriptors 1024
memorylocked unlimited
maxproc 1536
openfiles 1024
```

Setting system resource limits may sound draconian but is a much better alternative to the downward spiral of a user process gone amok.

See also:

- *http://www.tuxedo.org/~esr/jargon/html/entry/LART.html*

H A C K   Cleaning Up after Ex-Users
#19   Make sure you close the door all the way when a user takes their leave

It happens. Plans change, companies shift focus, and people move on. At some point, every admin has had to clean up shell access after someone has left the company, happily or otherwise.

I am personally of the opinion that if one doesn't trust one's users from the beginning, then they will one day prove themselves untrustworthy. (Of course, I've never had to admin an open shell server at an ISP, either.) At any rate, building trust with your users from the beginning will go a long way toward being able to sleep at night later on.

When you do have to lock old accounts up, it's best to proceed strategically. Don't assume that just because you ran a *passwd -l* that the user in question can't regain access to your machine. Let's assume that we're locking up after an account called *luser*. Here are some obvious (and some not so obvious) things to check on in the course of cleaning up:

```
passwd -l luser
```

Obviously, locking the user's password is a good first step.

```
chsh -s /bin/true luser
```

This is another popular step, changing the user's login shell to something that exits immediately. This generally prevents a user from gaining shell access to the server. But be warned, if *sshd* is running on this box, and you allow remote RSA or DSA key authentication, then *luser* can still forward ports to any machine that your server can reach! With a command like this:

```
luser@evil:~$ ssh -f -N -L8000:private.intranet.server.com:80 old.server.com
```

luser has just forwarded his local port 8000 to your internal intranet server's http port. This is allowed since *luser* isn't using a password (he is using an RSA key) and isn't attempting to execute a program on old.server.com (since he specified the -N switch).

Obviously, you should remove *~luser/.ssh/authorized_keys** and prevent *luser* from using his *ssh* key in the first place. Likewise, look for either of these files:

```
~luser/.shosts
~luser/.rhosts
```

This usually isn't a problem unless you're running *rsh*, or have enabled this functionality in *ssh*. But you never know if a future admin will decide to enable *.shosts* or *.rhosts* functionality, so it's better to remove them now, if they exist.

Did *luser* have any *sudo* privileges? Check *visudo* to be sure.

How about *cron* jobs or *at* jobs?

```
crontab -u luser -e
atq
```

For that matter, is *luser* running any jobs right now?

```
ps awux |grep -i ^luser
```

or as in "Manipulating Processes Symbolically with procps" **[Hack #17]**, you can use:

```
skill -KILL luser
```

Could *luser* execute cgi programs from his home directory (or somewhere else)?

```
find ~luser/public_html/ -perm +111
```

What about PHP or other embedded scripting languages?

```
find ~luser ~public_html/ -name '*.php*'
```

Does *luser* have any email forwarding set up? Forwarders can frequently be made to execute arbitrary programs.

```
less ~luser/.forward
grep -C luser /etc/mail/aliases
```

Finally, does *luser* own any files in strange places?

```
find / -user luser > ~root/luser-files.report
```

One safe (and quick) way of ensuring that all of *luser*'s personal configuration files are invalidated is to `mv /home/luser /home/luser.removed`. This will keep the contents of *luser*'s home directory intact, without worrying about having missed other possible points of entry. Note that this will break a legitimate *.forward* file (and also *~luser/public_html* and any other publicly accessible data that *luser* might have kept in his home directory), so if you go this route be sure to take that into account (say, by adding an appropriate entry to the system *aliases* file, and moving a cleaned version of *public_html/* back to */home/luser/public_html/*.

Look at configuration files for any system software to which *luser* had access, particularly services that run as privileged users. Even something as innocuous as a user-supplied Apache configuration file could be used to provide shell access later.

This list is by no means exhaustive but is meant to demonstrate that there is a lot more to revoking access than simply locking a user's password. If this user ever had root access, all bets are off. Access could later be granted by anything from a Trojan system binary to an invisible kernel module to having simply changed the root password.

Get to know your shell users long before the day you have to say goodbye. This job is difficult enough without having to worry about whom you can trust.

H A C K Eliminating Unnecessary Drivers from the
#20 Kernel
Keep your kernel optimized for quick booting and long-term stability

Linux will run on an enormous variety of computer hardware. There is support for all manner of hardware, from critical components (such as hard disk drives and RAM) to more exotic devices (such as USB scanners and video capture boards). The kernel that ships with most Linux distributions aims to be complete (and safe) at the expense of possibly being less efficient than it could be, by including support for as many devices as possible.

As your machine boots, take a look at the messages the kernel produces. You may find it probing for all sorts of hardware (particularly SCSI controllers and Ethernet cards) that you don't actually have installed. If your distribution hides the kernel boot messages, try the *dmesg* command (probably piped through *less*) to see what kernel messages were generated at boot.

To make your kernel boot quickly and at the same time eliminate the possibility that an unnecessary device driver might be causing problems with your installed hardware, you should trim down the drivers that the kernel attempts to load to fit your hardware.

There are two schools of thought on managing kernel drivers. Some people prefer to build a kernel with all of the functionality they need built into it, without using loadable kernel modules. Others prefer to build a more lightweight kernel and load the drivers they need when the system boots. Of course, both methods have their advantages and disadvantages.

For example, the monolithic kernel (without loadable modules) is guaranteed to boot, even if something happens to the drivers under */lib/modules*. Some admins even prefer to build a kernel with no loadable module support at all, to discourage the possibility of Trojan horse device drivers being loaded by a random miscreant down the road. On the other hand, if a new piece of hardware is added to the system, then you will need to rebuild your kernel to accommodate it.

If you use loadable modules, then you have enormous flexibility in how you load device drivers. You can alter the order that drivers load and even pass parameters to various modules as you load the driver, all without rebooting. The downside is that good copies of the modules must exist under */lib/ modules*, or else the system can't load its drivers. When you build a new kernel, you'll need to remember to run a make modules_install, and to keep your kernel module utilities (like *modprobe* and *lsmod*) up to date. Building a kernel with loadable modules can also help if your monolithic kernel is too large to boot (by loading extra device drivers after the kernel boots and the filesystems are mounted).

Regardless of the method that you choose for your system, you'll need to build a kernel with the minimal functionality that is required to boot. This includes drivers for the IDE, SCSI, or other bus (maybe floppy disk or even network card?) that your machine boots from. You will also need support for the filesystem that your root partition is installed on (likely *ext2*, *ext3*, or *reiserfs*). Make sure that you build a kernel with support for the amount of RAM that your machine has installed (see "Using Large Amounts of RAM" [Hack #21]). Select a processor that matches your hardware to be sure that all appropriate optimizations are turned on. Be sure to build an SMP kernel if you have more than one processor.

To build a customized kernel, unpack the kernel sources somewhere that has enough room (say, in */usr/local/src/linux*). Run a make menuconfig (or, if you're running X, make xconfig). Select your drivers carefully (hitting Y for built-in drivers, and M for loadable modules.) Remember that you're building a kernel for a server and don't include extraneous drivers. Does your server really need sound support, even if it is built into your motherboard? What about USB? Unless you have a specific use for a particular piece of hardware that is directly related to its job as a server, don't bother installing a driver for it. You should also consider disabling unused hardware in the BIOS, wherever possible, to conserve system resources and reduce the possibility of hardware resource conflicts.

After you're finished selecting which bits of the kernel to build, it will save your configuration to a file called *.config* at the top of the kernel source tree. Save this file for later, because it will make upgrading your kernel much easier down the road (by copying it to the top of the new kernel tree, and running make oldconfig). Now build the new kernel (and modules, if applicable), install it, and give it a try. Be sure to try out all of your devices after installing a new kernel, and watch your boot messages carefully. Track down any unexpected warnings or errors now, before they cause trouble at some future date.

Finally, if you're doing kernel work remotely, don't forget to build in support for your network devices! There's nothing quite like the pain of realizing that the network drivers aren't built just *after* you issue a shutdown -r now. Hopefully that console is accessible by someone on call (who will discretely boot your old kernel for you, without telling *too* many of your friends).

Building a kernel well-tailored to your hardware can be challenging, but is necessary to make your server run as efficiently as it can. Don't be discouraged if it takes a couple of tries to build the perfect Linux kernel, the effort is well worth it.

See also:

- *Running Linux*, Fourth Edition (O'Reilly)
- "Using Large Amounts of RAM" **[Hack #21]**

HACK #21 Using Large Amounts of RAM

Be sure that Linux is using all of your available system RAM

Linux is capable of addressing up to 64 GB of physical RAM on x86 systems. But if you want to accommodate more than 960 MB RAM, you'll have to let the system know about it.

First of all, your Linux kernel must be configured to support the additional RAM. Typically, the default kernel configuration will address up to 960 MB RAM. If you install more than that in a machine, it will simply be ignored. (The common complaint is that you've just installed 1 GB, and yet a 'free' only reports 960MB, even though it counts to 1024 MB at post time.)

The way that the kernel addresses its available system memory is dictated by the High Memory Support setting (a.k.a. the CONFIG_NOHIGH-MEM define.) Depending on the amount of RAM you intend to use, set it accordingly:

```
up to 960MB: off
up to 4GB: 4GB
more than 4GB: 64GB
```

Be warned that selecting 64 GB requires a processor capable of using Intel Physical Address Extension (PAE) mode. According to the kernel notes, all Intel processors since the Pentium Pro support PAE, but this setting won't work on older processors (and the kernel will refuse to boot, which is one reason that it isn't on by default). Make your selection and rebuild your kernel, as in "Eliminating Unnecessary Drivers from the Kernel" **[Hack #20]**.

Once the kernel is built and installed, you may have to tell your boot loader how much RAM is installed, so it can inform the kernel at boot time (as not every BIOS is accurate in reporting the total system RAM at boot.) To do this, add the *mem=* kernel parameter in your bootloader configuration. For example, suppose we have a machine with 2GB RAM installed.

If you're using Lilo, add this line to */etc/lilo.conf*:

```
append="mem=2048M"
```

If you're using Grub, try this in your */etc/grub.conf*:

```
kernel /boot/vmlinuz-2.4.19 mem=2048M
```

If you're running *loadlin*, just pass it on the *loadlin* line:

```
c:\loadlin c:\kernel\vmlinuz root=/dev/hda3 ro mem=2048M
```

Although, if you're running *loadlin*, why are you reading a book on Linux Server Hacks? ;)

hdparm: Fine Tune IDE Drive Parameters
Get the best possible performance from your IDE hardware

If you're running a Linux system with at least one (E)IDE hard drive, and you've never heard of *hdparm*, read on.

By default, most Linux distributions use the default kernel parameters when accessing your IDE controller and drives. These settings are very conservative and are designed to protect your data at all costs. But as many have come to discover, safe almost never equals fast. And with large volume data processing applications, there is no such thing as "fast enough."

If you want to get the most performance out of your IDE hardware, take a look at the *hdparm(8)* command. It will not only tell you how your drives are currently performing, but will let you tweak them to your heart's content.

It is worth pointing out that under some circumstances, these commands CAN CAUSE UNEXPECTED DATA CORRUPTION! Use them at your own risk! At the very least, back up your box and bring it down to single-user mode before proceeding.

Let's begin. Now that we're in single user mode (which we discussed in "Forgoing the Console Login" **[Hack #2]**), let's find out how well the primary drive is currently performing:

```
hdparm -Tt /dev/hda
```

You should see something like:

```
/dev/hda:
Timing buffer-cache reads: 128 MB in 1.34 seconds =95.52 MB/sec
Timing buffered disk reads: 64 MB in 17.86 seconds = 3.58 MB/sec
```

What does this tell us? The -T means to test the cache system (i.e., the memory, CPU, and buffer cache). The -t means to report stats on the disk in question, reading data not in the cache. The two together, run a couple of times in a row in single-user mode, will give you an idea of the performance of your disk I/O system. (These are actual numbers from a PII/350/128M Ram/EIDE HD; your numbers will vary.)

But even with varying numbers, 3.58 MB/sec is pathetic for the above hardware. I thought the ad for the HD said something about 66 MB per second!!?!? What gives?

Let's find out more about how Linux is addressing this drive:

```
# hdparm /dev/hda

/dev/hda:
 multcount    = 0 (off)
 I/O support  = 0 (default 16-bit)
 unmaskirq    = 0 (off)
 using_dma    = 0 (off)
 keepsettings = 0 (off)
 nowerr       = 0 (off)
 readonly     = 0 (off)
 readahead    = 8 (on)
 geometry     = 1870/255/63, sectors = 30043440, start = 0
```

These are the defaults. Nice, safe, but not necessarily optimal. What's all this about 16-bit mode? I thought that went out with the 386!

These settings are virtually guaranteed to work on any hardware you might throw at it. But since we know we're throwing something more than a dusty, 8-year-old, 16-bit multi-IO card at it, let's talk about the interesting options:

multcount

Short for multiple sector count. This controls how many sectors are fetched from the disk in a single I/O interrupt. Almost all modern IDE drives support this. The manpage claims:

> When this feature is enabled, it typically reduces operating system overhead for disk I/O by 30-50%. On many systems, it also provides increased data throughput of anywhere from 5% to 50%.

I/O support

This is a big one. This flag controls how data is passed from the PCI bus to the controller. Almost all modern controller chipsets support mode 3, or 32-bit mode w/sync. Some even support 32-bit async. Turning this on will almost certainly double your throughput (see below).

unmaskirq

Turning this on will allow Linux to unmask other interrupts while processing a disk interrupt. What does that mean? It lets Linux attend to other interrupt-related tasks (i.e., network traffic) while waiting for your disk to return with the data it asked for. It should improve overall system response time, but be warned: not all hardware configurations will be able to handle it. See the manpage.

using_dma

DMA can be a tricky business. If you can get your controller and drive using a DMA mode, do it. However, I have seen more than one machine hang while playing with this option. Again, see the manpage.

Let's try out some turbo settings:

```
# hdparm -c3 -m16 /dev/hda

/dev/hda:
 setting 32-bit I/O support flag to 3
 setting multcount to 16
 multcount = 16 (on)
 I/O support = 3 (32-bit w/sync)
```

Great! 32-bit sounds nice. And some multi-reads might work. Let's re-run the benchmark:

```
# hdparm -tT /dev/hda

/dev/hda:
 Timing buffer-cache reads: 128 MB in 1.41 seconds =90.78 MB/sec
 Timing buffered disk reads: 64 MB in 9.84 seconds = 6.50 MB/sec
```

Hmm, almost double the disk throughput without really trying! Incredible.

But wait, there's more: we're still not unmasking interrupts, using DMA, or even a using decent PIO mode! Of course, enabling these gets riskier. The manpage mentions trying Multiword DMA mode2, so let's try this:

```
# hdparm -X34 -d1 -u1 /dev/hda
```

Unfortunately this seems to be unsupported on this particular box (it hung like an NT box running a Java application) So, after rebooting it (again in single-user mode), I went with this:

```
# hdparm -X66 -d1 -u1 -m16 -c3 /dev/hda

/dev/hda:
 setting 32-bit I/O support flag to 3
 setting multcount to 16
 setting unmaskirq to 1 (on)
 setting using_dma to 1 (on)
 setting xfermode to 66 (UltraDMA mode2)
 multcount = 16 (on)
 I/O support = 3 (32-bit w/sync)
 unmaskirq = 1 (on)
 using_dma = 1 (on)
```

And then checked:

```
# hdparm -tT /dev/hda

/dev/hda:
 Timing buffer-cache reads:  128 MB in 1.43 seconds =89.51 MB/sec
 Timing buffered disk reads:  64 MB in 3.18 seconds =20.13 MB/sec
```

20.13 MB/sec. A far cry from the miniscule 3.58 with which we started.

Did you notice how we specified the *-m16* and *-c3* switch again? That's because it doesn't remember your *hdparm* settings between reboots. Be sure to add the above line to your */etc/rc.d/* * scripts once you're sure the system is stable (and preferably after your *fsck* runs; running an extensive filesystem check with your controller in a flaky mode may be a good way to generate vast quantities of entropy, but it's no way to administer a system. At least not with a straight face).

If you can't find *hdparm* on your system (usually in */sbin* or */usr/sbin*), get it from the source at *http://metalab.unc.edu/pub/Linux/system/hardware/*.

## CHAPTER TWO

Revision Control
Hacks #23–36

If you take administration seriously, you will likely spend untold hours fine-tuning your system to behave *just so*. Unfortunately, it isn't always possible to define when a given application is "working" and when it is "broken"; usually functionality is much more finely graded, somewhere in the grey area between up and down. Even making a small configuration change can bring about subtle effects that aren't seen for days (or weeks) down the road.

This is where Revision Control can be a powerful ally. Beyond providing simple backups, any revision control package worth its weight in bits will keep track of the changes in any file, when it was changed, who changed it, and why the change was made. This information can be of untold value when working on a complex system, particularly if more than one person is responsible for its upkeep. By keeping critical configuration files in systems such as RCS or CVS, you will be able to "roll back" to any previous revision of a file, and analyze the differences between what was present then and the version you have online right now.

In this section, the goal is to provide the specific syntax you need to make effective use of RCS and CVS, with useful examples of how you might use them. While RCS is extremely handy for maintaining file revisions on a single machine, CVS offers extensive archiving and merging capabilities, keeping a central repository somewhere on the network. Understandably, CVS is a much more complicated tool than RCS. Hacks 23 through 25 offer a crash course in RCS, while 26 through 36 will get you up to speed quickly on CVS, from simple commands to setting up your own anonymous CVS repository.

Naturally, this chapter assumes that you're already comfortable working with files from the command line, even if you haven't worked with RCS or CVS before. If you're looking for in-depth information about CVS, take a look at the excellent book *Open Source Development with CVS* by Karl Fogel (CoriolisOpen Press).

Getting Started with RCS

#23 Let RCS manage your system files, and keep a revision history

RCS is a revision control system, useful for keeping multiple revisions of configuration files, shell scripts, and any other text files you have lying around. Unlike CVS, there is no functionality for using RCS with remote machines; in RCS, everything is intended to be kept in the local filesystem.

RCS keeps all its revisions in a directory called *RCS/* (under the directory you're currently in). To start a new RCS repository, just make the directory:

```
root@catlin:/etc# mkdir RCS
```

Now, we'll need to initialize a file into the new RCS repository before working with it. Let's work with *syslog.conf*:

```
root@catlin:/etc# ci -i syslog.conf
RCS/syslog.conf,v <-- syslog.conf
enter description, terminated with single '.' or end of file:
NOTE: This is NOT the log message!
>> Here's the syslog.conf for Catlin
initial revision: 1.1
done
```

The initial *ci -i* does a "check in and initialize," to give RCS a good first copy of the file. RCS prompts for an initial description, and then removes the file from the current directory. You probably don't want to leave it like that for too long, so after you've initialized the file in RCS, check it out:

```
root@catlin:/etc# co syslog.conf
RCS/syslog.conf,v --> syslog.conf
revision 1.1
done
```

That copies the file back into the current directory. But we're not ready to start working on it just yet. First, let's check it out with a lock to prevent other people from making updates while we work on it.

```
root@catlin:/etc# co -l syslog.conf
RCS/syslog.conf,v --> syslog.conf
revision 1.1 (locked)
done
```

Now you can edit the file to your heart's content. Once you're finished with it, check it back in and unlock it with *ci -u*:

```
root@catlin:/etc# ci -u syslog.conf
syslog.conf,v <-- syslog.conf
new revision: 1.3; previous revision: 1.2
enter log message, terminated with single '.' or end of file:
>> Added remote logging to the new security log host
>> .
done
```

Be sure to use meaningful log entries, because you *won't* remember what you meant by "made a couple of edits" in six months, when your code starts doing strange things.

If you have trouble checking anything in or out, you've probably forgotten the -l (on co) or -u (on ci) switch at some point. You can usually start over by making a backup copy, then checking the file back out again, and copying it back, assuming that you've just edited *syslog.conf*:

```
root@catlin:/etc# ci -u syslog.conf
syslog.conf,v <-- syslog.conf
ci: syslog.conf,v: no lock set by root
root@catlin:/etc#
```

Uh-oh. Better back it up and start again from scratch:

```
root@catlin:/etc# cp syslog.conf syslog.conf.backup
root@catlin:/etc# co -l syslog.conf
syslog.conf,v --> syslog.conf
revision 1.4 (locked)
done
root@catlin:/etc# cp syslog.conf.backup syslog.conf
root@catlin:/etc# ci -u syslog.conf
syslog.conf,v <-- syslog.conf
new revision: 1.5; previous revision: 1.4
enter log message, terminated with single '.' or end of file:
>> commented out the FIFO line
>> .
done
```

We'll see some more fun things to do with RCS in the next couple of hacks.

Checking Out a Previous Revision in RCS
#24 Save yourself with RCS revisions

Inevitably, you will break things so horribly that you have no hope of getting them back again. Suppose you've just done a complicated edit to your *httpd.conf*, and you get the error message that strikes fear (and occasionally heartburn) in the heart of admins everywhere:

```
root@catlin:/usr/local/apache/conf# ../bin/apachectl restart
apachectl restart: httpd not running, trying to start
apachectl restart: httpd could not be started
```

Oh, dear. What have you done? With the web server down, people aren't even getting your friendly 404 page, they're seeing Connection Refused errors. You could dig into *httpd.conf* desperately with *vi* to figure out exactly what you (or perhaps the admin before you) did to deserve this.

But if you're using RCS, things aren't so bleak. To see what has changed between your last checkout and this one, use *rcsdiff*:

```
root@catlin:/usr/local/apache/conf# rcsdiff httpd.conf
=====================================================================
RCS file: RCS/httpd.conf,v
retrieving revision 1.1
diff -r1.1 httpd.conf
458c458
< ErrorLog /usr/local/apache/logs/error_log
---
> ErrorLog :wq/usr/local/apache/logs/error_log
```

There we are. Evidently, a :wq accidentally got inserted at line 458. Ah, must have missed that ESC key. Make your fix, start Apache, and check it back in.

But what if the changes were more extensive than that? Suppose you make a big change to a configuration file on Tuesday morning, and gremlins start to manifest themselves around Thursday afternoon. How can you get back to a known good copy?

Simple: check out a particular revision using the -r switch:

```
root@catlin:/etc# co -l -r1.2 syslog.conf
syslog.conf,v --> syslog.conf
revision 1.2
done
```

Presto, you're back to the state you were in when you checked the file in at rev 1.2. Remember with RCS, it makes sense to save early and often.

HACK #25   Tracking Changes with rcs2log

See at a glance who's been editing your files, and why

RCS really shows its strength when more than one person needs to edit a particular file. Having multiple admins can sometimes lead to a blame game when things aren't working properly. In these cases, it's obvious that somebody changed *something*, but nobody will admit to it. If you keep track of changes in RCS, then it's simple to tell who's been changing what:

```
root@www:/usr/local/apache/htdocs# rcs2log index.html
2002-08-14 rob <rob@mouse>

* index.html: meeting announcement

2002-07-30 rob <rob@mouse>

* index.html: gre.tunnel announcement

2002-07-12 sderle <sderle@mouse>

* index.html: added Marin and shuffled around a bit.

2002-07-10 rob <rob@mouse>
```

```
* index.html: meeting announcement + v0.81

2002-07-01 jim <jim@mouse>

* index.html: *** empty log message ***

2002-06-20 rob <rob@mouse>

* index.html: meeting reminder
```

Hmm, what's that empty log message doing there? It might be worth talking to Jim (and possibly doing an *rcsdiff* between it and the previous revision). But how can you tell which versions correspond to which log entries? Try the *-v* switch on *rcs2log*:

```
root@www:/usr/local/apache/htdocs# rcs2log -v index.html
2002-08-14 rob <rob@mouse>

* index.html 1.54: meeting announcement

2002-07-30 rob <rob@mouse>

* index.html 1.53: gre.tunnel announcement

2002-07-12 sderle <sderle@mouse>

* index.html 1.52: added Marin and shuffled around a bit.

2002-07-10 rob <rob@mouse>

* index.html 1.51: meeting announcement + v0.81

2002-07-01 jim <jim@mouse>

* index.html 1.50: *** empty log message ***

2002-06-20 rob <rob@mouse>

* index.html 1.49: meeting reminder
```

Now do a *diff* between whichever revisions you like:

```
root@www:/usr/local/apache/htdocs# rcsdiff -r1.49 -r1.50 index.html
===================================================================
RCS file: RCS/index.html,v
retrieving revision 1.49
retrieving revision 1.50
diff -r1.49 -r1.50
199a200,202
> <dt><a href="http://labs.google.com/">Google Labs</a></dt>
> <dd>Take a look at the strange and wondrous things that Google is up to...
</dd>
>
```

So it was just a link addition. Still, it might be easy to just hit that ^D when prompted, but it's generally considered bad form to not make *any* log entry.

At any rate, once you master the simple *ci*, *co*, *rcsdiff*, and *rcs2log* commands, you have some very flexible revision control tools at your disposal. Use them well, and they'll probably save your life one day. Or in the very least, they'll save the next best thing: your data.

Getting Started with CVS
#26 The ins and outs of the Concurrent Versioning System

Concurrent Versioning System (CVS) is a system for managing simultaneous development of files. It is commonly used in large programming projects and is also useful to system administrators, technical writers, and anyone who needs to manage files.

CVS stores files in a central repository. It is set up to be accessible to all users of the files, using standard Unix permissions. Commands are given to "check out" a copy of a file for development and "commit" changes back to the repository. It also scans the files as they are moved to and from the repository, to prevent one person's work from overwriting another's.

This system ensures that a history of the file is retained, which is extremely useful when the boss decides he wants a feature you trashed months ago. It also ensures that backing up the repository is enough to backup a project (providing all necessary files are kept in repository).

Typical Uses

CVS is designed for developers, either individually or in teams. For individuals, CVS provides a repository from which you can work from home, the office, or the client site without having to haul disks around. It also provides version control, allowing rollbacks without loss of data. For teams, it also keeps a record of who changed which lines of a file and prevents direct overwriting of each other's work.

System administrators can keep configuration files in CVS. You can make a change, *cvs commit* it, test it. If it fails, roll back the change, even if you only discover the failure six months down the track.

Administrators can keep a CVS tree of the configurations for server farms. Adding a new server? Just use *cvs* to checkout the config tree for that type of server. Committing all changes also helps you keep track of who did what, when.

In this section, we'll take a look at what you need to get CVS up and running quickly, both as a client and as a server.

Creating a Repository

The repository needs to be hosted on a machine with sufficient disk space to store all your files and all the data for the changes you expect. As a rule of thumb, put the repository on a partition with enough room for three times the expected final size of the module. Then use the "Scotty principle" and double your estimate—the project will expand. If you intend to store binary files, multiply by ten. After your first project, you'll have a feel for how much space to allow.

First, ensure that all CVS users have valid user accounts and can access the repository machine from all the machines they intend to use.

Now create your repository root directory. Repositories are often stored in /home/cvsroot or /usr/local/cvsroot. Use *cvs init* to set up the directory as a CVS repository.

```
cvs -d /home/cvsroot init
```

Debian Linux has a script, *cvs-makerepos*, that will build a repository based on pre-existing Debian configuration scripts. See man cvs-makerepos for more information and man cvsconfig for an automated system for configuring a Debian CVS repository.

In general, most CVS servers tend to use a single repository, with multiple Modules contained within it. For example, your repository might live in /home/cvsroot, but could contain many projects (such as *tools*, *email*, *dns*, *myproj*, etc.).

Importing a New Module

Before loading your project into CVS, consider its structure. Moving or renaming files and directories can damage the CVS record of the files' history. Deleting a directory can cost you the record of all its files and subdirectories. For this reason, CVS has no facility for moving or renaming files and directories, or removing directories.

Make your initial directory structure—even if it's just one directory. Add any initial files you want. From within the root directory of your project, use the command cvs -d repository import nameofmodule vendortag releasetag.

For most cases, you will not need to know about vendor tags and release tags. CVS requires them to be present, but you can simply use the name of the module as the vendor tag, and the current version as the release tag.

```
/home/jenn$ cd example
/home/jenn/example$ cvs -d /home/cvsroot import example example_project ver_
0-1
```

Environment Variables

If you are only working with one repository, and would like to save yourself some typing, set the $CVSROOT environment variable to the repository's full path, like this:

```
export CVSROOT=/home/cvsroot/
```

With $CVSROOT set, you can now omit the -d repository portion of any CVS command. If you need to temporarily work with another repository, either reset your $CVSROOT, or use the -d switch to override your existing $CVSROOT setting.

If the CVS repository resides on a different machine, then you need to tell CVS how to access it. For remote repositories, $CVSROOT is set to :method: user@host:path. It should look something like :ext:jenn@cvs.example.com. au:/home/cvs.

By default, CVS uses *rsh* to access a repository on a remote machine. While this may have been a very logical transport choice a few years ago, running *rsh* on a production server is now generally considered a Very Bad Idea. Fortunately, the *ext* access method tells CVS to look in the $CVS_RSH environment variable, and run that program to connect to the machine that contains the repository. Most people set the $CVS_RSH variable to *ssh*, and set up *ssh* client keys (as in "Quick Logins with ssh Client Keys" **[Hack #66]**) on the repository machine. This greatly simplifies working with your repository, as you won't have to type in a password every time you make an update.

Incidentally, the other common access method is *pserver*, and these days is generally used for accessing anonymous public CVS repositories. For an example of how to work with anonymous CVS (and set up your own public repository), see "Quick Logins with ssh Client Keys" **[Hack #66]**.

See Also:

- *CVS in a Nutshell* (O'Reilly)
- *Anonymous CVS*
- *Quick logins with ssh keys*

HACK #27 CVS: Checking Out a Module
How to get a working copy of a CVS Module

CVS stores the files in a central repository, but users work from a working copy of a file.

Make a directory to do your work in (I tend to use ~/cvs), then cd into that directory. The checkout syntax is cvs checkout module To checkout a module called example, try cvs checkout example.

The checkout will put a copy of that module's files and subdirectories into your *cvs* directory.

```
cvs$ ls
example
cvs$ cd example; ls
CVS src
cvs/example$ cd CVS; ls
Entries Repository Root
```

The *cvs* directory is a special directory that CVS uses for its own purposes. CVS/Entries lists files and subdirectories CVS knows about. CVS/Repository contains the path to the corresponding directory in the repository. CVS/Root contains the path to the repository, so you won't need to use the -d repository-path option again for these files.

Note that CVS/Root overrides the $CVSROOT environment variable, so if you change the repository, you should check out the module again. Alternately, if you're in the middle of a big edit when you realize that your repository needs to be changed, try this perl one-liner, as shown in "Global Search and Replace with Perl" [Hack #73]:

```
cvs/src$ ls
CVS Makefile sample.h sample.c
```

The *src* directory contains the source files for the example project. *sample.c*, *sample.h*, and *Makefile* are ordinary files in the working copy. In the repository, they are stored in a format that tracks the changes.

CVS: Updating Your Working Copy
HACK #28
Receiving recent changes in your CVS Module

Every day before you start work, and any time someone else may have made and committed changes, *cd* into your working directory and run *cvs update*. This checks your working copies against the repository files and imports any changed files for you. *cvs update -d* also gives you any new directories.

Update reports on the status of each file as it checks it:

U   File updated successfully

A   File added but not yet committed (need to run a *cvs commit*)

R   File removed but not yet committed (need to run a *cvs commit*)

M   File modified in your working directory; the file in the repository was changed and your working directory file was older than the last time

CVS checked it or the repository had changes that the system could safely merge

C   Conflict between the repository copy, and your copy, which requires human intervention

?   File the file is in your working directory but not the repository; CVS doesn't know what to do with it

HACK #29 CVS: Using Tags
Tagging a Module revision in CVS

Tags assign a symbolic name to a revision of a file or a set of files. *cvs tag* tags the repository versions of all the files in the current working directory and its subdirectories.

The *cvs tag* command is based on a timestamp. It assigns the symbolic name to the version of the file or directory that is closest to and older than the timestamp; it does not look at the working directory.

Note that CVS doesn't allow the '.' character in tags. Specify the filename after the tag name, as in the following example:

```
cvs tag tagname filename
cvs tag tagname
```

Otherwise, the command tags the repository versions of all files in the current working directory:

```
cvs tag -c tagname
```

Use the *-c* option to cause the process to abort if the repository copy differs from the working copy:

```
cvs/example$ cvs tag release-1-0 src/sample.c
cvs/example/src$ cvs tag release-1-0
cvs/example/src$ cvs tag -c release-1-0
```

To retrieve a tagged version, use the *-r* flag to checkout or update. If you checkout or update in your usual working directory, the tagged version will overwrite the existing files, as in:

```
cvs checkout -r tagname
cvs update -r tagname
```

Here's an example:

```
cvs$ mkdir example-rel-1.0
cvs/example-rel-1.0$ cvs checkout -r release-1-0
```

or:

```
cvs/example$ cvs update -r release-1-0
```

CVS: Making Changes to a Module
#30 Checking in your changes in CVS

Once your files are checked out, edit them and compile them normally. Apply the updates to the repository with *cvs commit*. This command needs to be run higher in the hierarchy than all the files you have changed—you can always run it from the base of your working copy.

You can also `cvs commit filename`, which will commit a single file or recursively commit a directory.

Different project teams have different opinions on how often to do a *cvs commit*. Good rules of thumb include "every time you have a clean compile," and "every day before lunch and before you leave."

```
cvs/example$ cvs commit
cvs commit: Examining .
cvs commit: Examining src
jenn@cvs.sample.com.au's password:
```

CVS examines each directory and subdirectory below the current working directory. Any file that CVS knows will be checked for changes. If your cvs repository is not on the local machine, CVS will ask for a password for the remote machine, unless you have already set up your ssh host keys (as shown in "Quick Logins with ssh Client Keys" **[Hack #66]**) and have eliminated the need for passwords.

CVS then opens whichever editor is the default in your environment—based on the $CVSEDITOR or $EDITOR environment variables. Add change-notes for the appropriate files, as in:

```
CVS:----------------------------------------------------------------
CVS: Enter Log. Lines beginning with 'CVS:' are removed automatically
CVS:
CVS: Committing in .
CVS:
CVS: Modified Files:
CVS: example/src/sample.h example/src/sample.c
CVS:----------------------------------------------------------------
```

I strongly recommend meaningful change-notes—if you're trying to do a rollback and all you have are messages that say "fixed a few bugs," you'll not know which version to roll back to without using *cvs diff*.

If there is a potential conflict, *cvs commit* fails. Correct this by running a *cvs update* on the repository—CVS will attempt to merge the files, and will ask for human help if it cannot do this without losing data:

```
cvs server: Up-to-date check failed for 'cvs_intro.html'
cvs [server aborted]: correct above errors first!
cvs commit: saving log message in /tmp/cvst7onmJ
```

CVS: Merging Files
Resolving update conflicts in CVS

If CVS can't merge a modified file successfully with the copy in the repository, it announces the conflict in the output of *cvs update*. The original file is stored in *.#file.version* in the file's working directory, and the results of the merge are stored as the original filename:

```
cvs/example$ cvs update
jenn@cvs.example.com.au's password:
cvs server: Updating .
RCS file: /home/cvs/example/sample.c,v
retrieving revision 1.3
retrieving revision 1.4
Merging differences between 1.3 and 1.4 into sample.c
rcsmerge: warning: conflicts during merge
cvs server: conflicts found in sample.c
C sample.c
```

CVS writes the merge with the conflicting lines surrounded by CVS tags. CVS can't automatically merge conflicts where the same line is changed in both versions of a file:

```
<<<<<<< sample.c
Deliberately creating a conflict.
=======
Let's make a conflict.
>>>>>>> 1.4
```

CVS: Adding and Removing Files and Directories
Adding and removing files in your Module

Files that CVS doesn't know what to do with are reported with a question mark after the commit process and during a *cvs update*. They need to be added to the repository before CVS will recognize them.

Use cvs add filename to mark a new file for inclusion. CVS doesn't put the file in the repository until you do a *cvs commit*.

Directories are added with the same command. Files within a directory can't be added until the directory is added.

Removing Files

To mark a file for removal from the working copies, use cvs remove filename. Before CVS will remove a file from the repository, you have to actually delete it from the filesystem. CVS doesn't actually remove the file entirely, it puts the file in a special subdirectory in the repository called *Attic*.

Removing Directories

Directories cannot be removed from the repository using CVS commands. If a directory is no longer required, empty the directory with *cvs remove*, and use cvs update -P and cvs checkout -P when retrieving a working copy. The *-P* flag ensures that empty directories are not retrieved.

If you must, you can remove a directory by using *rmdir* on the repository. Do this on a copy of the repository first and check that you aren't breaking anything: If the directory in the repository has an *Attic* subdirectory, you will lose archived copies of files formerly stored there.

If you remove a directory from the repository, you should have all your users remove their existing working copies, and check out fresh copies of the module.

CVS: Branching Development
Setting up a development branch in CVS

If you need to fix a bug in an older version of your code without changing current code, or modify a configuration set for staging servers without modifying the set for your production servers, you might need to branch your modules. A branch allows storage and retrieval of a variation of the main module, without affecting the main module. Changes on the branch can be merged in later. To make a branch, use cvs tag -b branchtag, as in:

```
cvs/example$ cvs tag -b release-1-0-patches
```

Retrieve a branch using either checkout or update. Checkout will create a new directory for the branch, and update will overwrite your current working directory with the branch.

```
cvs checkout -r branchtag
cvs update -r branchtag
```

Example:

```
cvs/example-rel-1.0$ cvs checkout -r release-1-0-patches
cvs/example$ cvs update -r release-1-0-patches
```

Branches can be merged back into the main trunk, using the conflict resolution system invoked by *cvs update* and *cvs commit*.

```
cvs checkout module
cvs update -j branchtag
```

Example:

```
/tmp/example$ cvs checkout example
/tmp/example$ cvs update -j release-1-0-patches
```

Or in a single command:

```
cvs checkout -j branchtag module
```

The following example:

```
/tmp/example$ cvs checkout -j release-1-0-patches example
```

resolves any conflicts the system reports, then use *cvs commit*.

HACK #34   CVS: Watching and Locking Files

Setting up an email watch on files in CVS

Unlike many versioning systems, CVS doesn't have file locking—it doesn't prevent simultaneous editing of files. However, you can set files to be watched, so CVS will mail watchers when a file is being edited. If files are being watched, developers need to use *cvs edit* and *cvs unedit* to release a file for editing. Unwatched files can be edited without notifying CVS in any way.

To set up files for being watched, use:

```
cvs watch on (files)
cvs watch off (files)
```

To set yourself as a watcher, use:

```
cvs watch add (files)
cvs watch remove (files)
```

or:

```
cvs watch add -a edit|unedit|commit|all (files)
cvs watch remove -a edit|unedit|commit|all (files)
```

The special CVS file notify determines what occurs when a watched file is changed. It defaults to sending mail to the user's username on the CVS server. If your users have other addresses, set up the file *users* in the repository's *CVSROOT* directory. Entries should be in the format user:email, one to a line.

```
jenn:jenn@cvs.example.com.au
```

HACK #35   CVS: Keeping CVS Secure

Protecting your users and your code base in CVS

Remote Repositories

If the repository is on the local machine, both access and security are fairly straightforward. You can set the $CVSROOT environment variable to the root directory of the CVS repository, or call checkout with the -d *directory* option.

If the repository is on a remote machine, it is necessary to tell CVS which machine it is on, and what method will be used to access the machine. There are several methods available, but for security and simplicity, I prefer SSH. The syntax for defining a remote $CVSROOT is :method:[[user]:[password]@]hostname[:[port]]:/path/to/repository. For example:

```
:ext:jenn@cvs.example.com.au:/usr/local/cvsroot
```

(Note that *info cvs* disagrees slightly with what my copy of CVS actually does. I have included the syntax that works for me—a colon between the host and the path. Use the syntax that works on your system.)

To use SSH, we use the *ext* method. This method uses an external-to-CVS *rsh* or *rsh*-compatible program to communicate with the CVS server. To tell CVS to use SSH instead of rsh, set the environment variable $CVS_RSH to SSH. Ensure that SSH is set up on the server and on all clients, that SSH keys are generated and that users have usernames and passwords on both machines. If the usernames are the same, the user@ part of the *CVSROOT* string is not necessary. If a standard SSH port is used, the port is not necessary.

```
cvs -d :ext:cvs.example.com.au:/usr/local/cvsroot checkout sample<code>
```

Permissions

The files in the repository are all read-only. Permissions to those files shouldn't be changed. To control access, use the directory permissions. Most administrators make a group for the people who should have access to the module, and ensure that the group has write access for the directory.

If using a remote repository, set the root directory of the module setgid to ensure that all directories beneath it are made with the correct permissions. If using a local repository, $CVSUMASK can be set to control the permissions of files and directories in the repository.

Developer Machines

Securing the project involves securing the repository and securing all checked out copies—typically your developer's machines. It's not enough to ensure that the repository is safe and all transmissions are properly encrypted if someone can walk into your developer's office on his day off and burn a CD of your code. Maintain the usual physical and Net-based security for your development machines, prototype and demonstration copies, and any other places the code gets checked out to.

HACK
#36
CVS: Anonymous Repositories

Create your own read-only anonymous CVS repository

Creating an Anonymous Repository

The *pserver* access method allows users to login to remote repositories by supplying a username and password that is checked against a password file that CVS maintains, or against the system's */etc/passwd*. The *pserver* method unfortunately passes all credentials in the clear, so at best an intervening snooper might capture a login to your CVS repository, or at worst could compromise the entire machine. For this reason, most people use ssh as their transport when using remote repositories. Please see "CVS: Keeping CVS Secure" [Hack #35], for further details.

Obviously, if you want to provide read-only access to your source tree to the public, using *ssh* as your transport would be unnecessary (and impractical). This is where *pserver* shows its real usefulness: allowing easy anonymous repository access.

Before we get anonymous CVS running, first we'll need to set the repository machine up to use the traditional pserver method.

Installing pserver

As we'll be using *pserver* for anonymous CVS access, we'll need to create a user that has no permissions to write to anything in your repository. Create a user called anonymous (or if 9-letter usernames bother you, cvsanon is another common choice.) Set its shell to */bin/true*, its home directory to something innocuous (like */var/empty*), put it in its own group, and lock its password (a *passwd -l* is a quick way to do that.) This user will never login; it's just a placeholder account for CVS to setuid to later.

Next we'll create a password file for CVS. Put the following in a file called *CVSROOT/passwd*, under your repository directory:

```
anonymous:23MLN3ne5kvBM
```

If you created a user account called cvsanon, use this line instead:

```
anonymous:23MLN3ne5kvBM:cvsanon
```

In the CVS *passwd* file, the left hand entry is the CVS login name, followed by the encrypted password, and finally ending in an optional system login name to map the CVS login to. If it is omitted, CVS will look up the first entry in the system's password file and use that. The encrypted string is the word *anonymous*.

To be absolutely sure that the anonymous user can't ever make changes to the repository, add the line anonymous to the *CVSROOT/readers* file under your repository. This file flags any users contained with in it (one per line) as read-only users.

Now we want to tell CVS to never accept regular system users under the *pserver* method (to prevent wayward users from habitually using their system logins with pserver.) This is set up in *CVSROOT/config*, under your repository directory. Uncomment the line that says SystemAuth=no and then only users specified in *CVSROOT/passwd* can login using pserver. Note that this will have no effect on CVS users that use *ext* and *ssh*; they still use simple filesystem permissions for access control, and never consult the CVS *passwd* file.

Finally, we can tell the system to actually accept *pserver* connections. CVS doesn't ever run as a daemon; it expects to be launched from *inetd*. It runs on port 2401, so add the following line to your */etc/services*:

```
pserver 2401/tcp
```

And add this entry to */etc/inetd.conf*:

```
pserver stream tcp nowait root /usr/bin/cvs cvs --allow-root=/usr/local/
cvsroot pserver
```

Substitute your repository's directory for */usr/local/cvsroot*. Now just skill -HUP inetd (and see "Getting Started with RCS" **[Hack #23]** if you don't have *skill* installed) and away you go.

Using a Remote pserver

To test your new anonymous repository, first set your $CVSROOT environment variable to this:

```
:pserver:anonymous@your.machine.here:/usr/local/cvsroot
```

Before you can do a *cvs checkout*, you'll first need to login to pserver with cvs login. When prompted for a password, enter *anonymous*. Now proceed with cvs checkout module, and you should see an update as normal. Verify that you can't perform a *cvs checkin*, and you're ready to publish your anonymous CVS details to the world.

## CHAPTER THREE

Backups
Hacks #37–44

Be assured that one day, the unthinkable *will* happen. Hard drives wear. Tapes stretch and break. You might even accidentally pass the wrong switch to a command (or be in the wrong directory, or on the wrong machine) and suddenly find yourself cursing at having hit the Enter key, as your data evaporates into the ether. It is at these moments that you learn the value of a properly designed and executed backup solution.

While we can get you started with some interesting approaches to backing up your data, this section is by no means comprehensive. As a systems administrator, you should design a backup plan that fits the needs of your organization, implement the plan, and continually revise it as necessary as time goes on. Definitely do not assume that just because you set up a *cron* job to run a backup that the backups themselves are good (or even that the job itself is running properly). Watch your logs. Buy new backup media before the old media develops problems. Make it a policy to test your backups by doing a full restore from backup as often as you deem necessary to sleep well at night. And even then, consider keeping another copy of your data, off-site if need be. For an extremely detailed look at everything that goes into building a secure data backup policy, be sure to check out *Unix Backups & Recovery* by W. Curtis Preston (O'Reilly).

In this section, we'll take a look at some methods for keeping copies of your data ready for when that day of reckoning comes. Every installation is different, and each site needs its own degree of backup functionality (ranging from weekly differentials to 5-minute snapshots). While we won't try to define the perfect backup policy for your site, we will see some tools you can use to develop your own.

Backing Up with tar over ssh

HACK #37 Copy arbitrary bits of the filesystem between servers using ssh and tar

Shuffling files between servers is simple with *scp*:

```
root@inky:~# scp some-archive.tgz blinky:/
```

Or even copying many files at once:

```
root@pinky:~/tmp# scp clyde:/usr/local/etc/* .
```

But *scp* isn't designed to traverse subdirectories and preserve ownership and permissions. Fortunately, *tar* is one of the very early (and IMHO, most brilliant) design decisions in *ssh* to make it behave exactly as any other standard Unix command. When it is used to execute commands without an interactive login session, *ssh* simply accepts data on STDIN and prints the results to STDOUT. Think of any pipeline involving *ssh* as an easy portal to the machine you're connecting to. For example, suppose you want to backup all of the home directories on one server to an archive on another:

```
root@inky~# tar zcvf - /home | ssh pinky "cat > inky-homes.tgz"
```

Or even write a compressed archive directly to a tape drive on the remote machine:

```
root@blinky~# tar zcvf - /var/named/data | ssh clyde "cat > /dev/tape"
```

Suppose you wanted to just make a copy of a directory structure from one machine directly into the filesystem of another. In this example, we have a working Apache on the local machine but a broken copy on the remote side. Let's get the two in sync:

```
root@clyde:~# cd /usr/local
root@clyde:/usr/local# tar zcf - apache/ \
    | ssh pacman "cd /usr/local; mv apache apache.bak; tar zpxvf -"
```

This moves */usr/local/apache/* on *pacman* to */usr/local/apache.bak/*, then creates an exact copy of */usr/local/apache/* from clyde, preserving permissions and the entire directory structure. You can experiment with using compression on both ends or not (with the z flag to *tar*), as performance will depend on the processing speed of both machines, the speed (and utilization) of the network, and whether you're already using compression in *ssh*.

Finally, let's assume that you have a large archive on the local machine and want to restore it to the remote side without having to copy it there first (suppose it's really huge, and you have enough space for the extracted copy, but not enough for a copy of the archive as well):

```
root@blinky~# ssh pinky "cd /usr/local/pacland; tar zpxvf -" \
    < really-big-archive.tgz
```

Or alternately, from the other direction:

```
root@pinky:/usr/local/pacland# ssh blinky "cat really-big-archive.tgz" \
  | tar zpvxf -
```

If you encounter problems with archives created or extracted on the remote end, check to make sure nothing is written to the terminal in your ~/.bashrc on the remote machine. If you like to run /usr/games/fortune or some other program that writes to your terminal, it's a better idea to keep it in ~/.bash_profile or ~/.bash_login than in ~/.bashrc, because you're only interested in seeing what fortune has to say when there is an actual human being logging in and definitely not when remote commands are executed as part of a pipeline. You can still set environment variables or run any other command you like in ~/.bashrc, as long as those commands are guaranteed never to print anything to STDOUT or STDERR.

Using *ssh* keys to eliminate the need for passwords makes slinging around arbitrary chunks of the filesystem even easier (and easily scriptable in cron, if you're so inclined). See the hacks listed below for an example of how to make it very easy (and secure) to connect to any of your servers with *ssh*.

See also:

- "Quick Logins with ssh Client Keys" [Hack #66]
- "Turbo-mode ssh Logins" (#67)
- "Using ssh-Agent Effectively" [Hack #68]

HACK #38 Using rsync over ssh
Keep large directory structures in sync quickly with rsync

While *tar* over *ssh* is ideal for making remote copies of parts of a filesystem, *rsync* is even better suited for keeping the filesystem in sync between two machines. Typically, *tar* is used for the initial copy, and *rsync* is used to pick up whatever has changed since the last copy. This is because *tar* tends to be faster than *rsync* when none of the destination files exist, but *rsync* is much faster than *tar* when there are only a few differences between the two filesystems.

To run an *rsync* over *ssh*, pass it the -e switch, like this:

```
root@rover:~# rsync -ave ssh greendome:/home/ftp/pub/ /home/ftp/pub/
```

Notice the trailing / on the file spec from the source side (on greendome.) On the source specification, a trailing / tells *rsync* to copy the *contents* of the directory, but not the directory itself. To include the directory as the top level of whatever is being copied, leave off the /:

```
root@village:~# rsync -ave ssh bcnu:/home/six .
```

This will keep a copy of the *~root/six/* directory on village in sync with whatever is present on *bcnu:/home/six/*.

By default, *rsync* will only copy files and directories, but not remove them from the destination copy when they are removed from the source. To keep the copies exact, include the *--delete* flag:

```
six@jammer:~/public_html# rsync -ave ssh --delete greendome:~one/reports .
```

Now when old reports are removed from *~one/reports/* on greendome, they're also removed from *~six/public_html/reports/* on jammer, every time this command is run. If you run a command like this in *cron*, leave off the *v* switch. This will keep the output quiet (unless *rsync* has a problem running, in which case you'll receive an email with the error output).

Using *ssh* as your transport for *rsync* traffic has the advantage of encrypting the data over the network and also takes advantage of any trust relationships you already have established using *ssh* client keys. For keeping large, complex directory structures in sync between two machines (especially when there are only a few differences between them), *rsync* is a very handy (and fast) tool to have at your disposal.

See also:

- man rsync
- "Quick Logins with ssh Client Keys" **[Hack #66]**
- "Using ssh-Agent Effectively" **[Hack #68]**
- "Automated Snapshot-Style Incremental Backups with rsync" **[Hack #42]**

HACK #39 Archiving with Pax
Make easy, portable archives using pax

pax stands for "portable archive exchange," as it was designed specifically to allow portability between different versions of Unix. There's also a bit of wry humor in the name, as *pax* attempts to bring some "peace" to the long-standing battle over which is better: *tar* or *cpio*. The *pax* utility can be used to create either type of archive, and during a restore, it automatically detects the type of archive for you. We'll start with some examples of basic *pax* usage, then move on to some fancier stuff.

Creating Archives

To back up the contents of your home directory, invoke write mode using the *w* switch:

```
cd
pax -wf home.pax .
```

In this example, I went to my home directory with *cd*, then told *pax* to write (w) to a file (f) named home.pax the contents of the current directory (.). When you use *pax*, it's very important to remember to include that *f* switch to indicate the name of the archive you'd like to create. If you forget the f, weird characters will be sent to your screen, accompanied by horrible, pained noises. Also, if you want to watch as *pax* does its thing, simply add the *v*, or verbose, switch to the switch portion of the command.

To see what type of file you've just created, use the *file* command:

```
file home.pax
home.pax: POSIX tar archive
```

To see the contents of that archive, tell *pax* which archive file you'd like to view, using the *f* switch:

```
pax -f home.pax |more
```

Since my archive file is rather large, I piped this output to the *more* command so I could read the contents of the archive one page at a time. If you also include the *v* switch, you'll get *ls -l*–type output of the archive contents. Again, don't forget to specify the name of the archive with the *f* switch, or nothing will happen, except that you'll lose your prompt until you press Ctrl-c.

Expanding Archives

To restore (or use read mode on) an archive, first *cd* into the *destination* directory, then use the *r* switch. For example, I'll restore the backup named *home.pax* into the *test* subdirectory of my home directory:

```
cd test
pax -rvf ~/home.pax
```

The *pax* utility can also restore *tar* and *cpio* archives. It is able to automatically detect the correct format for you; however, you should use the *file* utility before attempting the restore to determine whether or not the archive is compressed. If it is, you'll need to include the *z* switch.

As an example, I have a file called *backup.old* located in my home directory (~). I'll first use the *file* utility:

```
file backup.old
backup: gzip compressed data, deflated, last modified:
Sat Aug 17 14:21:12 2002, os: Unix
```

Since this backup is compressed, I'll use this command to restore it to the *test* directory:

```
cd test
pax -rvzf ~/backup.old
```

I have another file in my home directory called *backup*:

```
file ~/backup
backup: cpio archive
```

This file isn't compressed, so i'll restore it, like so:

```
pax -rvf ~/backup
```

The fact that the first backup happened to be a *tar* archive and the second a *cpio* archive didn't confuse *pax*; however, I would have received some strange error messages if I had forgotten to inform *pax* that the first archive was compressed.

Interactive Restores

You can do some pretty funky things when restoring with *pax*. For example, you can do an interactive rename/restore by including the *i* switch. Issuing the following command:

```
pax -rif ~/backup
```

will start an interactive restore of the archive named *backup* into the current directory. In interactive mode, *pax* will display the name of each file, one at a time, and prompt you to either rename it as it's restored, restore it with the original name, or to skip it and not restore it:

```
ATTENTION: pax interactive file rename operation.
drwxr-xr-x Aug 17 15:08 .
Input new name, or a "." to keep the old name, or a "return" to skip this
file.
Input >
Skipping file.
```

Here, I pressed Enter as I didn't want to change the name of "." or the current directory:

```
ATTENTION: pax interactive file rename operation.
drwxr-xr-x Jul 26 16:10 file1
input new name, or a "." to keep the old name, or a "return" to skip this
file.
input > old
Processing continues, name changed to: old

ATTENTION: pax interactive file rename operation.
-rw-r--r-- Jun 11 00:20 file2
input new name, or a "." to keep the old name, or a "return" to skip this
file.
input > .
Processing continues, name unchanged.
```

You'll note that I changed the name of *file1* to *old* and kept *file2* as is. A listing of the restored directory will show two files: one named *old* and one named *file2*.

Recursively Copy a Directory

One of the most powerful features of *pax* is that it is able to very quickly copy a complete directory structure to another portion of your hard drive, using copy mode. To use copy mode:

1. *cd* into the source directory
2. Ensure the destination directory exists; if it doesn't, use *mkdir* to create it
3. Issue this command: pax -rw . *destination_directory*

Note that you don't include the *f* switch in copy mode, as an archive file doesn't get created. Instead, the old directory structure is directly recreated into the new directory structure. This can be much easier to remember than the *tar* equivalent:

```
tar cf - . | (cd destination_directory; tar vpxf -)
```

Also note that **you never want to do this**:

```
cd
mkdir test
pax -rw . test
```

In the previous example, I *cd*'d into my home directory, made a subdirectory named *test*, then invoked copy mode. In doing so, I ended up in an endless loop of *test* subdirectories, each containing the contents of my home directory. If I hadn't interrupted this cycle with a Ctrl-c, *pax* would have continued ad infinitum, where infinitum is defined as the point where I run out of disk space. That's what this section of man pax refers to.

Warning: the *destination* directory must not be one of the file operands or a member of a file hierarchy rooted at one of the file operands. The result of a copy under these conditions is unpredictable.

However, this works beautifully and almost instantaneously:

```
su
Password:
cd ~user1/big_project
mkdir ~user2/big_project
chown user2 ~user2/big_project
pax -rw . ~user2/big_project
```

Voila, the entire *big_project* directory structure is now also in the second user's home directory. When using copy mode, you'll have to become the superuser as you'll be copying out of your home directory, so you can avoid the endless loop situation. If you have to make the new directory, it will be owned by root; if need be, use the *chown* command like I did to ensure that it has the desired ownership before doing the copy operation. You'll also want to take a look at man pax first to see how you want to handle the permissions of the copied directory structure.

It is also possible to interactively copy a directory structure by including the *i* switch:

```
pax -rwi . ~user2/big_project
```

Similarly to the previous interactive example, *pax* will display each filename, one at a time, so you can decide which files to copy over and which files to rename as you do so.

Incremental Backups

Now, let's do something useful with the *pax* command. I'll demonstrate how to create an incremental backup system. In this example, the user "genisis" would like to back up any changes she made to her home directory on a daily basis.

First, I'll become the superuser to create a directory to hold the backups:

```
su
Password:
mkdir /usr/backups
```

I'll then create a subdirectory and give the user "genisis" ownership of that subdirectory:

```
mkdir /usr/backups/genisis
chown genisis /usr/backups/genisis
```

I'll then leave the superuser account and as the user "genisis," *cd* into my home directory:

```
exit
cd
```

I'll then do a full backup of my home directory and save it to an archive file called *Monday*:

```
pax -wvf /usr/backups/genisis/Monday .
```

Now that I have a full backup, I can take daily incremental backups to just back up each day's changes. So when I'm finished with my work on Tuesday, I'll issue this command:

```
pax -wv -T 0000 -f /usr/backups/genisis/Tuesday .
```

Notice that I included the time switch (-T) and specified a time of midnight (0000). This tells *pax* to only back up the files that have changed since midnight, so it will catch all of the files that changed today. On Wednesday, I'll repeat that command but will change the archive name to Wednesday.

If you have the disk space and want to keep backups for longer than a week, modify your archive names to something like: Aug01, Aug02, etc. It's still a good idea to do a full backup once a week, followed by incremental backups the other days of that week. If disk space is an issue, include the *z* switch so the backups will be compressed. Also note that the *T* switch can be much pickier than I've demonstrated; see man pax for the details.

Skipping Files on Restore

To restore all of the files except *file3*, use this command:

```
pax -rvf ~/backup -c './file3'
```

The *c* switch is the exception switch. Note that your exception pattern (in my case, *file3*) needs to be enclosed in single quotes (the key next to your Enter key). Either use the literal pattern like I did (to *pax*, this file is known as *./file3*, not *file3*) or use a wildcard, like so:

```
pax -rvf ~/backup -c '*file3'
```

If you use a wildcard (*) at the beginning of your pattern as in the above example, you will exclude all files that end with "file3"—for example: *file3*, *myfile3*, *thatfile3*.

You can also specify which file to restore by using the *n*, or pattern matching, switch. The following will just restore *file2*:

```
pax -rvf ~/backup -n './file2'
```

The *n* switch differs from the *c* switch in that it will only restore the first file that matches the pattern. This means that this command will not restore *file3*, *myfile3*, and *thatfile3*:

```
pax -rvf ~/backup -n '*file3'
```

Since *file3* is the first file to match the expression, it will be the only file that will be restored.

The *c* and *n* switches are also useful when creating an archive; use them to specify which file you'd like to back up, or which file(s) you don't want to back up.

See also:

- Original article: *http://www.onlamp.com/pub/a/bsd/2002/08/22/freeBSD_Basics.html*
- *pax* source code (part of the ast-open package), *http://www.research.att.com/sw/download/*

Backing Up Your Boot Sector

#40   Keep a copy of your boot sector packed away for a rainy day

Installing a boot loader (such as LILO) can be trickier than one might like. Particularly when using IDE hardware, it's easy to get yourself into trouble and work a system into a state that makes it impossible to boot without a rescue disk.

One common mistake when using IDE hardware is to install a kernel on a partition that extends beyond the 1024th cylinder. The symptom is very strange, because a machine will boot fine at first, but installing a kernel later (after the machine has been used for some time) makes LILO throw an error and will refuse to come up on the next boot. This can be a very confusing symptom, since "it used to work." Most likely, the kernel that was installed when the system was built the first time happens to reside on a space on disk before cylinder 1024. After the system software and user data are installed, the disk begins to fill up. When the disk contains about 500 MB (or 1GB on some BIOS) of data, any new kernels will necessarily lie (at least in part) beyond cylinder 1024—which is inaccessible to the BIOS at boot time.

Modern versions of LILO will refuse to install such a kernel, but some older versions simply throw a warning, and install anyway. One way to deal with this is to make a small (say, 10 MB) partition at the beginning of your install process (as /dev/hda1, the first partition on the disk), and mount it under /boot. Now when you install new kernels, always copy them to /boot, and they are guaranteed to work with your BIOS, as they will necessarily be contained well before the 1024 cylinder limit.

At any rate, installing the boot loader shouldn't be taken lightly. Once you have your boot loader up and working as you want it, you should consider making a backup of the entire boot sector of your boot drive.

For IDE:

```
dd if=/dev/hda of=bootsector.bin bs=512 count=1
```

For SCSI:

```
dd if=/dev/sda of=bootsector.bin bs=512 count=1
```

Alternately, you can copy the boot sector directly to a floppy disk:

```
dd if=/dev/hda of=/dev/fd0 bs=512 count=1
```

Be extremely careful when specifying your if and of statements, as confusing them could obliterate your boot sector. It's probably a better idea to create a file and copy it to removable media as you would any other file. Trusting a floppy disk with critical system data may be a fun party trick, but after your first (or thousandth) floppy fails at a critical moment, you'll wish you had another copy.

Now if you ever end up with a munged boot sector, you can restore it quickly (after booting from rescue media) like this:

```
dd if=bootsector.bin of=/dev/hda
```

Or if you backed it up to floppy directly, against medical advice:

```
dd if=/dev/fd0 of=/dev/hda bs=512 count=1
```

Naturally, substitute *sda* for *hda* if you're using SCSI.

See also:

- Lilo's README (or other format of documentation under *doc/* from the lilo distribution)

HACK #41 Keeping Parts of Filesystems in sync with rsync

Use rsync over ssh to mirror exactly what you want, to any number of servers

For O'Reilly's web publishing system, we built a web "cluster" that spreads the work of one machine across several, increasing both performance and reliability. But how do you keep the actual data in the filesystem of each server in sync with each other?

One method is to use NFS to provide a common filesystem for your data. While making it simple to update content across all of the servers simultaneously, NFS has some significant drawbacks. File locking on NFS is notoriously tricky. Performance tuning on NFS is generally considered something of a black art. (When it works, it's very good, and when it doesn't...that's why we're on call, right?) But probably the biggest drawback to a monolithic NFS server is that it introduces a single point of failure for your entire enterprise. If the NFS server becomes unavailable (or overloaded) for any reason, all of the machines dependent on it will suffer.

One alternative approach is to asynchronously update servers using a tool such as *rsync*. With the cost of disk space at an all-time low, having a locally cached copy of your data makes sense: not only will the single point of failure be eliminated, but the files will be served much faster from the local disk than they could be from network storage.

It is very straightforward to add an *rsync* job to *cron* on each of the web servers, containing something like this:

```
rsync -ae ssh master.machine.com:/usr/local/apache/htdocs/ \
    /usr/local/apache/htdocs/
```

Assuming that you have your *ssh* keys set up in advance (see "Quick Logins with ssh Client Keys" **[Hack #66]**), this will update the local Apache document root with the current copy on *master.machine.com* over an encrypted *ssh* session. As long as updates are always made to *master.machine.com*, they will be copied faithfully to each of your other servers on the next pass.

The biggest drawback to this approach is that updates must happen asynchronously. If this job runs every five minutes, then the copy will be at most five minutes old (and about three minutes old, on average). As long as your application can tolerate the "be there in a minute" nature of *rsync*'ing large file structures, this method can buy you huge wins in terms of actual server performance and reliability. One strong caveat to using a bare *rsync* in *cron* is that you must take care that the job finishes before the next one is run. Otherwise, if a server gets particularly busy, it can enter a *downward spiral* where launching a new *rsync* drives up the load, which makes the running *rsync* take longer, which means that it is still running when the next one runs, which drives up the load.

Using *rsync* has a couple of advantages over using *tar* for this application. Using *tar* over *ssh* (see "Backing Up with tar over ssh" [Hack #37]) is generally quicker when making a full copy of a directory tree from scratch, but *rsync* is much faster when only a few files have changed on the master copy. It runs an analysis pass first to determine which files have been updated and then only transfers the changes.

But suppose that our web cluster has more complicated requirements. Assume that we are attempting to divide the load (see "Distributing Load with Apache RewriteMap" [Hack #99]) of serving pages into two groups: Application Servers (which run a heavy mod_perl-enabled Apache, driving our content management system) and lightweight front-end Apache servers, which only serve copies of static data (such as images and file archives). In this case, it would be a waste of space to copy the entire document tree to all of the servers, since the front-end machines will only ever serve a few particular types of files.

Using the *exclude-from* feature of *rsync*, you can supply a file that specifies what parts of the filesystem *rsync* will consider when syncing. Create a file that looks something like this in */usr/local/etc/balance.front* for your static servers:

```
### Stuff we definitely don't want to mirror.
#
- logs/

### the entire document root
#
+ /usr/
+ /usr/local/
+ /usr/local/apache/
+ /usr/local/apache/htdocs/
+ /usr/local/apache/htdocs/**

### user public_html directories
#
+ /home/
+ /home/*/
+ /home/*/public_html/
```

```
+ /home/*/public_html/**

# Images, archives, etc.
#
+ *.jpg
+ *.gif
+ *.png
+ *.pdf
+ *.mp3
+ *.zip
+ *.tgz
+ *.gz

# Exclude everything else.
#
- *
```

And create a similar file for syncing to your Application Servers:

```
### Stuff we definitely don't want to mirror.
#
- logs/
- *.tmp
- *.swp

### the entire document root
#
+ /usr/
+ /usr/local/
+ /usr/local/apache/
+ /usr/local/apache/htdocs/
+ /usr/local/apache/htdocs/**

# Exclude everything else.
#
- *
```

Now, create a list of each type of server (front and back), one machine per line. Call the files */usr/local/etc/servers.front* and */usr/local/etc/servers.back*, respectively.

For example, put this in *servers.front*:

```
tiberius
caligula
```

and this in *servers.back*:

```
augustus
claudius
germanicus
posthumous
castor
```

Finally, rather than calling *rsync* directly from cron on each of your web servers, try this bit of Perl in *cron* on the authoritative master machine.

Listing: Balance-push.sh

```
#!/bin/bash

#
# balance-push - Push content from the master server (localhost)
# to multiple front- and back-end servers, in parallel.
#

# $FRONT_END lists the servers that receive the front-end (e.g. static
content) updates.
#
FRONT_END=$(cat /usr/local/etc/servers.front)

# $BACK_END lists the hosts that receive the full back-end (e.g. everything)
updates.
#
BACK_END=$(cat /usr/local/etc/servers.back)

# $TARGET specifies the filesystem root on the remote host to push to.
# Normally, you want this to be /, unless you're doing testing.
#
TARGET=/

# $EXCLUDE specifies the prefix of the per-mode rsync exclude files.
# For example, if your exclude files are /usr/local/etc/balance.front and
# /usr/local/etc/balance.back, set this to "/usr/local/etc/balance". The
# per-mode extensions will be added.
#
EXCLUDE=/usr/local/etc/balance

# $LOCK_DIR specifies a path to put the lock files in.
#
LOCK_DIR=/var/tmp

######## Ignore the shell functions behind the curtain. ########

PATH=/bin:/usr/bin:/usr/local/bin

lock () {
local lockfile="$LOCK_DIR/balance.$1.lock"
if [ -f $lockfile ]; then
if kill -0 $(cat $lockfile); then
echo "$0 appears to be already running on $1."
echo "Please check $lockfile if you think this is in error."
exit 1
else
echo "$0 appears to have completed for $1 without cleaning up its lockfile."
fi
fi
echo $$ > $lockfile
}
```

```
unlock () {
rm -f $LOCK_DIR/balance.$1.lock
}

push_files () {
local mode=$1 host=$2

if [ ! "$mode" -o ! -r "$EXCLUDE.$mode" ]; then
echo "$0 $$: mode unset for $host!"
return
fi

if [ ! "$host" ]; then
echo "$0 $$: host unset for push $mode!"
return
fi

lock $host

rsync --archive --rsh=ssh --delete --ignore-errors --whole-file \
--exclude-from="$EXCLUDE.$mode" / ${host}:${TARGET}

unlock $host
}

push_tier () {
local mode=$1 host_list=$2

for host in $host_list; do
$SHELL -c "push_files $mode $host" &
done
}

export -f lock unlock push_files
export TARGET EXCLUDE LOCK_DIR PATH

[ "$FRONT_END" ] && push_tier front "$FRONT_END"
[ "$BACK_END" ] && push_tier back "$BACK_END"

#
# Fin.
#
```

This script (call it *balance-push*) will manage your *rsync* jobs for you, ensuring that servers don't "lap" themselves on each run. It will push the proper files to each group, depending on whatever you specify in the files in */usr/local/etc/*. If it finds a server that hasn't finished its last run, it will continue to skip the server until it has finished (and issue you an email to that effect via cron's MAILTO feature).

The load on your master will likely go up, depending on how many machines you're syncing to (as each server requires both an *rsync* and an *ssh* session.)

But practically speaking, on a production network serving millions of hits a day, the load introduced to each individual web server is negligible.

HACK #42 Automated Snapshot-Style Incremental Backups with rsync

Use rsync to create fast, small, and safe snapshots of your filesystem

Here is a method for generating automatic rotating snapshot-style backups on a Linux server. Snapshot backups are a feature of some high-end industrial strength file servers; they create the *illusion* of multiple full (up to ownership/permission) backups per day without the space or processing overhead. All of the snapshots are read-only and are accessible directly by users as special system directories.

Since making a full copy of a large filesystem can be a time-consuming and expensive process, it is common to make full backups only once a week or once a month, and store only changes on the other days. This technique is called making "incremental" backups, and is supported by the venerable old *dump* and *tar* utilities, along with many others.

The standard GNU fileutils *cp* command comes with a *-l* flag that causes it to create (hard) links instead of copies (it doesn't hard-link directories, though, which is good; you might want to think about why that is). Another handy switch for the *cp* command is *-a* (archive), which causes it to recurse through directories and preserve file owners, timestamps, and access permissions.

Together, the combination *cp -al* makes what appears to be a full copy of a directory tree but is really just an illusion that takes almost no space. If we restrict operations on the copy to adding or removing (unlinking) files—i.e., never changing one in place—then the illusion of a full copy is complete. To the end-user, the only differences are that the illusion-copy takes almost no disk space and almost no time to generate.

We can combine *rsync* and *cp -al* to create what appear to be multiple full backups of a filesystem without taking multiple disks' worth of space, as in:

```
rm -rf backup.3
mv backup.2 backup.3
mv backup.1 backup.2
cp -al backup.0 backup.1
rsync -a --delete source_directory/ backup.0/
```

If the above commands are run once every day, then backup.0, backup.1, backup.2, and backup.3 will appear to each be a full backup of *source_directory/* as it appeared today, yesterday, two days ago, and three days ago, respectively—complete, except that permissions and ownerships in old snapshots will get their most recent values (thanks to J.W. Schultz for pointing this out). In reality, the extra storage will be equal to the current size of *source_directory/* plus the total size of the changes over the last three days—exactly the same space that a full plus daily incremental backup with *dump* or *tar* would have taken.

This method is *much* better for network-based backups, since it's only necessary to do a full backup once, instead of once per week. Thereafter, only the changes need to be copied. Unfortunately, you can't *rsync* to a tape; you'll still need *dump* or *tar* for that.

If you have a spare machine, even a very low-end one, you can turn it into a dedicated backup server. Make it standalone, and keep it in a physically separate place—another room or even another building. Disable every single remote service on the backup server, and connect it only to a dedicated network interface on the source machine.

You can then perform backups from this machine using rsync over ssh (see "Keeping Parts of Filesystems in sync with rsync" **[Hack #41]**), and export the backups back to the original machine via read-only NFS. Then users can get to the snapshots themselves (without needing sysadmin intervention) and can't possibly change or delete them.

I'd consider this "pretty good" protection, but if you're (wisely) paranoid, or your job is on the line, build two backup servers. Then you can make sure that at least one of them is always offline.

Extensions: Hourly, Daily, and Weekly Snapshots

With a little bit of tweaking, you can make multiple-level rotating snapshots. On my system, for example, I keep the last four "hourly" snapshots (which are taken every four hours) as well as the last three "daily" snapshots (which are taken at midnight every day). You might also want to keep weekly or even monthly snapshots too, depending upon your needs and your available space.

I keep one script that runs every four hours to make and rotate hourly snapshots, and another script that runs once a day rotate the daily snapshots. There is no need to use *rsync* for the higher-level snapshots; just *cp -al* from the appropriate hourly one.

To make the automatic snapshots happen, I have added the following lines to root's *crontab*:

```
0 */4 * * * /usr/local/bin/make_snapshot.sh
0 13 * * * /usr/local/bin/daily_snapshot_rotate.sh
```

They cause make_snapshot.sh to be run every four hours on the hour and daily_snapshot_rotate.sh to be run every day at 13:00 (that is, 1:00 PM). Those scripts are included below.

Listing: make_snapshot.sh

```
#!/bin/bash
# ----------------------------------------------------------------------
# mikes handy rotating-filesystem-snapshot utility
# ----------------------------------------------------------------------
# RCS info: $Id: ch03,v 1.21 2003/03/07 20:16:38 ldolby Exp ldolby $
# ----------------------------------------------------------------------
# this needs to be a lot more general, but the basic idea is it makes
# rotating backup-snapshots of /home whenever called
# ----------------------------------------------------------------------


# ------------- system commands used by this script --------------------
ID=/usr/bin/id;
ECHO=/bin/echo;

MOUNT=/bin/mount;
RM=/bin/rm;
MV=/bin/mv;
CP=/bin/cp;
TOUCH=/bin/touch;

RSYNC=/usr/bin/rsync;


# ------------- file locations -----------------------------------------

MOUNT_DEVICE=/dev/hdb1;
SNAPSHOT_Rw=/root/snapshot;
EXCLUDES=/usr/local/etc/backup_exclude;


# ------------- the script itself --------------------------------------

# make sure we're running as root
if (( `$ID -u` != 0 )); then { $ECHO "Sorry, must be root. Exiting...";
exit; } fi

# attempt to remount the Rw mount point as Rw; else abort
$MOUNT -o remount,rw $MOUNT_DEVICE $SNAPSHOT_Rw ;
if (( $? )); then
{
$ECHO "snapshot: could not remount $SNAPSHOT_Rw readwrite";
exit;
}
fi;
```

```
# rotating snapshots of /home (fixme: this should be more general)

# step 1: delete the oldest snapshot, if it exists:
if [ -d $SNAPSHOT_Rw/home/hourly.3 ] ; then \
$RM -rf $SNAPSHOT_Rw/home/hourly.3 ; \
fi ;

# step 2: shift the middle snapshots(s) back by one, if they exist
if [ -d $SNAPSHOT_Rw/home/hourly.2 ] ; then \
$MV $SNAPSHOT_Rw/home/hourly.2 $SNAPSHOT_Rw/home/hourly.3 ; \
fi;
if [ -d $SNAPSHOT_Rw/home/hourly.1 ] ; then \
$MV $SNAPSHOT_Rw/home/hourly.1 $SNAPSHOT_Rw/home/hourly.2 ; \
fi;

# step 3: make a hard-link-only (except for dirs) copy of the latest
snapshot,
# if that exists
if [ -d $SNAPSHOT_Rw/home/hourly.0 ] ; then \
$CP -al $SNAPSHOT_Rw/home/hourly.0 $SNAPSHOT_Rw/home/hourly.1 ; \
fi;

# step 4: rsync from the system into the latest snapshot (notice that
# rsync behaves like cp --remove-destination by default, so the destination
# is unlinked first. If it were not so, this would copy over the other
# snapshot(s) too!
$RSYNC \
-va --delete --delete-excluded \
--exclude-from="$EXCLUDES" \
/home/ $SNAPSHOT_Rw/home/hourly.0 ;

# step 5: update the mtime of hourly.0 to reflect the snapshot time
$TOUCH $SNAPSHOT_Rw/home/hourly.0 ;

# and thats it for home.

# now remount the Rw snapshot mountpoint as readonly

$MOUNT -o remount,ro $MOUNT_DEVICE $SNAPSHOT_Rw ;
if (( $? )); then
{
$ECHO "snapshot: could not remount $SNAPSHOT_Rw readonly";
exit;
} fi;
```

If you notice above, I have added an excludes list to the rsync call. This is just to prevent the system from backing up garbage like web browser caches, which change frequently (so they'd take up space in every snapshot) but would be no loss if they were accidentally destroyed.

Listing: Daily_snapshot_rotate.sh

```
#!/bin/bash
# -------------------------------------------------------------------
# mikes handy rotating-filesystem-snapshot utility: daily snapshots
# -------------------------------------------------------------------
# RCS info: $Id: daily_snapshot_rotate.sh,v 1.2 2002/03/25 21:53:27 mrubel
Exp $
# -------------------------------------------------------------------
# intended to be run daily as a cron job when hourly.3 contains the
# midnight (or whenever you want) snapshot; say, 13:00 for 4-hour snapshots.
# -------------------------------------------------------------------


# ------------ system commands used by this script -------------------
ID=/usr/bin/id;
ECHO=/bin/echo;

MOUNT=/bin/mount;
RM=/bin/rm;
MV=/bin/mv;
cp=/bin/cp;


# ------------- file locations ------------------------------------------

MOUNT_DEVICE=/dev/hdb1;
SNAPSHOT_Rw=/root/snapshot;


# ------------- the script itself -------------------------------------

# make sure we're running as root
if (( `$ID -u` != 0 )); then { $ECHO "Sorry, must be root. Exiting...";
exit; } fi

# attempt to remount the Rw mount point as Rw; else abort
$MOUNT -o remount,rw $MOUNT_DEVICE $SNAPSHOT_Rw ;
if (( $? )); then
{
$ECHO "snapshot: could not remount $SNAPSHOT_Rw readwrite";
exit;
}
fi;


# step 1: delete the oldest snapshot, if it exists:
if [ -d $SNAPSHOT_Rw/home/daily.2 ] ; then \
$RM -rf $SNAPSHOT_Rw/home/daily.2 ; \
fi ;

# step 2: shift the middle snapshots(s) back by one, if they exist
if [ -d $SNAPSHOT_Rw/home/daily.1 ] ; then \
$MV $SNAPSHOT_Rw/home/daily.1 $SNAPSHOT_Rw/home/daily.2 ; \
fi;
if [ -d $SNAPSHOT_Rw/home/daily.0 ] ; then \
```

```
$MV $SNAPSHOT_Rw/home/daily.0 $SNAPSHOT_Rw/home/daily.1; \
fi;

# step 3: make a hard-link-only (except for dirs) copy of
# hourly.3, assuming that exists, into daily.0
if [ -d $SNAPSHOT_Rw/home/hourly.3 ] ; then \
$cp -al $SNAPSHOT_Rw/home/hourly.3 $SNAPSHOT_Rw/home/daily.0 ; \
fi;

# note: do *not* update the mtime of daily.0; it will reflect
# when hourly.3 was made, which should be correct.

# now remount the Rw snapshot mountpoint as readonly

$MOUNT -o remount,ro $MOUNT_DEVICE $SNAPSHOT_Rw ;
if (( $? )); then
{
$ECHO "snapshot: could not remount $SNAPSHOT_Rw readonly";
exit;
} fi;
```

Sample Output of ls -l /snapshot/home

```
total 28
drwxr-xr-x 12 root root 4096 Mar 28 00:00 daily.0
drwxr-xr-x 12 root root 4096 Mar 27 00:00 daily.1
drwxr-xr-x 12 root root 4096 Mar 26 00:00 daily.2
drwxr-xr-x 12 root root 4096 Mar 28 16:00 hourly.0
drwxr-xr-x 12 root root 4096 Mar 28 12:00 hourly.1
drwxr-xr-x 12 root root 4096 Mar 28 08:00 hourly.2
drwxr-xr-x 12 root root 4096 Mar 28 04:00 hourly.3
```

Notice that the contents of each of the subdirectories of */snapshot/home/* is a complete image of */home* at the time the snapshot was made. Despite the *w* in the directory access permissions, no one—not even root—can write to this directory; it's mounted read-only.

See also:

- "Keeping Parts of Filesystems in sync with rsync" **[Hack #41]**
- See the version at *http://www.mikerubel.org/computers/rsync_snapshots/)*

Working with ISOs and CDR/CDRWs

HACK #43   The command line makes working with ISOs a snap

There are a number of graphical CD-ROM utilities for Linux. Most of these are simply front-ends that call command line tools to do the actual work of building ISOs and burning disks. And graphical tools aren't much help if you're working on servers that don't have a console attached, unless you are running X remotely, perhaps over *ssh* (as in "X over ssh" **[Hack #70]**). With the *mkisofs* and *cdrecord* utilities installed, working with ISO images from the command line is very straightforward.

If you've never heard of an ISO, it's slang for an image of an ISO9660 filesystem. The ISO9660 format (along with a couple of common extensions) is the common format of data CD-ROMs.

To make an ISO image to prepare for burning in a CD burner, use *mkisofs*:

```
mkisofs -r /home/rob/ > /tmp/rob-home.iso
```

The *-r* tells *mkisofs* to build Rock Ridge extensions into the resulting image file. This means that long filenames and file permissions will be preserved when the disk is mounted on systems that support Rock Ridge. Linux has great support for RR, and using *-r* generally makes your life much easier when building disks designed to be used with Linux. Anyone can make an ISO of files they have read access to; you don't have to be root to run *mkisofs*. But for the rest of the commands in this hack, you'll likely need root privileges.

Note that *mkisofs* stores the contents of the directories you specify on the command line, not the directories themselves. In the above example, the ISO will have */home/rob/* mapped to its */*, with the contents of */home/rob/* filling the root of the CD.

If you need to make an ISO from an existing data CD, try this:

```
# dd if=/dev/cdrom of=image.iso
```

This will create an ISO image of the CD, in all glorious 650+MB, so be sure you have plenty of space before trying this. You may be able to make this go faster by manipulating the *bs* parameter of *dd*:

```
# dd if=/dev/cdrom of=image.iso bs=10k
```

The optimal setting is usually dependent on your drive and IDE controller, so try a couple of values to see what works best on your system.

To mount an ISO that you've made (either with *mkisofs* or straight from *dd*), try this:

```
# mkdir /mnt/iso
# mount -o loop,ro -t iso9660 ./image.iso /mnt/iso
```

If the *mount* command complains about Could not find any loop device, you might need to load the loopback driver:

```
# modprobe loop
```

Once the ISO is mounted, you should be able to cd /mnt/iso and look around at the filesystem contained in the image. If you find problems with it, simply umount /mnt/iso, remove the image file, and try again.

When you're ready to burn an ISO to CDR, try something like this:

```
# cdrecord -v speed=12 dev=0,0,0 -data image.iso
```

You should specify the writing speed of your burner (or slower) in the *speed=* option. If you need to erase a CDRW before burning the ISO, try passing the *blank=* parameter:

```
# cdrecord -v speed=12 dev=0,0,0 blank=fast -data image.iso
```

Getting a burner running under Linux isn't as hard as it used to be, thanks to the *ide-scsi* driver. This is a kernel module that makes IDE (and other) CD burners appear to be SCSI burners, which are much easier to program.

See also:

- For help on getting your burner running under Linux, check out the CD Writing HOWTO available at The Linux Documentation Project at *http://www.tldp.org/HOWTO/CD-Writing-HOWTO.html*

HACK #44   Burning a CD Without Creating an ISO File
Create a CD from another CD, the live filesystem, or even an http download

The safest method for making a copy of a CD is to first make an ISO and then burn the ISO (as in "Working with ISOs and CDR/CDRWs" **[Hack #43]**). But sometimes you don't have the space (or time) for the interim step of making a copy.

If you have a fast enough machine, you can usually burn straight from one CD to another. This usually works best when the source CD and the burner are on separate device chains (like primary and secondary IDE, or IDE and SCSI).

To make a real-time copy of a CD, give this a try:

```
# dd if=/dev/hdb | cdrecord -v speed=12 dev=0,0,0 fs=8m -data -
```

The - argument to *cdrecord* means that the data track should be read from STDIN instead of from a file. The *dd* line is feeding the *cdrecord* pipe with a copy of the CD in the slave drive on the primary IDE chain (*hdb*). The *fs=8m* parameter makes the write FIFO a bit bigger, to help offset any momentary pipeline hiccups. As long as your bus is up to the task (and your machine isn't otherwise too occupied) then this method will work fine.

Likewise, there is no real need to make an ISO before burning a copy of data from the filesystem. Give this a try:

```
# mkisofs -r /home/ftp/ | cdrecord -v speed=12 dev=0,0,0 fs=8m -data -
```

Like the *dd* above, *mkisofs* writes to STDOUT by default. This is then fed to STDIN of the *cdrecord* process, burning the ISO as it is created, in real time. This saves the need to keep a copy of the ISO file lying around your filesystem. Be warned, if your data source is greater than the size of your CDR (somewhere between 650 and 700MB) then you'll end up with a coaster but not a usable disk.

Get an idea of how much space you'll need with *du* first:

```
# du -hs /home/ftp/
412M /home/ftp
```

Perfect. A 412M ISO will fit nicely.

Anything that can print ISO data to STDOUT is a candidate for the left-hand side of a pipeline. How about doing a real-time network burn?

```
root@catlin:~# mkisofs -r backup/ \
  | ssh florian "cdrecord -v speed=12 dev=0,0,0 fs=8m -data -"
```

Or copying a local CD to a remote burner over the network?

```
root@catlin:~# dd if=/dev/cdrom \
  | ssh florian "cdrecord -v speed=12 dev=0,0,0 fs=8m -data -"
```

Or even downloading an ISO and burning it, all in one pass?

```
# curl http://my.server.com/slackware-8.1-install.iso \
  | cdrecord -v speed=0 dev=0,0,0 fs=8m -data -
```

I wouldn't recommend attempting to do a network burn over wireless; you'll want a nice, solid 100Mbps Ethernet cable for this job. And the download example might look silly, but it does illustrate the power of the Unix pipeline: any program can be plugged into nearly any other, to make things happen that the designer of either program likely hadn't ever thought.

Networking
Hacks #45–53

There was once a time when a network admin was a person who spent all of his time trying to figure out how to make machines talk to each other over a network. It seems that lately, much of a network admins' time is spent trying to figure out how to restrict access to their machines via the network, thus keeping out undesirables while still allowing legitimate traffic to pass through.

Fortunately, the netfilter firewall in Linux provides a very flexible interface to the kernel's networking decisions. Using the *iptables* command, you can create firewall rules that let you create a rich and very flexible access policy. It can not only match packets based on port, interface and MAC addresses, but also on data contained within the packet and even by the rate that packets are received. This information can be used to help weed out all sorts of attempted attacks, from port floods to virii.

But locking users out isn't nearly as much fun as connecting users together. After all the whole point of a computer network is to allow people to communicate with each other! We'll take a look at some more unusual methods for controlling the flow of network traffic, from the remote port forwarding to various forms of IP tunnelling. By the time we've explored IP encapsulation and user space tunnels like *vtun*, we'll see how it is possible to build networks on top of the Internet that behave in all sorts of unexpected and surprisingly useful ways.

HACK #45 Creating a Firewall from the Command Line of any Server

You don't have to have a dedicated firewall to benefit from using iptables

The netfilter firewall (available in Linux 2.4 and later) allows for very flexible firewall manipulation from the command line. Using *iptables* can take a while to get used to, but it allows for a very expressive syntax that lets you create complex (and hopefully useful ;) firewall rules.

Even if your machine isn't a "real" firewall (that is, it only has one network interface and isn't protecting other machines) the filter functionality can be very useful. Suppose you want to allow telnet access to this machine (just in case something happens to *ssh* or its libraries) but don't want to permit it from just anywhere on the Net. You could use a tcpwrapper (by populating */etc/hosts.allow* and */etc/hosts.deny*, and setting up */etc/inetd.conf* appropriately). Or, you could use *iptables* with a line like this:

```
iptables -A INPUT -t filter -s ! 208.201.239.36 -p tcp --dport 23 -j DROP
```

Generally, most people want to permit unrestricted access from trusted hosts, block all access from known problem hosts, and allow something in between for everyone else. Here is one method for using a whitelist, blacklist, and restricted port policy simultaneously.

```
#!/bin/sh
#
# A simple firewall initialization script
#
WHITELIST=/usr/local/etc/whitelist.txt
BLACKLIST=/usr/local/etc/blacklist.txt
ALLOWED="22 25 80 443"


#
# Drop all existing filter rules
#
iptables -F


#
# First, run through $WHITELIST, accepting all traffic from the hosts and
networks
# contained therein.
#
for x in `grep -v ^# $WHITELIST | awk '{print $1}'`; do
echo "Permitting $x..."
iptables -A INPUT -t filter -s $x -j ACCEPT
done


#
# Now run through $BLACKLIST, dropping all traffic from the hosts and
networks
# contained therein.
#
for x in `grep -v ^# $BLACKLIST | awk '{print $1}'`; do
echo "Blocking $x..."
iptables -A INPUT -t filter -s $x -j DROP
done


#
# Next, the permitted ports: What will we accept from hosts not appearing
# on the blacklist?
#
```

```
for port in $ALLOWED; do
echo "Accepting port $port..."
iptables -A INPUT -t filter -p tcp --dport $port -j ACCEPT
done


#
# Finally, unless it's mentioned above, and it's an inbound startup request,
# just drop it.
#
iptables -A INPUT -t filter -p tcp --syn -j DROP
```

Be sure to specify all of the ports you'd like to include in the $ALLOWED variable at the top of the script. If you forget to include 22, you won't be able to *ssh* into the box!

The */usr/local/etc/blacklist.txt* file is populated with IP addresses, host names, and networks like this:

```
1.2.3.4 # Portscanned on 8/15/02
7.8.9.0/24 # Who knows what evil lurks therein
r00tb0y.script-kiddie.coop # $0 s0rR33 u 31337 h4x0r!
```

Likewise, */usr/local/etc/whitelist.txt* contains the "good guys" that should be permitted no matter what the other rules specify:

```
11.22.33.44 # My workstation
208.201.239.0/26 # the local network
```

Since we're only grabbing lines that don't start with #, you can comment out an entire line if you need to. The next time you run the script, any commented entries will be ignored. We run an *iptables -F* at the beginning to flush all existing filter entries, so you can simply run the script again when you make changes to *blacklist.txt*, *whitelist.txt*, or the ports specified in $ALLOWED.

Also note that this script only allows for TCP connections. If you need to also support UDP, ICMP, or some other protocol, run another pass just like the $ALLOWED for loop, but include your additional ports and protocols (passing *-p udp* or *-p icmp* to *iptables*, for example).

Be careful about using whitelists. Any IPs or networks appearing on this list will be permitted to access all ports on your machine. In some circumstances, a clever miscreant may be able to send forged packets apparently originating from one of those IPs, if they can find out ahead of time (or logically deduce) what IPs appear on your whitelist. This kind of attack is difficult to perform, but it is possible. If you are particularly paranoid, you might only allow whitelist addresses from networks that aren't routable over the Internet but are used on your internal network.

It is extremely useful to have console access while working with new firewall rules (you can't lock yourself out of the console with *iptables*!) If you get confused about where you are when working with *iptables*, remember that you can always list out all rules with *iptables -L*, and start over by issuing *iptables -F*. If *iptables -L* seems to hang, try *iptables -L -n* to show the rules without doing any DNS resolution—your rules might accidentally be prohibiting DNS requests.

You can do a lot with simple filtering, but there's much more to *iptables* than just the filter target.

See also:

- Netfilter HOWTO at *www.netfilter.org*
- "iptables Tips & Tricks" **[Hack #47]**

HACK #46 Simple IP Masquerading
Set up NAT on your gateway in ten seconds

If you have a private network that needs to share an Internet connection with one IP address, you'll want to use IP Masquerading on your gateway machine. Luckily, with *iptables* this is a simple two-liner:

```
# echo "1" > /proc/sys/net/ipv4/ip_forward
# iptables -t nat -A POSTROUTING -o $EXT_IFACE -j MASQUERADE
```

where $EXT_IFACE is the outside interface of your gateway. Now any machines that reside on a network on any of the other interfaces in your gateway will be able to "get out" to the Internet. As far as the Net is concerned, all traffic originates from your gateway's external IP address.

There was a time when one had to worry about miscreants on the external network sending forged packets to your gateway, claiming to be originating from the internal network. These packets would obligingly be masqueraded by the kernel, and leave your network as if they were legitimate traffic. This made it possible for anyone to launch attacks that apparently originated from your network, making very bad times for the hapless gateway owner.

I say that this was a problem, because recent kernels give you a free firewall rule to deal with exactly this problem, called *rp_filter*. With *rp_filter* enabled, if a packet that arrives on an interface has a source address that doesn't match the corresponding routing table entry, it is dropped. This effectively prevents IP spoofing and allows simple (and safe) masquerading with the example above.

In the very unlikely event that *rp_filter* is causing problems for you, you can deactivate it very easily:

```
# echo "0" > /proc/sys/net/ipv4/conf/all/rp_filter
```

See also:

- "iptables Tips & Tricks" [Hack #47]

iptables Tips & Tricks

#47   Make your firewall do far more than filter packets with iptables

iptables is the next generation of firewall software for the netfilter project. It provides all of the functionality of its predecessor, ipchains, in addition to support for stateful firewalling. *iptables* also supports a framework for extending its capabilities with loadable modules. Here are a few tricks you can use with the base distribution of *iptables*, as well as some of the extensible modules available for *iptables*.

For these examples, we'll assume that the following environment variables are already set:

$EXT_IFACE
: The external (public) interface of the firewall

$INT_IFACE
: The inside (private) interface of the firewall

$DEST_IP
: The ultimate requested destination of this packet

You can use *iptables* to limit new inbound TCP packets to prevent a Denial of Service attack. This is accomplished with the following rules:

```
# Create syn-flood chain for detecting Denial of Service attacks
iptables -t nat -N syn-flood

# Limit 12 connections per second (burst to 24)
iptables -t nat -A syn-flood -m limit --limit 12/s --limit-burst 24 \
  -j RETURN
iptables -t nat -A syn-flood -j DROP

# Check for DoS attack
iptables -t nat -A PREROUTING -i $EXT_IFACE -d $DEST_IP -p tcp --syn \
  -j syn-flood
```

These rules limit new inbound TCP connections (packets with SYN bit set) to 12 per second after 24 connections per second have been seen.

Using *iptables*, a transparent Squid proxy can be set up. This will transparently cache and log all outbound HTTP requests to the Internet. It requires no modification to the user's browser and is useful for blocking unwanted content. This is accomplished with the following *iptables* rule at the top of the PREROUTING chain:

```
# Setup transparent Squid proxy for internal network
#
# For details on setting up Squid, see:
# http://www.linuxdoc.org/HOWTO/mini/TransparentProxy.html
#
iptables -t nat -A PREROUTING -i $INT_IFACE -p tcp --dport 80 \
  -j REDIRECT --to-port 3128
```

This rule redirects outgoing requests on TCP port 80 to a Squid proxy running on TCP port 3128 on the firewall.

Arbitrary TCP flags can be matched with iptables. This means you can block XMAS-tree (all flags set) and NULL packets with the following rules:

```
# DROP XMAS & NULL TCP packets
iptables -t nat -A PREROUTING -p tcp --tcp-flags ALL ALL -j DROP
iptables -t nat -A PREROUTING -p tcp --tcp-flags ALL NONE -j DROP
```

Advanced iptables Features

iptables has introduced several advanced firewall features that are available by patching the Linux kernel. These patches can be obtained from *http://www. netfilter.org/* by downloading the patch-o-matic version corresponding to the *iptables* version you are using. Patch-o-matic patches are *iptables* patches that are not yet available in the mainstream Linux kernel. Some of the patches are experimental and should be used with caution.

Using the experimental netfilter *psd* patch, *iptables* can detect and block inbound port scans with the following rule:

```
# DROP inbound port scans
iptables -t nat -A PREROUTING -i $EXT_IFACE -d $DEST_IP -m psd -j DROP
```

Using the experimental netfilter *iplimit* patch, iptables can limit the number of connections received from a particular IP address with the following rule:

```
# DROP packets from hosts with more than 16 active connections
iptables -t nat -A PREROUTING -i $EXT_IFACE -p tcp --syn -d $DEST_IP -m
iplimit --iplimit-above 16 -j DROP
```

One of the most powerful netfilter patches allows you to match packets based on their content. The experimental string-matching patch allows you to filter out packets that match a certain string. This is helpful to filter out the CodeRed or Nimda viruses before they hit your web server. The following rules achieve this:

```
# DROP HTTP packets related to CodeRed and Nimda viruses silently
iptables -t filter -A INPUT -i $EXT_IFACE -p tcp -d $DEST_IP --dport http \
  -m string --string "/default.ida?" -j DROP
```

```
iptables -t filter -A INPUT -i $EXT_IFACE -p tcp -d $DEST_IP --dport http \
  -m string --string ".exe?/c+dir" -j DROP
iptables -t filter -A INPUT -i $EXT_IFACE -p tcp -d $DEST_IP --dport http \
  -m string --string ".exe?/c+tftp" -j DROP
```

Port forwarding is now native to *iptables*. The nat table uses a feature called Destination NAT in the PREROUTING chain to accomplish this. The following rule can be used to port forward HTTP requests to a system (10.0.0.3) on the internal network:

```
# Use DNAT to port forward http
iptables -t nat -A PREROUTING ! -i $INT_IFACE -p tcp --destination-port \
  80 -j DNAT --to 10.0.0.3:80
```

You can also port forward UDP packets. If you port forward traffic for a particular port, you do not need to have a corresponding rule in the INPUT chain to accept inbound connections on that port. This will only work if the destination is on a network on a locally attached interface (that is, not to destinations on foreign networks). Take a look at tools like *rinetd* ("Forwarding TCP Ports to Arbitrary Machines" **[Hack #48]**) or *nportredird* if you need traffic to forward to remote networks.

If you port forward your HTTP requests to an internal host, you can filter out the CodeRed virus in the FORWARD chain with this rule:

```
iptables -t filter -A FORWARD -p tcp --dport http \
  -m string --string "/default.ida?" -j DROP
```

Using *iptables* can be challenging at first, but its flexibility makes it a tremendously useful tool. If you ever get stuck while developing your rule set (and you will), remember that your two best friends are *iptables -L -n* and *tcpdump* (maybe followed by a quick session with *ethereal*).

See also:

- "Forwarding TCP Ports to Arbitrary Machines" **[Hack #48]**
- The Linux Firewall HOWTO

Forwarding TCP Ports to Arbitrary Machines

#48   Make non-local services appear to come from local ports

As we saw in "iptables Tips & Tricks" **[Hack #47]**, it is simple to forward TCP and UDP ports from a firewall to internal hosts using *iptables*. But what if you need to forward traffic from arbitrary addresses to a machine that isn't even on your network? Try an application layer port forwarder, like *rinetd*.

This simple bit of code is a couple of years old but is small, efficient, and perfect for just this sort of problem. Unpack the archive and simply run *make*, and you'll be presented with a tiny *rinetd* binary that will let you forward TCP ports to your heart's content. Unfortunately, UDP ports aren't supported by *rinetd*.

The configuration file is dead simple:

```
[Source Address] [Source Port] [Destination Address] [Destination Port]
```

Each port to be forwarded is specified on a separate line. The source and destination addresses can be either host names or IP addresses, and an IP address of 0.0.0.0 binds *rinetd* to every available local IP:

```
0.0.0.0 80 some.othersite.gov 80
216.218.203.211 25 123.45.67.89 25
0.0.0.0 5353 my.shellserver.us 22
```

Save the file to */etc/rinetd.conf*, and copy *rinetd* to somewhere handy (like */usr/local/sbin/*, for example.) Then start it by simply running *rinetd*.

The first example forwards all web traffic destined for any local address to *some.othersite.gov*. Note that this will only work if there isn't another process (like Apache) already bound to local port 80.

The next forwards inbound SMTP traffic destined for 216.218.203.211 to the mail server at 123.45.67.89 (but doesn't interfere with any SMTP agents bound to other local IPs). The final example will forward any inbound traffic on port 5353 to the *ssh* server on *my.shellserver.us*. These all work without NAT or any special kernel configuration. Simply run *rinetd*, and it daemonizes and starts listening on the ports you have specified.

This utility can really help ease the transition when renumbering or physically relocating servers, as services can appear to remain up on the original IP (even though they are actually coming from another network entirely). *rinetd* doesn't even need to run as root, if you're only binding to ports higher than 1024. There are also extensive options for providing access control and keeping logs. This tiny tool is well worth having handy for when TCP port indirection is called.

See also:

- *http://www.boutell.com/rinetd/*
- "iptables Tips & Tricks" [Hack #47]

Using Custom Chains in iptables
Keep your firewall rules under control with custom chains

By default, the *iptables* filter table consists of three chains: INPUT, FOR-WARD, and OUTPUT. You can add as many custom chains as you like to help simplify managing large rule sets. Custom chains behave just as built-in chains, introducing logic that must be passed before the ultimate fate of a packet is determined.

To create a new chain, use the *-N* switch:

```
root@mouse:~# iptables -N fun-filter
```

You can see which chains are defined at any time with the standard *-L* switch:

```
root@mouse:~# iptables -L
Chain INPUT (policy ACCEPT)
target prot opt source destination

Chain FORWARD (policy ACCEPT)
target prot opt source destination

Chain OUTPUT (policy ACCEPT)
target prot opt source destination

Chain fun-filter (0 references)
target prot opt source destination
```

In order to make use of your custom chain, you'll have to jump to it from somewhere. Let's add a jump to the fun-filter chain we've just created straight from the INPUT chain:

```
root@mouse:~# iptables -t filter -A INPUT -j fun-filter
```

Now your custom chain can grow to any sort of complexity you like. For example, you may want to match packets based on the source MAC address:

```
root@mouse:~# iptables -A fun-filter -m mac --mac-source 11:22:33:aa:bb:cc \
  -j ACCEPT
root@mouse:~# iptables -A fun-filter -m mac --mac-source de:ad:be:ef:00:42 \
  -j ACCEPT
root@mouse:~# iptables -A fun-filter -m mac --mac-source 00:22:44:fa:ca:de
  -j REJECT --reject-with icmp-host-unreachable
root@mouse:~# iptables -A fun-filter -j RETURN
```

The RETURN jump at the end of the table makes processing resume back in the chain that called this one (in this case, back in the INPUT chain). Again, show what all of your tables look like with the *-L* switch:

```
root@mouse:~# iptables -L
Chain INPUT (policy ACCEPT)
target prot opt source destination
fun-filter all -- anywhere anywhere

Chain FORWARD (policy ACCEPT)
target prot opt source destination

Chain OUTPUT (policy ACCEPT)
target prot opt source destination

Chain fun-filter (0 references)
target prot opt source destination
ACCEPT all -- anywhere anywhere MAC 11:22:33:AA:BB:CC
ACCEPT all -- anywhere anywhere MAC DE:AD:BE:EF:00:42
REJECT all -- anywhere anywhere MAC 00:22:44:FA:CA:DE reject-with icmp-host-
unreachable
RETURN all -- anywhere anywhere
```

You can jump into any number of custom defined chains and even jump
between them. This helps to isolate rules that you're developing from the
standard system policy rules, and enable and disable them easily. If you
want to stop using your custom chain temporarily, you can simply delete the
jump from the INPUT chain (rather than flushing the entire custom chain):

```
root@mouse:~# iptables -t filter -D INPUT -j fun-filter
```

If you decide to delete your custom chain, use -X:

```
root@mouse:~# iptables -X fun-filter
```

Note that there can be no references to your custom chain if you try to
delete it; use -F to flush the chain first if there are still rules referring to your
chain.

When properly managed, even the most complex iptables rulesets can be
easily read, if you use intuitively named custom chains.

See also:

- "iptables Tips & Tricks" [Hack #47]

HACK #50 Tunneling: IPIP Encapsulation
IP tunneling with the Linux IPIP driver

If you have never worked with IP tunneling before, you might want to take a
look at the Advanced Router HOWTO before continuing. Essentially, an IP
tunnel is much like a VPN, except that not every IP tunnel involves encryption. A machine that is "tunneled" into another network has a virtual interface configured with an IP address that isn't local, but exists on a remote

network. Usually, all (or most) network traffic is routed down this tunnel, so remote clients appear to exist on the network services, or more generally, to connect to any two private networks together using the Internet to carry the tunnel traffic.

If you want to perform simple IP-within-IP tunneling between two machines, you might want to try IPIP. It is probably the simplest tunnel protocol available and will also work with *BSD, Solaris, and even Windows. Note that IPIP is simply a tunneling protocol and does not involve any sort of encryption. It is also only capable of tunneling unicast packets; if you need to tunnel multicast traffic, take a look at GRE tunneling in "Tunneling: IPIP Encapsulation" [Hack #50].

Before we rush right into our first tunnel, you'll need a copy of the advanced routing tools (specifically the *ip* utility). You can get the latest authoritative copy at *ftp://ftp.inr.ac.ru/ip-routing/*. Be warned, the advanced routing tools aren't especially friendly, but they allow you to manipulate nearly any facet of the Linux networking engine.

Assume that you have two private networks (10.42.1.0/24 and 10.42.2.0/24) and that these networks both have direct Internet connectively via a Linux router at each network. The "real" IP address of the first network router is 240.101.83.2, and the "real" IP of the second router is 251.4.92.217. This isn't very difficult, so let's jump right in.

First, load the kernel module on both routers:

```
# modprobe ipip
```

Next, on the first network's router (on the 10.42.1.0/24 network), do the following:

```
# ip tunnel add mytun mode ipip remote 251.4.92.217 \
    local 240.101.83.2 ttl 255
# ifconfig mytun 10.42.1.1
# route add -net 10.42.2.0/24 dev mytun
```

And on the second network's router (on the 10.42.2.0/24), reciprocate:

```
# ip tunnel add mytun mode ipip remote 240.101.83.2 \
    local 251.4.92.217 ttl 255
# ifconfig tun10 10.42.2.1
# route add -net 10.42.1.0/24 dev mytun
```

Naturally, you can give the interface a more meaningful name than mytun if you like. From the first network's router, you should be able to ping 10.42.2.1, and from the second network router, you should be able to ping 10.42.1.1. Likewise, every machine on the 10.42.1.0/24 network should be able to route to every machine on the 10.42.2.0/24 network, just as if the Interent weren't even there.

If you're running a Linux 2.2x kernel, you're in luck: here's a shortcut that you can use to avoid having to use the Advanced Router tools package at all. After loading the module, try these commands instead:

```
# ifconfig tun10 10.42.1.1 pointopoint 251.4.92.217
# route add -net 10.42.2.0/24 dev tun10
```

And on the second network's router (on the 10.42.2.0/24):

```
# ifconfig tun10 10.42.2.1 pointopoint 240.101.83.2
# route add -net 10.42.1.0/24 dev tun10
```

That's all there is to it.

If you can ping the opposite router but other machines on the network don't seem to be able to pass traffic beyond the router, make sure that both routers are configured to forward packets between interfaces:

```
# echo "1" > /proc/sys/net/ipv4/ip_forward
```

If you need to reach networks beyond 10.42.1.0 and 10.42.2.0, simply add additional route add -net... lines. There is no configuration needed on any of your network hosts, as long as they have a default route to their respective router (which they definitely should, since it is their router, after all).

To bring the tunnel down: On both routers, bring down the interface and delete it, if you like:

```
# ifconfig mytun down
# ip tunnel del mytun
```

(or, in Linux 2.2):

```
# ifconfig tun10 down
```

The kernel will very politely clean up your routing table for you when the interface goes away.

See also:

- Advanced Routing HOWTO, *http://www.tldp.org/HOWTO/ Adv-Routing-HOWTO/*
- Advanced Routing Tools (*iproute2*), *ftp://ftp.inr.ac.ru/ip-routing/*

HACK #51 Tunneling: GRE Encapsulation

IP tunnels with Generic Routing Encapsulation

GRE stands for Generic Routing Encapsulation. Like IPIP tunneling (see "Tunneling: IPIP Encapsulation" [Hack #50]), GRE is an unencrypted encapsulation protocol. The main advantages of using GRE instead of IPIP are it supports multicast packets, and it will interoperate with Cisco routers.

Just as with the IPIP tunneling hack, we'll assume that you have two private networks (10.42.1.0/24 and 10.42.2.0/24) and that these networks both have direct Internet connectivity via a Linux router at each network. The "real" IP address of the first network router is 240.101.83.2, and the "real" IP of the second router is 251.4.92.217.

Again, as with IPIP tunneling ("Tunneling: IPIP Encapsulation" [Hack #50]), you will need a copy of the advanced routing tools package (there is no shortcut for GRE tunnels in Linux 2.2 that I've been able to find). Once you have the *iproute2* package installed, we'll begin by loading the GRE kernel module on both routers:

```
# modprobe ip_gre
```

On the first network's router, set up a new tunnel device:

```
# ip tunnel add gre0 mode gre remote 251.4.92.217 local 240.101.83.2 ttl 255
# ip addr add 10.42.1.254 dev gre0
# ip link set gre0 up
```

Note that you can call the device anything you like; gre0 is just an example. Also, that 10.42.1.254 address can be any available address on the first network, but shouldn't be 10.42.1.1 (the IP already bound to its internal interface). Now, add your network routes via the new tunnel interface:

```
# ip route add 10.42.2.0/24 dev gre0
```

The first network is finished. Now for the second:

```
# ip tunnel add gre0 mode gre remote 240.101.83.2 local 251.4.92.217 ttl 255
# ip addr add 10.42.2.254 dev gre0
# ip link set gre0 up
# ip route add 10.42.1.0/24 dev gre0
```

Again, the 10.42.2.254 address can be any available address on the second network. Feel free to add as many ip route add ... dev gre0 commands as you need.

That's it! You should now be able to pass packets between the two networks as if the Internet didn't exist. A tracroute from the first network should show just a couple of hops to any host in the second network (although you'll probably notice a fair bit of latency when crossing the 10.42.2.254 hop, unless you're really well connected). If you're having trouble, check the notes in the IPIP example and don't panic. Your best friend when debugging new network configurations is probably a packet sniffer like *tcpdump* or *ethereal*. Running a tcpdump 'proto \icmp' on both routers while pinging will give you a very detailed overview of what's going on.

To bring the tunnel down, run this on both routers:

```
# ip link set gre0 down
# ip tunnel del gre0
```

See also:

- Advanced Routing HOWTO, *http://www.tlpd.org/HOWTO/ Adv-Routing-HOWTO/*

- Advanced Routing Tools (*iproute2*), *ftp://ftp.inr.ac.ru/ip-routing/*

Using vtun over ssh to Circumvent NAT

Connect two networks together using vtun and a single ssh connection

vtun is a user space tunnel server, allowing entire networks to be tunneled to each other using the *tun* universal tunnel kernel driver. Connections can be made directly over IP or even over PPP or serial. this technique can be particularly useful when general network access is restricted by an intervening firewall, as all IP traffic will be encryted and forwarded over a single TCP port (that is, over a single *ssh* connection).

The procedure described below will allow a host with a private IP address (10.42.4.6) to bring up a new tunnel interface with a real, live routed IP address (208.201.239.33) that works as expected, as if the private network weren't even there. We'll do this by bringing up the tunnel, dropping the default route, then adding a new default route via the other end of the tunnel.

To begin with, here is the (pre-tunneled) configuration of the network.

```
root@client:~# ifconfig eth2
eth2 Link encap:Ethernet HWaddr 00:02:2D:2A:27:EA
inet addr:10.42.3.2 Bcast:10.42.3.63 Mask:255.255.255.192
UP BROADCAST RUNNING MULTICAST MTU:1500 Metric:1
RX packets:662 errors:0 dropped:0 overruns:0 frame:0
TX packets:733 errors:0 dropped:0 overruns:0 carrier:0
collisions:0 txqueuelen:100
RX bytes:105616 (103.1 Kb) TX bytes:74259 (72.5 Kb)
Interrupt:3 Base address:0x100

root@client:~# route
Kernel IP routing table
Destination Gateway Genmask Flags Metric Ref Use Iface
10.42.3.0 * 255.255.255.192 U 0 0 0 eth2
loopback * 255.0.0.0 U 0 0 0 lo
default 10.42.3.1 0.0.0.0 UG 0 0 0 eth2
```

As you can see, our local network is 10.42.3.0/26, our IP is 10.42.3.2, and our default gateway is 10.42.3.1. This gateway provides network address translation (NAT) to the internet. Here's what our path looks like to yahoo.com:

```
root@client:~# traceroute -n yahoo.com
traceroute to yahoo.com (64.58.79.230), 30 hops max, 40 byte packets
1 10.42.3.1 2.848 ms 2.304 ms 2.915 ms
```

```
 2 209.204.179.1 16.654 ms 16.052 ms 19.224 ms
 3 208.201.224.194 20.112 ms 20.863 ms 18.238 ms
 4 208.201.224.5 213.466 ms 338.259 ms 357.7 ms
 5 206.24.221.217 20.743 ms 23.504 ms 24.192 ms
 6 206.24.210.62 22.379 ms 30.948 ms 54.475 ms
 7 206.24.226.104 94.263 ms 94.192 ms 91.825 ms
 8 206.24.238.61 97.107 ms 91.005 ms 91.133 ms
 9 206.24.238.26 95.443 ms 98.846 ms 100.055 ms
10 216.109.66.7 92.133 ms 97.419 ms 94.22 ms
11 216.33.98.19 99.491 ms 94.661 ms 100.002 ms
12 216.35.210.126 97.945 ms 93.608 ms 95.347 ms
13 64.58.77.41 98.607 ms 99.588 ms 97.816 ms
```

In this example, we'll be connecting to a tunnel server on the Internet at 208.201.239.5. It has two spare live IP addresses (208.201.239.32 and 208. 201.239.33) to be used for tunneling. We'll refer to that machine as the *server*, and our local machine as the *client*.

Now, let's get the tunnel running. To begin with, load the *tun* driver on both machines:

```
# modprobe tun
```

It is worth noting that the *tun* driver will sometimes fail if the kernel version on the server and client don't match. For best results, use a recent kernel (and the same version, e.g., 2.4.19) on both machines.

On the server machine, install this file to */usr/local/etc/vtund.conf*:

```
options {
port 5000;
ifconfig /sbin/ifconfig;
route /sbin/route;
syslog auth;
}

default {
compress no;
speed 0;
}

home {
type tun;
proto tcp;
stat yes;
keepalive yes;

pass sHHH; # Password is REQUIRED.

up {
ifconfig "%% 208.201.239.32 pointopoint 208.201.239.33";

program /sbin/arp "-Ds 208.201.239.33 %% pub";
program /sbin/arp "-Ds 208.201.239.33 eth0 pub";
```

```
route "add -net 10.42.0.0/16 gw 208.201.239.33";
};

down {
program /sbin/arp "-d 208.201.239.33 -i %%";
program /sbin/arp "-d 208.201.239.33 -i eth0";

route "del -net 10.42.0.0/16 gw 208.201.239.33";
};
}
```

and launch the *vtund* server with this command:

```
root@server:~# vtund -s
```

Now, you'll need a *vtund.conf* for the client side. Try this one, again in */usr/ local/etc/vtund.conf*:

```
options {
port 5000;
ifconfig /sbin/ifconfig;
route /sbin/route;
}

default {
compress no;
speed 0;
}

home {
type tun;
proto tcp;
keepalive yes;

pass sHHH; # Password is REQUIRED.

up {
ifconfig "%% 208.201.239.33 pointopoint 208.201.239.32 arp";

route "add 208.201.239.5 gw 10.42.3.1";
route "del default";
route "add default gw 208.201.239.32";

};

down {
route "del default";
route "del 208.201.239.5 gw 10.42.3.1";
route "add default gw 10.42.3.1";
};
}
```

Finally, run this command on the client:

```
root@client:~# vtund -p home server
```

Presto! You now not only have a tunnel up between client and server, but have added a new default route via the other end of the tunnel. Take a look at what happens when we traceroute to yahoo.com with the tunnel in place:

```
root@client:~# traceroute -n yahoo.com
traceroute to yahoo.com (64.58.79.230), 30 hops max, 40 byte packets
1 208.201.239.32 24.368 ms 28.019 ms 19.114 ms
2 208.201.239.1 21.677 ms 22.644 ms 23.489 ms
3 208.201.224.194 20.41 ms 22.997 ms 23.788 ms
4 208.201.224.5 26.496 ms 23.8 ms 25.752 ms
5 206.24.221.217 26.174 ms 28.077 ms 26.344 ms
6 206.24.210.62 26.484 ms 27.851 ms 25.015 ms
7 206.24.226.103 104.22 ms 114.278 ms 108.575 ms
8 206.24.238.57 99.978 ms 99.028 ms 100.976 ms
9 206.24.238.26 103.749 ms 101.416 ms 101.09 ms
10 216.109.66.132 102.426 ms 104.222 ms 98.675 ms
11 216.33.98.19 99.985 ms 99.618 ms 103.827 ms
12 216.35.210.126 104.075 ms 103.247 ms 106.398 ms
13 64.58.77.41 107.219 ms 106.285 ms 101.169 ms
```

This means that any server processes running on client are now fully available to the Internet, at IP address 208.201.239.33. This has happened all without making a single change (e.g., port forwarding) on the gateway 10.42.3.1.

Here's what the new tunnel interface looks like on the client:

```
root@client:~# ifconfig tun0
tun0 Link encap:Point-to-Point Protocol
inet addr:208.201.239.33 P-t-P:208.201.239.32 Mask:255.255.255.255
UP POINTOPOINT RUNNING MULTICAST MTU:1500 Metric:1
RX packets:39 errors:0 dropped:0 overruns:0 frame:0
TX packets:39 errors:0 dropped:0 overruns:0 carrier:0
collisions:0 txqueuelen:10
RX bytes:2220 (2.1 Kb) TX bytes:1560 (1.5 Kb)
```

and here's the updated routing table. Note that we still need to keep a host route to the tunnel server's IP address via our old default gateway, otherwise the tunnel traffic couldn't get out:

```
root@client:~# route
Kernel IP routing table
Destination Gateway Genmask Flags Metric Ref Use Iface
208.201.239.5 10.42.3.1 255.255.255.255 UGH 0 0 0 eth2
208.201.239.32 * 255.255.255.255 UH 0 0 0 tun0
10.42.3.0 * 255.255.255.192 U 0 0 0 eth2
10.42.4.0 * 255.255.255.192 U 0 0 0 eth0
loopback * 255.0.0.0 U 0 0 0 lo
default 208.201.239.32 0.0.0.0 UG 0 0 0 tun0
```

To bring down the tunnel, simply kill the *vtund* process on the client. This will restore all network settings back to their original state.

This method works fine, if you trust *vtun* to use strong encryption and to be free from remote exploits. Personally, I don't think you can be too paranoid when it comes to machines connected to the Internet. To use *vtun* over *ssh* (and therefore rely on the strong authentication and encryption that *ssh* provides) simply forward port 5000 on client to the same port on server. Give this a try:

```
root@client:~# ssh -f -N -c blowfish -C -L5000:localhost:5000 server
root@client:~# vtund -p home localhost
root@client:~# traceroute -n yahoo.com
traceroute to yahoo.com (64.58.79.230), 30 hops max, 40 byte packets
 1 208.201.239.32 24.715 ms 31.713 ms 29.519 ms
 2 208.201.239.1 28.389 ms 36.247 ms 28.879 ms
 3 208.201.224.194 48.777 ms 28.602 ms 44.024 ms
 4 208.201.224.5 38.788 ms 35.608 ms 35.72 ms
 5 206.24.221.217 37.729 ms 38.821 ms 43.489 ms
 6 206.24.210.62 39.577 ms 43.784 ms 34.711 ms
 7 206.24.226.103 110.761 ms 111.246 ms 117.15 ms
 8 206.24.238.57 112.569 ms 113.2 ms 111.773 ms
 9 206.24.238.26 111.466 ms 123.051 ms 118.58 ms
10 216.109.66.132 113.79 ms 119.143 ms 109.934 ms
11 216.33.98.19 111.948 ms 117.959 ms 122.269 ms
12 216.35.210.126 113.472 ms 111.129 ms 118.079 ms
13 64.58.77.41 110.923 ms 110.733 ms 115.22 ms
```

In order to discourage connections to *vtund* on port 5000 of the server, add a netfilter rule to drop connections from the outside world:

```
root@server:~# iptables -A INPUT -t filter -i eth0 -p tcp --dport 5000 -j
DROP
```

This will allow local connections to get through (since they use loopback), and therefore require an *ssh* tunnel to server before accepting a connection.

As you can see, this can be an extremely handy tool to have around. In addition to giving live IP addresses to machines behind a NAT, you can effectively connect any two networks together if you can obtain a single *ssh* connection between them (originating from either direction).

If your head is swimming from the *vtund.conf* configuration previously, or if you're terminally lazy and don't want to figure out what to change when setting up your own client's *vtund.conf*, take a look at the Automatic *vtund.conf* generator, in "Automatic vtund.conf Generator" [Hack #53].

Notes:

- The session name (*home* in the above example) must match on the client AND server sides, or you'll get an ambiguous "server disconnected" message.

- The same goes for the *password* field in the *vtund.conf*. It must be present AND match on both sides, or the connection won't work.

- If you're having trouble connecting, make sure you're using the same kernel version on both sides, and that the server is up and running (try `telnet server 5000` from the client side to verify that the server is happy).
- Try the direct method first, then get ssh working once you are happy with your *vtund.conf* settings.
- If you're still having trouble, check */etc/syslog.conf* to see where your *auth* facility messages are going, and watch that log on both the client and server when trying to connect.

See also:

- *vtun*'s homepage: *http://vtun.sourceforge.net/*
- */usr/src/linux/Documentation/networking/tuntap.txt*
- man vtund; man vtund.conf
- "Automatic vtund.conf Generator" **[Hack #53]**
- "Creating a Firewall from the Command Line of any Server" **[Hack #45]**
- "Forwarding Ports over ssh" **[Hack #71]**

Automatic vtund.conf Generator
#53   Generate a vtund.conf on the fly to match changing network conditions

If you've just come from "Tunneling: GRE Encapsulation" **[Hack #51]**, this script will generate a working *vtund.conf* for the client side automatically.

If you haven't read "Tunneling: GRE Encapsulation" **[Hack #51]** (or if you've never used *vtun*), then go back and read it before attempting to grok this bit of Perl. Essentially, it attempts to take the guesswork out of changing the routing table around on the client side by auto-detecting the default gateway and building the *vtund.conf* accordingly.

To configure the script, take a look at the Configuration section. The first line of $Config contains the addresses, port, and secret that we used in "Tunneling: GRE Encapsulation" **[Hack #51]**. The second is there simply as an example of how to add more.

To run the script, either call it as *vtundconf home*, or set $TunnelName to the one to which you want to default. Or better yet, make symlinks to the script like this:

```
# ln -s vtundconf home
# ln -s vtundconf tunnel2
```

Then generate the appropriate *vtund.conf* by calling the symlink directly:

```
# vtundconf home > /usr/local/etc/vtund.conf
```

You might be wondering why anyone would go to all of the trouble to make a script to generate a *vtund.conf* in the first place. Once you get the settings right, you'll never have to change them, right?

Well, usually that is the case. But consider the case of a Linux laptop that uses many different networks in the course of the day (say a DSL line at home, Ethernet at work, and maybe a wireless connection at the local coffee shop). By running *vtund.conf* once at each location, you will have a working configuration instantly, even if your IP and gateway is assigned by DHCP. This makes it very easy to get up and running quickly with a live, routable IP address, regardless of the local network topology.

Incidentally, *vtund* and *vtund.conf* currently runs great on Linux, FreeBSD, OS X, Solaris, and a few others.

Listing: vtundconf

```perl
#!/usr/bin/perl -w

# vtund wrapper in need of a better name.
#
# (c)2002 Schuyler Erle & Rob Flickenger
#
################ CONFIGURATION

# If TunnelName is blank, the wrapper will look at @ARGV or $0.
#
# Config is TunnelName, LocalIP, RemoteIP, TunnelHost, TunnelPort, Secret
#
my $TunnelName = "";
my $Config = q{
home 208.201.239.33 208.201.239.32 208.201.239.5 5000 sHHH
tunnel2 10.0.1.100 10.0.1.1 192.168.1.4 6001 foobar
};


################ MAIN PROGRAM BEGINS HERE

use POSIX 'tmpnam';
use IO::File;
use File::Basename;
use strict;

# Where to find things...
#
$ENV{PATH} = "/bin:/usr/bin:/usr/local/bin:/sbin:/usr/sbin:/usr/local/sbin";
my $IP_Match = '((?:\d{1,3}\.){3}\d{1,3})'; # match xxx.xxx.xxx.xxx
my $Ifconfig = "ifconfig -a";
my $Netstat = "netstat -rn";
my $Vtund = "/bin/echo";
my $Debug = 1;
```

```
# Load the template from the data section.
#
my $template = join( "", <DATA> );

# Open a temp file -- adapted from Perl Cookbook, 1st Ed., sec. 7.5.
#
my ( $file, $name ) = ("", "");
$name = tmpnam( ) until $file = IO::File->new( $name, O_RDWR|O_CREAT|O_EXCL
);
END { unlink( $name ) or warn "Can't remove temporary file $name!\n"; }

# If no TunnelName is specified, use the first thing on the command line,
# or if there isn't one, the basename of the script.
# This allows users to symlink different tunnel names to the same script.
#
$TunnelName ||= shift(@ARGV) || basename($0);
die "Can't determine tunnel config to use!\n" unless $TunnelName;

# Parse config.
#
my ($LocalIP, $RemoteIP, $TunnelHost, $TunnelPort, $Secret);
for (split(/\r*\n+/, $Config)) {
my ($conf, @vars) = grep( $_ ne "", split( /\s+/ ));
next if not $conf or $conf =~ /^\s*#/o; # skip blank lines, comments
if ($conf eq $TunnelName) {
($LocalIP, $RemoteIP, $TunnelHost, $TunnelPort, $Secret) = @vars;
last;
}
}

die "Can't determine configuration for TunnelName '$TunnelName'!\n"
unless $RemoteIP and $TunnelHost and $TunnelPort;

# Find the default gateway.
#
my ( $GatewayIP, $ExternalDevice );

for (qx{ $Netstat }) {
# In both Linux and BSD, the gateway is the next thing on the line,
# and the interface is the last.
#
if ( /^(?:0.0.0.0|default)\s+(\S+)\s+.*?(\S+)\s*$/o ) {
$GatewayIP = $1;
$ExternalDevice = $2;
last;
}
}

die "Can't determine default gateway!\n" unless $GatewayIP and
$ExternalDevice;

# Figure out the LocalIP and LocalNetwork.
#
```

```perl
my ( $LocalNetwork );
my ( $iface, $addr, $up, $network, $mask ) = "";

sub compute_netmask {
($addr, $mask) = @_;
# We have to mask $addr with $mask because linux /sbin/route
# complains if the network address doesn't match the netmask.
#
my @ip = split( /\./, $addr );
my @mask = split( /\./, $mask );
$ip[$_] = ($ip[$_] + 0) & ($mask[$_] + 0) for (0..$#ip);
$addr = join(".", @ip);
return $addr;
}

for (qx{ $Ifconfig }) {
last unless defined $_;

# If we got a new device, stash the previous one (if any).
if ( /^([^\s:]+)/o ) {
if ( $iface eq $ExternalDevice and $network and $up ) {
$LocalNetwork = $network;
last;
}
$iface = $1;
$up = 0;
}

# Get the network mask for the current interface.
if ( /addr:$IP_Match.*?mask:$IP_Match/io ) {
# Linux style ifconfig.
compute_netmask($1, $2);
$network = "$addr netmask $mask";
} elsif ( /inet $IP_Match.*?mask 0x([a-f0-9]{8})/io ) {
# BSD style ifconfig.
($addr, $mask) = ($1, $2);
$mask = join(".", map( hex $_, $mask =~ /(..)/gs ));
compute_netmask($addr, $mask);
$network = "$addr/$mask";
}

# Ignore interfaces that are loopback devices or aren't up.
$iface = "" if /\bLOOPBACK\b/o;
$up++ if /\bUP\b/o;
}

die "Can't determine local IP address!\n" unless $LocalIP and $LocalNetwork;

# Set OS dependent variables.
#
my ( $GW, $NET, $PTP );
if ( $^O eq "linux" ) {
$GW = "gw"; $PTP = "pointopoint"; $NET = "-net";
} else {
```

```
$GW = $PTP = $NET = "";
}

# Parse the config template.
#
$template =~ s/(\$\w+)/$1/gee;

# Write the temp file and execute vtund.
#
if ($Debug) {
print $template;
} else {
print $file $template;
close $file;
system("$Vtund $name");
}

__DATA__

options {
port $TunnelPort;
ifconfig /sbin/ifconfig;
route /sbin/route;
}

default {
compress no;
speed 0;
}

$TunnelName { # 'mytunnel' should really be `basename $0` or some such
# for automagic config selection
type tun;
proto tcp;
keepalive yes;

pass $Secret;

up {
ifconfig "%% $LocalIP $PTP $RemoteIP arp";
route "add $TunnelHost $GW $GatewayIP";
route "delete default";
route "add default $GW $RemoteIP";
route "add $NET $LocalNetwork $GW $GatewayIP";
};

down {
ifconfig "%% down";
route "delete default";
route "delete $TunnelHost $GW $GatewayIP";
route "delete $NET $LocalNetwork";
route "add default $GW $GatewayIP";
};
}
```

## CHAPTER FIVE

Monitoring
Hacks #54–65

It is difficult to know how to tune a running system if you have no idea how a system "normally" runs. By asking careful questions of the system (and interpreting the answers correctly), you can avoid poking around at variables in the dark and make effective changes exactly where they need to be made.

This is where log files can be your best friend. Treat them well, and pay them the attention they're due; you will learn volumes about how your system is being used. But if you simply let them fill up your disks, they can be a source of much confusion. With the proper tools and techniques, your system logs will be concise and detailed enough to tell you exactly what you need to know.

But sometime, the information you're after doesn't get logged anywhere, but is expressed in the running Linux system, either as a pinpoint check of system resources or data on the network itself. Incidentally, we won't examine full-blown system monitoring and trending packages (such as Nagios or MRTG) in this chapter but instead will look at ways to interrogate your system to get specific information about what's going on *right now*. We'll also see a couple of ways of to detect potential problems before they happen and even how to automatically deal with catastrophic failures when they do occur.

HACK
#54 Steering syslog

Make syslog work harder, and spend less time looking through huge log files

The default syslog installation on many distributions doesn't do a very good job of filtering classes of information into separate files. If you see a jumble of messages from *sendmail*, *sudo*, *bind*, and other system services in */var/log/ messages*, then you should probably review your */etc/syslog.conf*.

There are a number of facilities and priorities on which syslog can filter. For easy reference, here they are:

Steering syslog

Facilities	Priorities
auth	debug
auth-priv	info
cron	notice
daemon	warning
kern	err
lpr	crit
mail	alert
news	emerg
syslog	
user	
uucp	
local0 - local7	

Note that applications decide for themselves at what facility and priority to log (and the best applications let you choose), so they may not always be logged as you expect. Here's a sample */etc/syslog.conf* that attempts to shuffle around what gets logged where:

```
auth.warning /var/log/auth
mail.err /var/log/maillog
kern.* /var/log/kernel
cron.crit /var/log/cron
*.err;mail.none /var/log/syslog
*.info;auth.none;mail.none /var/log/messages

#*.=debug /var/log/debug

local0.info /var/log/cluster
local1.err /var/log/spamerica
```

All of the above lines will log the specified priority (or higher) to the respective file. The special priority none tells syslog not to bother logging the specified facility at all. The local0 through local7 facilities are supplied for use with your own programs, however you see fit. For example, the */var/log/ spamerica* file fills with *local1.err* (or higher) messages that are generated by our spam processing job. It's nice to have those messages separate from the standard mail delivery log (in */var/log/maillog.*)

That commented *.=debug line is useful when debugging daemonized services. It tells syslog to specifically log only debug priority messages of any facility and generally shouldn't be running (unless you don't mind filling your disks with debug logs). Another approach is to log debug information to a fifo. This will make debug logs take up no space but will disappear unless a process is watching it. To log to a fifo, first create it in the filesystem:

```
# mkfifo -m 0664 /var/log/debug
```

Then amend the debug line in *syslog.conf* to include a | like this:

```
*.=debug |/var/log/debug
```

Now debug information is constantly logged to the fifo, and can be viewed with a command like less -f /var/log/debug. This is also handy to set up if you want a process to constantly watch all system messages and perhaps notify you via email when a critical system message is seen. Try making a fifo called */var/log/monitor*, and add a rule like this to your *syslog.conf*:

```
*.* |/var/log/monitor
```

Now every message (at every priority) is passed to the */var/log/monitor* fifo, and any process watching it can react accordingly, all without taking up any disk space.

Mark Who?

Do you notice a bunch of lines like this in */var/log/messages*?

```
Dec 29 18:33:35 catlin -- MARK --
Dec 29 18:53:35 catlin -- MARK --
Dec 29 19:13:35 catlin -- MARK --
Dec 29 19:33:35 catlin -- MARK --
Dec 29 19:53:35 catlin -- MARK --
Dec 29 20:13:35 catlin -- MARK --
Dec 29 20:33:35 catlin -- MARK --
Dec 29 20:53:35 catlin -- MARK --
Dec 29 21:13:35 catlin -- MARK --
```

These are generated by the mark functionality of syslog, as a way of "touching base" with the system, so that you can theoretically tell if syslog has unexpectedly died. Most times, this only serves to fill your logfiles, and unless you are having problems with syslog, you probably don't need it. To turn this off, pass the *-m 0* switch to syslogd (after first killing any running syslogd), like this:

```
# killall syslogd; /usr/sbin/syslogd -m 0
```

Remote Logging

Modern versions of syslogd disable the ability to receive logs from remote machines and for good reason. Without safeguards in place, it is entirely possible for a random miscreant to fill up your disk with bogus syslog messages, as there is no host authentication available in syslog. Still, it is very handy to have a centralized syslog, particularly when dealing with a cluster of machines.

To turn on remote reception on the master, start syslogd with *-r*:

```
# /usr/sbin/syslogd -m 0 -r
```

On each of the machines you'd like to log from, add this to the *syslog.conf*:

```
*.* @master.syslog.host.com
```

(Naturally, with your own hostname or IP address after the @.) It is a very good idea to protect the syslog port on your syslog server. It listens on UDP port 514 and is easily filtered with this *iptables* command:

```
# iptables -A INPUT -t filter -p udp --dport 514 -s ! $LOCAL_NET -j DROP
```

where $LOCAL_NET is the network (or host) that you would like to receive sylog messages from (e.g., 192.168.1.0/24 or florian.nocat.net).

Once your system logs are better organized, it becomes much easier to find the information you're looking for. Even then, system logs can get a bit overwhelming. For even more help dealing with log files, check out "Colorized Log Analysis in Your Terminal" **[Hack #75]**.

HACK #55   Watching Jobs with watch
Use watch to repeatedly run any command, and show you the results

If you have ever had a long-running background process, chances are you are used to repeatedly checking to see if the command has finished using *ps* and *grep*:

```
mc@escher:~$ ps ax |grep tar
10303 ? S 0:00 bash -c cd /; tar cf - home
10304 ? S 0:42 tar cf - home
mc@escher:~$ ps ax |grep tar
10303 ? S 0:00 bash -c cd /; tar cf - home
10304 ? S 0:43 tar cf - home
```

Or maybe you're *ftp*ing a file and forget the *hash* command (and for some reason, aren't using *ncftp, scp,* or *wget* or *curl*), so you have no idea how far along your transfer is. Naturally, you log in again and take a look at the file with *ls*:

```
mc@escher:~$ ls -l xfree86.tgz
-rw-r--r-- 1 rob users 12741812 Jun 13 2001 xfree86.tgz
mc@escher:~$ ls -l xfree86.tgz
-rw-r--r-- 1 rob users 12744523 Jun 13 2001 xfree86.tgz
```

Any time you find yourself running a command over and over again, try the *watch* command. It will repeatedly cycle over any command you give it, and whatever interval you'd like (defaulting to 2 seconds). It clears the screen on each pass, making a nice, easy to read display.

```
mc@escher:~$ watch 'ps ax |grep tar'

Every 2s: ps ax |grep tar|grep -v pts/0 Fri Sep 6 00:22:01 2002

10303 ? S 0:00 bash -c cd /; tar cf - home
10304 ? S 0:42 tar cf - home
```

You'll only need to enclose the command in single quotes if you're using pipes (or other special characters that you don't want interpolated before *watch* runs). To specify a different time interval, try the *-n* switch:

```
mc@escher:~$ watch -n1 ls -l xfree86.tgz

Every 1s: ls -l xfree86.tgz Fri Sep 6 00:31:41 2002

-rw-r--r-- 1 rob users 12756042 Jun 13 2001 xfree86.tgz
```

It will even highlight the differences on each pass, making changes leap out in reverse type. Try the *-d* switch for that (it's especially nice for watching the output of a netstat -a | grep ESTAB, to watch network connections come and go. Think of *watch* as your obsessive-compulsive little buddy. It obsesses at your slightest whim, so you don't have to. To exit, hit ^C.

See also:

- man watch

What's Holding That Port Open?
#56   Associate a process with the port it is bound to easily with netstat

Generating a list of network ports that are in the Listen state on a Linux server is simple with netstat:

```
root@catlin:~# netstat -ln
Active Internet connections (only servers)
Proto Recv-Q Send-Q Local Address Foreign Address State
tcp 0 0 0.0.0.0:5280 0.0.0.0:* LISTEN
tcp 0 0 0.0.0.0:80 0.0.0.0:* LISTEN
tcp 0 0 10.42.3.2:53 0.0.0.0:* LISTEN
tcp 0 0 10.42.4.6:53 0.0.0.0:* LISTEN
tcp 0 0 127.0.0.1:53 0.0.0.0:* LISTEN
tcp 0 0 0.0.0.0:22 0.0.0.0:* LISTEN
udp 0 0 10.42.3.2:53 0.0.0.0:*
udp 0 0 10.42.4.6:53 0.0.0.0:*
udp 0 0 127.0.0.1:53 0.0.0.0:*
udp 0 0 0.0.0.0:67 0.0.0.0:*
raw 0 0 0.0.0.0:1 0.0.0.0:* 7
```

So, we see the usual services (a web server on port 80, DNS on port 53, *ssh* on port 22, *dhcp* on port 67), but what's that process listening on 5280?

Finding out which programs are actually bound to those ports is simple with recent versions of netstat. As long as you're root, just add the *-p* switch (for programs):

```
root@catlin:~# netstat -lnp
Active Internet connections (only servers)
Proto Recv-Q Send-Q Local Address Foreign Address State PID/Program name
```

```
tcp 0 0 0.0.0.0:5280 0.0.0.0:* LISTEN 698/perl
tcp 0 0 0.0.0.0:80 0.0.0.0:* LISTEN 217/httpd
tcp 0 0 10.42.3.2:53 0.0.0.0:* LISTEN 220/named
tcp 0 0 10.42.4.6:53 0.0.0.0:* LISTEN 220/named
tcp 0 0 127.0.0.1:53 0.0.0.0:* LISTEN 220/named
tcp 0 0 0.0.0.0:22 0.0.0.0:* LISTEN 200/sshd
udp 0 0 0.0.0.0:32768 0.0.0.0:* 220/named
udp 0 0 10.42.3.2:53 0.0.0.0:* 220/named
udp 0 0 10.42.4.6:53 0.0.0.0:* 220/named
udp 0 0 127.0.0.1:53 0.0.0.0:* 220/named
udp 0 0 0.0.0.0:67 0.0.0.0:* 222/dhcpd
raw 0 0 0.0.0.0:1 0.0.0.0:* 7 222/dhcpd
```

Ah, that's better. PID 698 is a Perl process that is bound to port 5280. We now hunt it down with *ps*:

```
root@catlin:~# ps auwex |grep -w 698
nocat 698 0.0 2.0 5164 3840 ? S Aug25 0:00 /usr/bin/perl -w ./bin/gateway
PWD=/usr/local/nocat HOSTNAME=catlin.r
```

The ps aweux shows us all (a) non-interactive (x) processes with user information (u) in wide format (w) with some environment bits appended (e). We then *grep* on word boundaries (-w) for the PID.

That's better: now we know that the nocat user is in the */usr/local/nocat/* running *bin/gateway*, a Perl process that is listening on port 5280. Without the *-p* switch on *netstat*, associating an open port with a particular process is much trickier.

Incidentally, if you're not root, then the system won't disclose which programs are running on which ports. If you see an error like this:

```
(No info could be read for "-p": geteuid( )=1000 but you should be root.)
```

then come back when you're root! (Or see "Make sudo Work Harder" **[Hack #12]** for how to *sudo* yourself into an amazing simulation of root.)

Checking On Open Files and Sockets with lsof

Easily see which files, directories, and sockets your running processes are holding open

Have you ever tried to *umount* a filesystem, only to find that some process was still using it?

```
root@mouse:~# umount /mnt
umount: /mnt: device is busy
```

To quickly hunt down what processes are still using */mnt*, try the *lsof* tool:

```
root@mouse:~# lsof /mnt
COMMAND PID USER FD TYPE DEVICE SIZE NODE NAME
```

```
bash 30951 rob cwd DIR 7,0 1024 2 /mnt
```

Ah, apparently rob is *cd*'d to */mnt* (since his *bash* process has it set as its *cwd*). *lsof* will list all open files, directories, libraries, sockets, and devices associated with a particular process. In the above example, we specified a mount point and had *lsof* show us the associated processes. To do the reverse (show files associated with a PID), use the *-p* switch:

```
root@mouse:~# lsof -p 30563
COMMAND PID USER FD TYPE DEVICE SIZE NODE NAME
inetd 30563 root cwd DIR 3,3 408 2 /
inetd 30563 root rtd DIR 3,3 408 2 /
inetd 30563 root txt REG 3,3 21432 39140 /usr/sbin/inetd
inetd 30563 root mem REG 3,3 432647 11715 /lib/ld-2.2.3.so
inetd 30563 root mem REG 3,3 4783716 11720 /lib/libc-2.2.3.so
inetd 30563 root mem REG 3,3 19148 11708 /lib/libnss_db-2.2.so
inetd 30563 root mem REG 3,3 238649 11728 /lib/libnss_files-2.2.3.so
inetd 30563 root mem REG 3,3 483324 11710 /lib/libdb-3.1.so
inetd 30563 root 0u CHR 1,3 647 /dev/null
inetd 30563 root 1u CHR 1,3 647 /dev/null
inetd 30563 root 2u CHR 1,3 647 /dev/null
inetd 30563 root 4u IPv4 847222 TCP *:telnet (LISTEN)
inetd 30563 root 5u IPv4 560439 TCP *:cvspserver (LISTEN)
```

If you'd rather specify the process by name, use *-c*:

```
root@mouse:~# lsof -c syslogd
COMMAND PID USER FD TYPE DEVICE SIZE NODE NAME
syslogd 25627 root cwd DIR 3,3 408 2 /
syslogd 25627 root rtd DIR 3,3 408 2 /
syslogd 25627 root txt REG 3,3 27060 5538 /usr/sbin/syslogd
syslogd 25627 root mem REG 3,3 432647 11715 /lib/ld-2.2.3.so
syslogd 25627 root mem REG 3,3 4783716 11720 /lib/libc-2.2.3.so
syslogd 25627 root mem REG 3,3 238649 11728 /lib/libnss_files-2.2.3.so
syslogd 25627 root mem REG 3,3 75894 11719 /lib/libnss_dns-2.2.3.so
syslogd 25627 root mem REG 3,3 225681 11724 /lib/libresolv-2.2.3.so
syslogd 25627 root mem REG 3,3 19148 11708 /lib/libnss_db-2.2.so
syslogd 25627 root mem REG 3,3 483324 11710 /lib/libdb-3.1.so
syslogd 25627 root 0u unix 0xdcc2d5b0 775254 /dev/log
syslogd 25627 root 1w REG 3,3 135744 5652 /var/log/debug
syslogd 25627 root 2w REG 3,3 107459 5651 /var/log/syslog
syslogd 25627 root 3w REG 3,3 107054 58317 /var/log/maillog
syslogd 25627 root 4w REG 3,3 4735 16 /var/log/authlog
```

You can also specify special devices on the command line. For example, let's see what the user on *pts/0* is up to:

```
rob@mouse:~# lsof /dev/pts/0
COMMAND PID USER FD TYPE DEVICE SIZE NODE NAME
bash 29816 rob 0u CHR 136,0 2 /dev/pts/0
bash 29816 rob 1u CHR 136,0 2 /dev/pts/0
bash 29816 rob 2u CHR 136,0 2 /dev/pts/0
bash 29816 rob 255u CHR 136,0 2 /dev/pts/0
lsof 30882 root 0u CHR 136,0 2 /dev/pts/0
```

```
lsof 30882 root 1u CHR 136,0 2 /dev/pts/0
lsof 30882 root 2u CHR 136,0 2 /dev/pts/0
```

If you need to specify multiple switches, they are ORed with each other by default. To require all switches (that is, to AND them) include the -*a* flag on each switch you want to AND. For example, to see all of the open files associated with *vi* processes that rob is running, try this:

```
root@mouse:~# lsof -u rob -ac vi
COMMAND PID USER FD TYPE DEVICE SIZE NODE NAME
vi 31059 rob cwd DIR 3,3 2824 39681 /home/rob
vi 31059 rob rtd DIR 3,3 408 2 /
vi 31059 rob txt REG 3,3 554504 9799 /usr/bin/vim
vi 31059 rob mem REG 3,3 432647 11715 /lib/ld-2.2.3.so
vi 31059 rob mem REG 3,3 282178 2825 /lib/libncurses.so.5.2
vi 31059 rob mem REG 3,3 76023 2831 /usr/lib/libgpm.so.1.18.0
vi 31059 rob mem REG 3,3 4783716 11720 /lib/libc-2.2.3.so
vi 31059 rob mem REG 3,3 249120 11721 /lib/libnss_compat-2.2.3.so
vi 31059 rob mem REG 3,3 357644 11725 /lib/libnsl-2.2.3.so
vi 31059 rob 0u CHR 136,1 3 /dev/pts/1
vi 31059 rob 1u CHR 136,1 3 /dev/pts/1
vi 31059 rob 2u CHR 136,1 3 /dev/pts/1
vi 31059 rob 3u REG 3,3 4096 15 /home/rob/.sushi.c.swp
```

If you'd like to examine open sockets and their associated processes (like a *netstat -p*), try the -*i* switch:

```
rob@mouse:~# lsof -i
COMMAND PID USER FD TYPE DEVICE SIZE NODE NAME
sshd 69 root 3u IPv4 61 TCP *:ssh (LISTEN)
mysqld 126 mysql 3u IPv4 144 TCP *:3306 (LISTEN)
mysqld 128 mysql 3u IPv4 144 TCP *:3306 (LISTEN)
mysqld 129 mysql 3u IPv4 144 TCP *:3306 (LISTEN)
httpd 24905 root 22u IPv4 852520 TCP *:443 (LISTEN)
httpd 24905 root 23u IPv4 852521 TCP *:www (LISTEN)
httpd 28383 www 4u IPv4 917713 TCP nocat.net:www->65.192.187.158:8648
(ESTABLISHED)
httpd 28389 www 4u IPv4 917714 TCP nocat.net:www->65.192.187.158:9832
(ESTABLISHED)
httpd 28389 www 22u IPv4 852520 TCP *:443 (LISTEN)
httpd 28389 www 23u IPv4 852521 TCP *:www (LISTEN)
exim 29879 exim 0u IPv4 557513 TCP *:smtp (LISTEN)
inetd 30563 root 4u IPv4 847222 TCP *:telnet (LISTEN)
inetd 30563 root 5u IPv4 560439 TCP *:cvspserver (LISTEN)
sshd 30973 root 4u IPv4 901571 TCP nocat.net:ssh->some.where.net:52543
(ESTABLISHED)
sshd 30991 rob 4u IPv4 901577 TCP nocat.net:ssh->some.where.else.net:52544
(ESTABLISHED)
```

Note that you must be root to run *lsof* for many functions, including retrieving open socket information. *lsof* is a complex and very flexible tool, giving you as much (or as little) detail as you need about what files are in use by every running process on your system.

See also:

- The latest version of *lsof* can be downloaded at *ftp://vic.cc.purdue.edu/pub/tools/unix/lsof/*.

Monitor System Resources with top

Use the top utility to get a better overview of what your system is up to

The *top* command can give you up-to-the-second reporting of system load, memory usage, and CPU utilization. It is distributed as part of the *procps* package. The simplest way to get started is to simply run *top* from the command line:

```
$ top
```

You'll be presented with a screenful of information updated every two seconds.

```
3:54pm up 1 day, 16 min, 2 users, load average: 0.00, 0.00, 0.00
38 processes: 37 sleeping, 1 running, 0 zombie, 0 stopped
CPU states: 0.0% user, 0.7% system, 0.0% nice, 99.2% idle
Mem: 189984K av, 155868K used, 34116K free, 0K shrd, 42444K buff
Swap: 257032K av, 0K used, 257032K free 60028K cached

PID USER PRI NI SIZE RSS SHARE STAT %CPU %MEM TIME COMMAND
6195 rob 14 0 1004 1004 800 R 0.5 0.5 0:00 top
1 root 8 0 212 212 180 S 0.0 0.1 0:13 init
2 root 9 0 0 0 SW 0.0 0.0 0:00 keventd
3 root 9 0 0 0 SW 0.0 0.0 0:00 kswapd
4 root 9 0 0 0 SW 0.0 0.0 0:00 kreclaimd
5 root 9 0 0 0 SW 0.0 0.0 0:00 bdflush
6 root 9 0 0 0 SW 0.0 0.0 0:00 kupdated
8 root -1 -20 0 0 SW< 0.0 0.0 0:00 mdrecoveryd
176 root 9 0 788 788 680 S 0.0 0.4 0:00 syslogd
179 root 9 0 1228 1228 444 S 0.0 0.6 0:00 klogd
182 root 8 0 1228 1228 1104 S 0.0 0.6 0:06 sshd
184 root 8 0 616 616 520 S 0.0 0.3 0:00 crond
186 daemon 9 0 652 652 560 S 0.0 0.3 0:00 atd
197 root 9 0 2544 2544 2396 S 0.0 1.3 0:00 httpd
200 root 9 0 3740 3740 1956 S 0.0 1.9 0:00 named
202 root 9 0 1004 1004 828 S 0.0 0.5 0:00 dhcpd
203 root 9 0 504 504 444 S 0.0 0.2 0:00 agetty
```

Hit ? while top is running to get a list of available commands. A couple of very useful display keys are M (which sorts on resident memory size), P (which sorts by CPU usage again), S (to toggle cumulative runtime, that is, how long each process and all of its children have been running, in CPU seconds), and i (to stop displaying idle processes.)

If you're running *top* as root, there are a couple of other interactive and sorting commands that you'll likely find useful. The u key lets you filter out all processes except those owned by a given user. Follow that up with k, which lets you interactively kill a given PID (with any signal you like.) This can be really handy for hunting down runaway processes, and killing them from inside top (maybe even copying-and-pasting the offending PID to avoid the dreaded kill typo).

It can be handy to leave *top* running in a terminal window on busy machines that you're logged into, but aren't otherwise working on. If you'd like to see a continual load average display in the title bar of a login window (for a sort of mini-top while remaining in your shell), check out "Constant Load Average Display in the Titlebar" **[Hack #59]**.

See also:

- "Manipulating Processes Symbolically with procps" **[Hack #17]**
- "Constant Load Average Display in the Titlebar" **[Hack #59]**
- *procps* home: *ftp://people.redhat.com/johnsonm/procps/*

H A C K
#59
Constant Load Average Display in the Titlebar

Make your title bar work harder, so you don't have to.

If you have managed a Linux server for any length of time, you're probably intimately familiar with the *top* utility. (If not, stop reading and immediately go type top in the nearest terminal window, and hit ? when you get bored.) If you've managed a number of Linux servers, then you probably know what it's like to have several *top*s running in multiple windows, all competing for desktop real estate.

In computing, wasted resources are resources that could be better spent helping you. Why not run a process that updates the titlebar of your terminal with the current load average in real time, regardless of what else you're running?

Save this as a script called *tl*, and save it to your *~/bin* directory:

Listing: tl

```
#!/usr/bin/perl -w

use strict;
$|++;

my $host=`/bin/hostname`;
chomp $host;

while(1) {
```

```
open(LOAD,"/proc/loadavg") || die "Couldn't open /proc/loadavg: $!\n";

my @load=split(/ /,<LOAD>);
close(LOAD);

print "\033]0;";
print "$host: $load[0] $load[1] $load[2] at ", scalar(localtime);
print "\007";

sleep 2;
}
```

When you'd like to have your titlebar replaced with the name, load average, and current time of the machine you're logged into, just run *tl&*. It will happily go on running in the background, even if you're running an interactive program like *vim*. If you have your titlebar already set to show the current working directory, no problem. When you *cd*, the current working directory is flashed momentarily, and then replaced with the time and load average again. Need to see that directory one more time? Just hit Enter on a blank line, and it will flash again.

Now instead of spreading terminals around and completely covering your desktop, you can stack a pile of them together (leaving only your titlebars showing), and enjoy an "at a glance" view of how hard each machine is working. When you need to work on a machine, just bring that window to the foreground, and immediately begin working. Of course, this is all available to you without installing a single piece of software on your local machine.

When you're finished, don't forget to killall tl before logging out. Or if you're terminally lazy, try this:

```
$ echo 'killall tl > /dev/null 2>&1' >> ~/.bash_logout
```

That will kill all of your running *tl* jobs on logout, without even having to lift a finger. System administration just keeps getting easier, doesn't it?

Network Monitoring with ngrep
#60

See who's doing what, with a grep for your network interface

The *ngrep* utility is an interesting packet capture tool, similar to *tcpdump* or *snoop*. It is unique in that it attempts to make it as easy as possible to match which captured packets to print, by using a *grep* compatible format (complete with regular expressions and a bunch of GNU grep's switches). It also converts the packets to ASCII (or hex) before printing.

For example, to see the contents of all http GET requests that pass through your router, try this:

```
# ngrep -q GET
```

If you're only interested in a particular host, protocol, or port (or other packet matching criteria), you can specify a bpf filter as well as a data pattern. It uses a syntax similar to *tcpdump*:

```
# ngrep -qi rob@nocat.net port 25

T 10.42.4.7:65174 -> 209.204.146.26:25 [AP]
RCPT TO:<rob@nocat.net>..

T 209.204.146.26:25 -> 10.42.4.7:65174 [AP]
250 2.1.5 <rob@nocat.net>... Recipient ok..

T 10.42.4.7:65174 -> 209.204.146.26:25 [AP]
Date: Sun, 8 Sep 2002 23:55:18 -0700..Mime-Version: 1.0 (Apple Message fram
ework v543)..Content-Type: text/plain; charset=US-ASCII; format=flowed..Sub
ject: Greetings.....From: John Doe <johnd@somewhere.else.com>..To: rob@noca
t.net..Content-Transfer-Encoding: 7bit..Message-Id: <19DB8C16-C3C1-11D6-B23
9-0003936D6AE0@somewhere.else.com>..X-Mailer: Apple Mail v2)....What does t
hat pgp command you mentioned do again?....Thanks,.....--A Friend....
```

Since *ngrep* prints to STDOUT, you can do post-processing on the output to make a nice printing filter. If you process the output yourself, add the *-l* switch to make the output line buffered. For example, if you're interested in what people on your network are searching for online, try something like this bit of Perl.

Listing: go-ogle

```perl
#!/usr/bin/perl
use Socket;
$|++;

open(NG,"ngrep -lqi '(GET|POST).*/(search|find)' |");
print "Go ogle online.\n";
my ($go,$i) = 0;
my %host = ( );

while(<NG>) {

if(/^T (\d+\.\d+.\d+\.\d+):\d+ -> (\d+\.\d+\.\d+\.\d+):80/) {
$i = inet_aton($1);
$host{$1} ||= gethostbyaddr($i, AF_INET) || $1;
$i = inet_aton($2);
$host{$2} ||= gethostbyaddr($i, AF_INET) || $2;
print "$host{$1} -> $host{$2} : ";
$go = 1;
next;
}
if(/(q|p|query|for)=(.*)?(&|HTTP)/) {
next unless $go;
my $q = $2;
```

```
$q =~ s/(\+|&.*)/ /g;
$q =~ s/%(\w+)/chr(hex($1))/ge;
print "$q\n";
$go = 0;
}
}
```

I call the script *go-ogle*. This will run an *ngrep* looking for any GET or POST request that includes *search* or *find* somewhere in the URL. The results look something like this:

```
Go ogle online.
caligula.nocat.net -> www.google.com : o'reilly mac os x conference
caligula.nocat.net -> s1.search.vip.scd.yahoo.com : junk mail $$$
tiberius.nocat.net -> altavista.com : babel fish
caligula.nocat.net -> 166-140.amazon.com : Brazil
livia.nocat.net -> 66.161.12.119 : lart
```

It will unescape encoded strings in the query (note the ' in the google query and the $$$ from yahoo). It will also convert IP addresses to hostnames for you (since *ngrep* doesn't seem to have that feature, probably so it can optimize capturing for speed). The last two results are interesting: the Brazil query was actually run on *http://www.imdb.com/*, and the last one was to *http://www.dictionary.com/*. Evidently IMDB is now in a partnership with Amazon, and Dictionary.com's search machine doesn't have a PTR record. It's amazing how much you can learn about the world by watching other people's packets.

Note that you must be root to run *ngrep*, and for best results, it should be run from the router at the edge of your network.

See also:

- man ngrep
- *http://www.packetfactory.net/Projects/ngrep/*

Scanning Your Own Machines with nmap
Find out when servers and services come online anywhere on your network

If you haven't used it before, nmap is a tremendously useful tool for identifying machines and services on your network. It will perform a number of different types of network scanning (from standard TCP and UDP to more exotic scans like stealth TCP SYN scans, Xmas Tree and NULL probes, and a bunch of other fun options).

Even more interesting is the OS fingerprinting code, which analyzes packets returned by the target machine and compares the results against a database of known operating systems. This is a fascinating bit of code, in that it can typically identify the remote side's operating system without connecting to any actual services, and even return an estimated uptime for the machine being scanned.

To perform a standard port sweep with OS fingerprinting, try the -O switch:

```
rob@catlin:~# nmap -O caligula

Starting nmap V. 3.00 ( www.insecure.org/nmap/ )
Interesting ports on caligula.rob.nocat (10.42.4.7):
(The 1600 ports scanned but not shown below are in state: closed)
Port State Service
22/tcp open ssh
Remote operating system guess: Mac OS X 10.1 - 10.1.4
Uptime 5.760 days (since Tue Sep 3 19:14:36 2002)

Nmap run completed -- 1 IP address (1 host up) scanned in 31 seconds
```

If you'd like to *nmap* your entire network and have a bit of time to kill, you can specify a network and subnet on the command line. This performs a TCP SYN scan and fingerprinting for the first 64 addresses of 10.42.4.0:

```
root@catlin:~# nmap -OsS 10.42.4.0/26
```

Since *nmap* prints to STDOUT, you can save the output of a scan run and compare it against previous runs for a differential report, quite easily. We'll run an Xmas tree scan and *grep* out a couple of lines (like the run time) to eliminate false positives:

```
root@catlin:~# nmap -sX 10.42.4.0/26 | egrep -v '^(Nmap|Starting)' \
> nmap.output
```

Let's run the same command again (say, the next day, at a random hour):

```
root@catlin:~# nmap -sX localhost | egrep -v '^(Nmap|Starting)' \
> nmap.output2
```

and let's do a context *diff* to see what changed:

```
root@catlin:~# diff -c nmap.output*
*** nmap.output Mon Sep 9 14:45:06 2002
--- nmap.output2 Mon Sep 9 14:45:21 2002
**************
*** 1,7 ****

Interesting ports on catlin.rob.nocat (10.42.4.6):
! (The 1598 ports scanned but not shown below are in state: closed)
Port State Service
22/tcp open ssh
53/tcp open domain
80/tcp open http
--- 1,8 ----

Interesting ports on catlin.rob.nocat (10.42.4.6):
! (The 1597 ports scanned but not shown below are in state: closed)
```

```
Port State Service
+ 21/tcp open ftp
22/tcp open ssh
53/tcp open domain
80/tcp open http
root@catlin:~#
```

Fascinating. It looks like catlin has picked up an *ftp* server at some point. This technique will find new (and dead) hosts and services each time it is run. By keeping an archive of *nmap* output (perhaps logged to time and date encoded files, or even to a database) you can keep a log of the state of all machines on your network. Turning it into a shell script and running it from *cron* is left as an exercise (a hopefully fun, and definitely worthwhile exercise) for the reader.

See also:

* nmap's home: *http://www.insecure.org/nmap/*

Disk Age Analysis
HACK #62 Easily identify which parts of your disk change frequently

How can you quickly tell which parts of your filesystem are modified frequently and which haven't changed in months? It's very straightforward, with a proper application of Perl.

Here is a Perl script that will perform disk aging analysis on a filesystem. The program breaks down disk space two ways, by last modified date and last accessed date. A sample run looks like:

```
% diskage /usr/local

Disk aging analysis for /usr/local:

last num last num
Age (days) modified files accessed files
0 - 30 260403 Kb 817 140303 Kb 6968
31 - 60 11789 Kb 226 23140 Kb 199
61 - 90 40168 Kb 1126 1087585 Kb 31625
91 - 180 118927 Kb 995 0 Kb 0
181 - 365 85005 Kb 1889 0 Kb 0
366 - 9999 734735 Kb 33739 0 Kb 0
----------- ----- ----------- -----
Total 1251029 Kb 38792 1251029 Kb 38792
```

You can run the script with the *-v* option to list the last modified and last accessed days for every file in the filesystem.

Listing: diskage

```perl
#!/usr/local/bin/perl
#
# Disk aging report generator
# Written by Seann Herdejurgen
#
# May 1998

use File::Find;

# Initialize variables
@levels=(30,60,90,180,365,9999);

# Check for verbose flag
if ($ARGV[0] eq "-v") {
$verbose++;
shift(@ARGV);
}

$ARGV[0]=$ENV{'PWD'} if ($ARGV[0] eq "");

foreach $dir (@ARGV) {
foreach $level (@levels) {
$modified{$level}=0;
$accessed{$level}=0;
$mfiles{$level}=0;
$afiles{$level}=0;
}
print("\nDisk aging analysis for $dir:\n\n");
print (" mod acc size file\n") if ($verbose);

# Traverse desired filesystems
find(\&wanted,$dir);

print(" last num last num\n");
print(" Age (days) modified files accessed files\n");
$msize=$asize=$mtotal=$atotal=$lastlevel=0;

foreach $level (@levels) {
printf("%4d - %4d %8d Kb %5d %8d Kb %5d\
n",$lastlevel,$level,$modified{$level}/
1024,$mfiles{$level},$accessed{$level}/1024,$afiles{$level});
$msize+=$modified{$level}/1024;
$asize+=$accessed{$level}/1024;
$mtotal+=$mfiles{$level};
$atotal+=$afiles{$level};
$lastlevel=$level+1;
}

printf(" ----------- ----- ----------- -----\n");
printf(" Total %8d Kb %5d %8d Kb %5d\n",$msize,$mtotal,$asize,$atotal);
}
```

```
exit;

sub wanted {
(($dev,$ino,$mode,$nlink,$uid,$gid,$rdev,$size) = lstat($_));
$mod=int(-M _);
$acc=int(-A _);
foreach $level (@levels) {
if ($mod<=$level) { $modified{$level}+=$size; $mfiles{$level}++; last; }
}
foreach $level (@levels) {
if ($acc<=$level) { $accessed{$level}+=$size; $afiles{$level}++; last; }
}
printf("%4d %4d %6d %s\n",$mod,$acc,$size,$_) if ($verbose);
}
```

HACK #63 Cheap IP Takeover

Accomplish IP takeover with ping, bash, and a simple network utility

Directing traffic to one of several machines is fairly straightforward when using round-robin DNS, as discussed in "Distributing Server Load with Round-Robin DNS" [Hack #79]. But what happens when one of those servers becomes unavailable? Here's one scheme for monitoring the health of another server and standing in for it if it fails.

First, we need to make a distinction between the server's "real" IP address, and the IP (or IPs) that it actually serves public content from. For this example, we'll be referring to two servers, Pinky and Brain. Pinky uses the IP address 208.201.239.12 for its "real" IP on eth0, and also has an IP alias of 208.201.239.36 on eth0:0. Brain uses 208.201.239.13 on eth0, and 208.201. 239.37 on eth0:0. If you've never used IP aliases before, here's the very quick HOWTO:

```
# ifconfig eth0:0 1.2.3.4
```

Voila, you have another IP address (1.2.3.4) bound to eth0, called eth0:0. You used to have to specifically compile IP aliasing into the kernel, but this option seems to have gone away in recent kernels and is apparently on by default. One important thing to remember about IP aliases is that if the interface to which it is bound (in this case, eth0) is ever brought down, then all of its associated aliases are also brought down. You can also make the alias any alphanumeric string, although some versions of *ifconfig* only display the first four or five characters of the alias when displaying interfaces.

Once Pinky and Brain have their respective eth0:0 set, bind a service (like Apache) to their aliased IPs, and set up round-robin DNS to point to both with a single hostname (see "Distributing Server Load with Round-Robin DNS" [Hack #79]). We'll assume that we're setting up redundant web service for www.oreillynet.com, resolving to either 208.201.239.36 or 208.201.239.37.

Now that roughly half of the traffic is going to each server, we'll need Pinky and Brain to monitor the health of each other. This can be done by pinging each other's real IP address, and watching the results. Save the following into a script, and install it on Pinky.

Listing: takeover

```
#!/bin/bash
OTHER="brain"
PUBLIC="208.201.239.37"

PAUSE=3

PATH=/bin:/usr/bin:/sbin:/usr/sbin:/usr/local/sbin
MISSED=0

while true; do
if ! ping -c 1 -w 1 $OTHER > /dev/null; then
((MISSED++))
else
if [ $MISSED -gt 2 ]; then
ifconfig eth0:$OTHER down
fi
MISSED=0
fi;

if [ $MISSED -eq 2 ]; then
ifconfig eth0:$OTHER $PUBLIC
#
# ...but see discussion below...
#
fi
sleep $PAUSE;
done
```

Naturally, set OTHER to "pinky" and PUBLIC to "208.201.239.36" on the copy that runs on Brain.

Let's suppose that Brain suddenly stops responding on 208.201.239.17 (say a network tech accidentally pulled the wrong plug when working on the rack). After missing 3 pings in a row, Pinky will leap into action, bringing up eth0: brain up as 208.201.239.37, the public IP that Brain is supposed to be serving. It will then continue to watch Brain's real IP address, and relinquish control when it is back online. The ping -c 1 -w 1 means "send one ping packet, and time out after one second, no matter what happens." ping will return non-zero if the packet didn't come back in the one second time limit.

But this isn't quite the entire solution. Although Pinky is now answering for Brain, any machines on the same network as the two servers (notably, the router just upstream at your ISP) will have the wrong MAC address cached for

208.201.239.37. With the wrong MAC address cached, no traffic will flow to Pinky, since it will only respond to packets that bear its own MAC address. How can we tell all of the machines on the 208.201.239.0 network that the MAC address for 208.201.239.37 has been updated?

One way is to use the *send_arp* utility from the High Availability Linux project. This very handy (and tiny) utility will craft an ARP packet to your specifications and send it to a MAC address of your choice on the local network. If we specify all ones (i.e., `ff:ff:ff:ff:ff:ff`) for the destination, then it effectively becomes a broadcast ARP packet. While most routers won't update their ARP tables when they see unrequested ARP broadcasts, such a packet will signal them to resend an ARP request, to which Pinky will obligingly reply. The advantage of using broadcast is that it will signal all machines on the subnet simultaneously, instead of having to track all of the MAC addresses of machines that need updating.

The syntax of *send_arp* is send_arp [Source IP] [Source MAC] [Target IP] [Target MAC]. For example, our simple monitoring script above should run the following when it detects that Brain is down:

```
send_arp 208.201.239.37 00:11:22:aa:bb:cc 208.201.239.37 ffffffffffff
```

(Where `00:11:22:aa:bb:cc` is the hardware MAC address of Pinky's eth0.) The script can continue to watch to watch when Brain's real IP address (208.201.239.17) becomes available. When it does, we can bring eth0:brain back down and let Brain worry about updating the ARP cache again (which it should be set to do on boot).

There are a number of improvements that could be made to this technique. For one thing, just because 208.201.239.17 is up doesn't guarantee that 208. 201.239.37 is also available. Also, ping isn't the best test for service availability (a better test might be to actually request a web page from the other machine and make sure that it has a closing </html> tag).

These improvements are left as an exercise to you, dear reader. Every site is different, so you'll need to find the technique that works best with the tools that you at hand. After all, that's exactly what a hack is, isn't it?

See also:

- The *Fake* package from High Availability Linux, *http://www.linux-ha.org/failover/*
- "Distributing Server Load with Round-Robin DNS" [Hack #79]

HACK
#64

Running ntop for Real-Time Network Stats

See who's doing what on your network over time with ntop

If you're looking for real-time network statistics, you should check out the terrific *ntop* tool. It is a full-featured protocol analyzer with a web front-end, complete with SSL and GD graphing support. *ntop* isn't lightweight (requiring more resources depending on the size of your network and the volume of net traffic) but can give you a very nice overview (and some critical details) about who's talking to whom on your network.

ntop needs to initially run as root (to throw your interfaces into promiscuous mode and start capturing packets), but then releases its privileges to a user that you specify. If you decide to run *ntop* for long periods of time, you'll probably be happiest running it on a dedicated monitoring box (with few other services running on it for security and performance reasons.)

Here's a quick reference on how to get *ntop* up and running quickly. First, create an *ntop* user and group:

```
root@gemini:~# groupadd ntop
root@gemini:~# useradd -c "ntop user" -d /usr/local/etc/ntop \
  -s /bin/true -g ntop ntop
```

Then unpack and build *ntop* as per the instructions in *docs/BUILD-NTOP. txt*. We'll assume that you have the source tree unpacked in */usr/local/src/ ntop-2.1.3/*.

Create a directory for *ntop* in which to keep its capture database:

```
root@gemini:~# mkdir /usr/local/etc/ntop
```

(Note that it should be owned by root, and *not* by the *ntop* user.)

If you'd like to use SSL for https (instead of standard http), then copy the default SSL key to */usr/local/etc/ntop*:

```
root@gemini:# cp /usr/local/src/ntop-2.1.3/ntop/*pem /usr/local/etc/ntop
```

Note that the default SSL key will not be built with the correct hostname for your server. If you'd like to make your own (and eliminate the SSL warnings in your browser), check out "Generating an SSL cert and Certificate Signing Request" **[Hack #93]** and "Creating Your Own CA" **[Hack #94]** for an example of how to make your own key and sign it with your own CA.

Now we initialize the *ntop* databases and set an administrative password:

```
root@gemini:~# ntop -A -u ntop -P /usr/local/etc/ntop
21/Sep/2002 20:30:23 Initializing GDBM...
21/Sep/2002 20:30:23 Started thread (1026) for network packet analyser.
21/Sep/2002 20:30:23 Started thread (2051) for idle hosts detection.
21/Sep/2002 20:30:23 Started thread (3076) for DNS address resolution.
```

```
21/Sep/2002 20:30:23 Started thread (4101) for address purge.
```

```
Please enter the password for the admin user:
Please enter the password again:
21/Sep/2002 20:30:29 Admin user password has been set.
```

Finally, run *ntop* as a daemon, and start the SSL server on your favorite port (4242, for example):

```
root@gemini:~# ntop -u ntop -P /usr/local/etc/ntop -W4242 -d
```

By default, *ntop* will also run a standard http server on port 3000. You should strongly consider locking down access to these ports at your firewall, or by using command line iptables rules, as in "Creating a Firewall from the Command Line of any Server" **[Hack #45]**. Let *ntop* run for a while, then connect to *https://your.server.here:4242/*. You can find out all sorts of details about what traffic has been seen on your network, as in Figure 5-1.

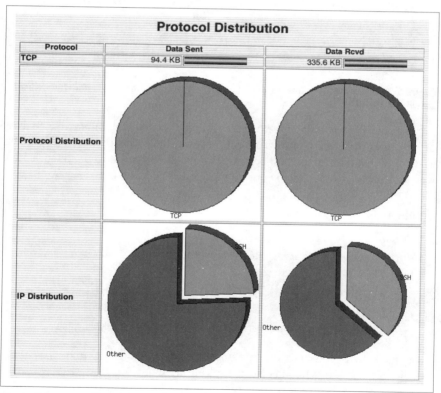

Figure 5-1. ntop will generate real-time statistical graphs of your network traffic

And even look at various statistics graphically, as an easy-to-read (and pretty-to-print) pie chart, as in Figure 5-2.

Info about host nocat.net

IP Address	208.201.239.5 ■ [unicast]
First/Last Seen	09/21/02 21:27:16 - 09/21/02 21:35:20 [8:04]
Domain	net
Last MAC Address/Router ■■	00:01:30:B8:23:D0
Host Location	Remote (outside specified/local subnet)
IP TTL (Time to Live)	54:54 [~10 hop(s)]
Total Data Sent	110.8 KB/1,159 Pkts/0 Retran. Pkts [0%]
Broadcast Pkts Sent	0 Pkts
Data Sent Stats	Local (100 %)
IP vs. Non-IP Sent	IP (100 %)
Total Data Rcvd	384.4 KB/1,372 Pkts/0 Retran. Pkts [0%]
Data Rcvd Stats	Local (100 %)
IP vs. Non-IP Rcvd	IP (100 %)
Sent vs. Rcvd Pkts	Sent (45.8 %) Rcvd (54.2 %)
Sent vs. Rcvd Data	Sent (22.4 %) Rcvd (77.6 %)
Further Host Information	[Whois]

Host Traffic Stats

Time	Tot. Traffic Sent	% Traffic Sent	Tot. Traffic Rcvd	% Traffic Rcvd
Midnight - 1AM	0	0.0 %	0	0.0 %
1AM - 2AM	0	0.0 %	0	0.0 %
2AM - 3AM	0	0.0 %	0	0.0 %
3AM - 4AM	0	0.0 %	0	0.0 %
4AM - 5AM	0	0.0 %	0	0.0 %
5AM - 6AM	0	0.0 %	0	0.0 %
6AM - 7AM	0	0.0 %	0	0.0 %

Figure 5-2. When run overtime, ntop will reveal great detail about how individual clients use your network

While tools like *tcpdump* and *ethereal* will give you detailed, interactive analysis of network traffic, *ntop* delivers a wealth of statistical information in a slick and easy-to-use web interface. When properly installed and locked down, it may well become a favorite tool in your network analysis tool chest.

See also:

- *http://www.ntop.org/*
- *http://www-serra.unipi.it/~ntop/ntop.html*

HACK #65 Monitoring Web Traffic in Real Time with httptop

See who's hitting your web server the hardest up to the second with httptop

Advanced http log analysis packages like *analog* can give you very detailed report on who has been looking at what on your site. Unfortunately, log processing jobs can take quite a long time to run on a busy site, giving you detailed retrospective reporting but nothing about what's happening right *now*.

Another approach is to log all relevant web activity to a database and perform queries on it for real-time statistics. This method can give you instantaneous, to-the-hit reporting, as long as you have a database and web server powerhouse capable of supporting the additional load. On a very busy site, this simply isn't practical.

Somewhere in between lies *httptop*, a Perl script that attempts to give *top*-like reporting in real time, without the overhead of a database server. It expects to be given the path to an *access_log* file. Run the command like this:

```
$ httptop -f combined /usr/local/apache/logs/access_log
```

You'll be presented with a screen that refreshes every couple of seconds, sorted on hits per second. Just as with *top*, hit **?** for a listing of available keys. They include such niceties as sorting by most recent hits or total hits, and optionally displaying the referring URL or domain, the requested URI, or remote requesting host.

If you have a bunch of VirtualHosts and would like to be able to simultaneously run *httptop* across all of them, try this:

Add a line like this to each of your VirtualHost entries:

```
CustomLog /usr/local/apache/logs/combined-log vhost
```

and the following log definition (which should appear all on one line) somewhere in your global configuration:

```
LogFormat "%v %h %l %u %t \"%r\" %>s %b \"%{Referer}i\" \"%{User-Agent}i\""
vhost
```

Now you can watch activity on all of your hosts simultaneously with a command, as:

```
$ httptop -f vhost /usr/local/apache/logs/combined-log
```

Note that *httptop* requires the Time::HiRes and File::Tail Perl modules to be installed first. If you don't feel like typing all of this in, *httptop* (and most of the examples in this book) are available from the *examples.oreilly.com* web site. See the introduction for the exact URL.

Listing: httptop

```perl
#!/usr/bin/perl -w
#

=head1 NAME

httptop - display top(1)-like per-client HTTP access stats

=head1 SYNOPSIS
```

```
httptop [-f <format>] [-r <refresh_secs>] [-b <backtrack_lines>] <logdir |
path_to_log>

=cut

use Time::HiRes qw( time );
use File::Tail ();
use Term::ReadKey;
use Getopt::Std;

use strict;

### Defaults you might be interested in adjusting.

my $Update = 2; # update every n secs
my $Backtrack = 250; # backtrack n lines on startup
my @Paths = qw(
%
/title/%/logs/access_log
/var/log/httpd/%/access_log
/usr/local/apache/logs/%/access_log
);

my $Log_Format = "combined";
my %Log_Fields = (
combined => [qw/ Host x x Time URI Response x Referer Client /],
vhost => [qw/ VHost Host x x Time URI Response x Referer Client /]
);

### Constants & other thingies. Nothing to see here. Move along.

my $Version = "0.4.1";

sub by_hits_per () { $b->{Rate} <=> $a->{Rate} }
sub by_total () { $b->{Total} <=> $a->{Total} }
sub by_age () { $a->{Last} <=> $b->{Last} }

my $last_field = "Client";
my $index = "Host";
my $show_help = 0;

my $order = \&by_hits_per;
my $Help = "htlwufd?q";
my %Keys = (
h => [ "Order by hits/second" => sub { $order = \&by_hits_per } ],
t => [ "Order by total recorded hits" => sub { $order = \&by_total } ],
l => [ "Order by most recent hits" => sub { $order = \&by_age } ],
w => [ "Show remote host" => sub { $index = "Host" } ],
u => [ "Show requested URI" => sub { $index = "URI" } ],
f => [ "Show referring URL" => sub { $index = "Referer" } ],
d => [ "Show referring domain" => sub { $index = "Domain" } ],
'?' => [ "Help (this thing here)" => sub { $show_help++ } ],
q => [ "Quit" => sub { exit } ]
```

```
    );

    my @Display_Fields = qw/ Host Date URI Response Client Referer Domain /;
    my @Record_Fields = qw/ Host URI Referer Domain /;
    my $Max_Index_Width = 50;
    my $Initial_TTL = 50;

    my @Months = qw/ Jan Feb Mar Apr May Jun Jul Aug Sep Nov Dec /;
    my %Term = (
    HOME => "\033[H",
    CLS => "\033[2J",
    START_TITLE => "\033]0;", # for xterms etc.
    END_TITLE => "\007",
    START_RV => "\033[7m",
    END_RV => "\033[m"
    );

    my ( %hist, %opt, $spec );

    $SIG{INT} = sub { exit };
    END { ReadMode 0 };

    ### Subs.

    sub refresh_output
    {
    my ( $cols, $rows ) = GetTerminalSize;
    my $show = $rows - 3;
    my $count = $show;
    my $now = (shift || time);

    for my $type ( values %hist ) {
    for my $peer ( values %$type ) {
    # if ( --$peer->{_Ttl} > 0 ) {
    my $delta = $now - $peer->{Start};
    if ( $delta >= 1 ) {
    $peer->{ Rate } = $peer->{ Total } / $delta;
    } else {
    $peer->{ Rate } = 0
    }

    $peer->{ Last } = int( $now - $peer->{ Date } );
    # } else {
    # delete $type->{$peer}
    # }
    }
    }

    $count = scalar( values %{$hist{$index}} ) - 1 if $show >= scalar values
    %{$hist{$index}};
    my @list = ( sort $order values %{$hist{$index}} )[ 0 .. $count ];

    my $first = 0;
```

```
$first = ( $first <= $_ ? $_ + 1 : $first ) for map { $_ ? length($_->
{$index}) : 0 } @list;
$first = $Max_Index_Width if $Max_Index_Width < $first;

print $Term{START_TITLE}, "Monitoring $spec at: ", scalar localtime,
$Term{END_TITLE} if $ENV{TERM} eq "xterm"; # UGLY!!!

my $help = "Help/?";
my $head = sprintf( "%-${first}s %6s %4s %4s %s (%d total)",
$index, qw{ Hits/s Tot Last }, $last_field,
scalar keys %{$hist{$index}}
);

#
# Truncate status line if need be
#
$head = substr($head, 0, ($cols - length($help)));
print @Term{"HOME", "START_RV"}, $head, " " x ($cols - length($head) -
length($help)), $help, $Term{END_RV}, "\n";

for ( @list ) {
# $_->{_Ttl}++;

my $line = sprintf( "%-${first}s %6.3f %4d %3d %s",
substr( $_->{$index}, 0, $Max_Index_Width ), @$_{(qw{ Rate Total Last },
$last_field)} );
if ( length($line) > $cols ) {
substr( $line, $cols - 1 ) = "";
} else {
$line .= " " x ($cols - length($line));
}
print $line, "\n";
}

print " " x $cols, "\n" while $count++ < $show;
}

sub process_line
{
my $line = shift;
my $now = ( shift || time );
my %hit;

chomp $line;
@hit{@{$Log_Fields{$Log_Format}}} = grep( $_, split( /"([^"]+)"|\[([^\]]+)\
]|\s/o, $line ) );

$hit{ URI } =~ s/HTTP\/1\S+//gos;

$hit{ Referer } = "<unknown>" if not $hit{Referer} or $hit{Referer} eq "-";
( $hit{Domain} = $hit{Referer} ) =~ s#^\w+://([^/]+).*$#$1#os;

$hit{ Client } ||= "<none>";
$hit{ Client } =~ s/Mozilla\/[\w.]+ \(compatible; /(/gos;
$hit{ Client } =~ s/[^\x20-\x7f]//gos;
```

```perl
# if $now is negative, try to guess how old the hit is based on the time
stamp.
if ( $now < 0 ) {
my @hit_t = ( split( m![:/\s]!o, $hit{ Time } ))[ 0 .. 5 ];
my @now_t = ( localtime )[ 3, 4, 5, 2, 1, 0 ];
my @mag = ( 3600, 60, 1 );

# If the hit didn't parse right, or didn't happen today, the hell with it.
return unless $hit_t[2] == ( $now_t[2] + 1900 )
and $hit_t[1] eq $Months[ $now_t[1] ]
and $hit_t[0] == $now_t[0];

splice( @hit_t, 0, 3 );
splice( @now_t, 0, 3 );

# Work backward to the UNIX time of the hit.
$now = time;
$now -= (shift( @now_t ) - shift( @hit_t )) * $_ for ( 3600, 60, 1 );
}

$hit{ Date } = $now;

for my $field ( @Record_Fields ) {
my $peer = ( $hist{$field}{$hit{$field}} ||= { Start => $now, _Ttl =>
$Initial_TTL } );
@$peer{ @Display_Fields } = @hit{ @Display_Fields };
$peer->{ Total }++;
}
}

sub display_help {
my $msg = "httptop v.$Version";
print @Term{qw/ HOME CLS START_RV /}, $msg, $Term{END_RV}, "\n\n";
print " " x 4, $_, " " x 8, $Keys{$_}[0], "\n" for ( split "", $Help );
print "\nPress any key to continue.\n";
}


### Init.

getopt( 'frb' => \%opt );

$Backtrack = $opt{b} if $opt{b};
$Update = $opt{r} if $opt{r};
$Log_Format = $opt{f} if $opt{f};
$spec = $ARGV[0];

die <<End unless $spec and $Log_Fields{$Log_Format};
Usage: $0 [-f <format>] [-r <refresh_secs>] [-b <backtrack_lines>] <logdir |
path_to_log>
Valid formats are: @{[ join ", ", keys %Log_Fields ]}.
End

for ( @Paths ) {
```

```
last if -r $spec;
( $spec = $_ ) =~ s/%/$ARGV[0]/gos;
}
die "No access_log $ARGV[0] found.\n" unless -r $spec;

my $file = File::Tail->new(
name => $spec,
interval => $Update / 2,
maxinterval => $Update,
tail => $Backtrack,
nowait => 1
) or die "$spec: $!";

my $last_update = time;
my ( $line, $now );

# Backtracking.
while ( $Backtrack-- > 0 ) {
last unless $line = $file->read;
process_line( $line, -1 );
}
$file->nowait( 0 );

ReadMode 4; # Echo off.
print @Term{"HOME", "CLS"}; # Home & clear.
refresh_output;

### Main loop.

while (defined( $line = $file->read )) {
$now = time;

process_line( $line, $now );

while ( $line = lc ReadKey(-1) ) {
$show_help = 0 if $show_help;
$Keys{$line}[1]->() if $Keys{$line};
}

if ( $show_help == 1 ) {
display_help;
$show_help++; # Don't display help again.
} elsif ( $now - $last_update > $Update and not $show_help ) {
$last_update = $now;
refresh_output( $now );
}
}

__END__

=head1 DESCRIPTION

httptop is intended to be a top(1)-equivalent for httpd access activity.
```

httptop should be invoked with the path to an Apache access_log, or alternately a string that uniquely identifies the directory in which to find the access_log. The search paths can be configured in the source.

httptop has limited flexibility for dealing with logs of different formats. Run 'httptop' without options to see which format names are available.

While httptop is running, you can obtain a list of terminal commands by pressing '?'. As with top(1), pressing 'q' quits.

To use public keys with an *ssh* server, you'll first need to generate a public/private key pair:

```
$ ssh-keygen -t rsa
```

You can also use *-t dsa* for DSA keys, or *-t rsa1* if you're using Protocol v1. (And shame on you if you are! Upgrade to v2 as soon as you can!)

After you enter the above command, you should see something like this:

```
Generating public/private rsa key pair.
Enter file in which to save the key (/home/rob/.ssh/id_rsa):
```

Just hit Enter there. It will then ask you for a pass phrase; just hit enter twice (but read the Security note below). Here's what the results should look like:

```
Enter passphrase (empty for no passphrase):
Enter same passphrase again:
Your identification has been saved in /home/rob/.ssh/id_rsa.
Your public key has been saved in /home/rob/.ssh/id_rsa.pub.
The key fingerprint is:
a6:5c:c3:eb:18:94:0b:06:a1:a6:29:58:fa:80:0a:bc rob@localhost
```

This created two files, *~/.ssh/id_rsa* and *~/.ssh/id_rsa.pub*. To use this key-pair on a server, try this:

```
$ ssh server "mkdir .ssh; chmod 0700 .ssh"
$ scp .ssh/id_rsa.pub server:.ssh/authorized_keys2
```

Of course, substitute your server name for server. It should ask for your password both times. Now, simply *ssh server* and it should log you in automagically without a password. And yes, it will use your shiny new public key for *scp*, too.

If that didn't work for you, check your file permissions on both *~/.ssh/** and *server:~/.ssh/**. Your private key (id_rsa) should be 0600 (and only be present on your local machine), and everything else should be 0655 or better.

Terrific. So you can now *ssh server* quickly and with a minimum of fuss. Is it possible to make it even quicker to connect to machines you frequently touch? You bet, just check out "'Turbo-mode' ssh Logins" **(#67)**.

Security Concerns

Some consider the use of public keys a potential security risk. After all, one only has to steal a copy of your private key to obtain access to your servers. While this is true, the same is certainly true of passwords.

Ask yourself, how many times a day do you enter a password to gain shell access to a machine (or *scp* a file)? How frequently is it the same password on many (or all) of those machines? Have you ever used that password in a way that might be questionable (on a web site, on a personal machine that isn't quite up to date, or possibly with an *ssh* client on a machine that you don't directly control). If any of these possibilities sound familiar, then consider that an *ssh* key in the same setting would make it virtually impossible for an attacker to later gain unauthorized access (providing, of course, that you keep your private key safe).

See Also:

- *SSH: The Definitive Guide* (O'Reilly)
- "'Turbo-mode' ssh Logins" **(#67)**
- "Running the ssh-Agent in a GUI" **[Hack #69]**

HACK #67   Turbo-mode ssh Logins
Even faster logins from the command line

If you've just come from the previous hack, you've only seen half of the solution! Even with client keys, you still have to needlessly type ssh server every time you want to *ssh* in. Back in the dark, insecure, unenlightened days of *rsh*, there was an obscure feature that I happened to love that hasn't (yet) been ported to *ssh*. It used to be possible to symlink */usr/bin/rsh* to a file of the same name as your server, and *rsh* was smart enough to realize that if it wasn't called as *rsh*, that it should *rsh* to whatever name it was called as.

Of course, this is trivial to implement in shell. Create a file called *ssh-to* with these two lines in it:

```
#!/bin/sh
ssh `basename $0` $*
```

(Those are backticks around basename $0.) Now put that in your PATH (if *~/bin* doesn't exist or isn't in your PATH already, it should be) and set up symlinks to all of your favorite servers to it:

```
$ cd bin
$ ln -s ssh-to server1
$ ln -s ssh-to server2
$ ln -s ssh-to server3
```

Now, to *ssh* to server1 (assuming you've copied your public key over as described previously) you can simply type "server1" and you'll magically end up with a shell on server1, without typing "ssh," and without entering your password. That $* at the end allows you to run arbitrary commands in a single line (instead of spawning a shell), like this:

```
server1 uptime
```

(This will simply show the uptime, number of users, and load average on server1, then exit. Wrap it in a *for* loop and iterate over a list of servers to get a pinpoint status of all of your machines.)

I believe that this is the quickest way of using *ssh*, short of setting up single character aliases to do it for you (which is excessively hackish, unmaintainable, and unnecessary, although it does seem to impress some people):

```
$ alias a='ssh alice'
$ alias b='ssh bob'
$ alias e='ssh eve'
...
```

At any rate, *ssh* has many options that make it a very flexible tool for securely navigating between any number of servers. Now if we can just find a way to make it log in and actually fix the machine for you, we'd have a real hack.

See also:

- "Quick Logins with ssh Client Keys" **[Hack #66]**
- "Using ssh-Agent Effectively" **[Hack #68]**

Using ssh-Agent Effectively

#68 Use ssh-agent to automatically manage your ssh client keys

The *ssh*-agent is a very handy component of *ssh* that manages your private keys for you, passing your credentials along whenever they are required.

The *ssh*-agent manpage tells us the following:

> *ssh*-agent is a program to hold private keys used for public key authentication (RSA, DSA). The idea is that *ssh*-agent is started in the beginning of an X-session or a login session, and all other windows or programs are started as clients to the *ssh*-agent program. Through use of environment variables the agent can be located and automatically used for authentication when logging in to other machines using *ssh*(1).

Practically, this means that with an agent running (and with properly configured *ssh* clients), it is possible to *ssh* to multiple machines without requiring a copy of your private key on each intervening machine (or typing in your password on every connection).

Assume we already have an authorized *ssh* key (see "Quick Logins with ssh Client Keys" **[Hack #66]**) installed on each homer, bart, and lisa. If you *ssh* to each machine from your local machine, there's no problem:

```
rob@caligula:~$ ssh homer
rob@homer:~$ exit
logout
```

```
Connection to homer.oreillynet.com closed.
rob@caligula:~$ ssh bart
rob@bart:~$ exit
logout
Connection to bart.oreillynet.com closed.
rob@caligula:~$ ssh lisa
rob@lisa:~$ exit
```

But what happens when we try to *ssh* from homer directly to bart?

```
rob@caligula:~$ ssh homer
rob@homer:~$ ssh bart
rob@bart's password:
```

This is where *ssh*-agent comes in handy. Rather than expose your private key to unnecessary risk by placing a copy on all of your servers, simply start the agent on your local machine like this:

```
rob@caligula:~$ eval `ssh-agent`
Agent pid 8450
```

Then add your default *ssh* keys with the *ssh*-add command:

```
rob@caligula:~$ ssh-add
Identity added: /home/rob/.ssh/id_rsa (/home/rob/.ssh/id_rsa)
Identity added: /home/rob/.ssh/id_dsa (/home/rob/.ssh/id_dsa)
Identity added: /home/rob/.ssh/identity (rob@caligula)
```

You'll also need to check that homer, bart, and lisa are configured to forward agent requests along. This is usually denied by default, but is controlled with a line like this:

```
ForwardAgent yes
```

in your *~/.ssh/config* or */usr/local/etc/ssh_config* file. You can also specify it from the command line with the *-A* switch.

Now, when you *ssh* from homer directly to bart, homer will first ask your agent for any available credentials. Likewise, *ssh*ing from bart to lisa will first cause bart to check with homer, who will forward the request back to your agent. This makes it easy to skate from machine to machine very quickly:

```
rob@caligula:~$ ssh homer
rob@homer:~$ ssh bart
rob@bart:~$ ssh lisa
rob@lisa:~$
```

Congratulations. You now have very simple network navigation, without the worry of giving away your private *ssh* keys. Even copying files between machines (with *scp*) is faster and easier than before.

But what happens if you have no opportunity to start an agent in the first place? (This is frequently the case if your login is a graphical XDM prompt, or if you're running OS X.) Fear not. At least, not before reading "Running the ssh-Agent in a GUI" [Hack #69].

Surely, there is no way to make it even faster and easier to *ssh* to a machine, without making it less secure. Or is there? For the answer, check out "'Turbo-mode' ssh Logins" **(#67)**.

Running the ssh-Agent in a GUI
Running ssh-agent in windowing environments

This *ssh*-agent method described in "Using ssh-Agent Effectively" **[Hack #68]** works fine as long as that initial eval ssh-agent can be run before your window environment starts. One place to do this is at login, in your *~/.bash_login* (or *~/.login* if running *tcsh*). But this can be a less than optimal solution if you're using pass phrases on your keys (which you probably should be). Your window system won't start until you enter your key passwords, after logging in. Another side effect to this approach is that if your *ssh*-agent ever gets killed, you'll have to quit X, start a new agent, and log in again. And in some environments (such as OS X) there is never even an opportunity to run commands before the graphical environment starts.

Rather than wastefully running an agent for every window you have open (or copy-and-pasting the environment settings between them), try this code in your *~/.profile*:

```
if [ -f ~/.agent.env ]; then
. ~/.agent.env > /dev/null

if ! kill -0 $SSH_AGENT_PID > /dev/null 2> then
echo "Stale agent file found. Spawning new agent..."
eval `ssh-agent | tee ~/.agent.env`
ssh-add
fi
else
echo "Starting ssh-agent..."
eval `ssh-agent | tee ~/.agent.env`
ssh-add
fi
```

This will maintain a *~/.agent.env* file for you, with an environment pointing at your currently running *ssh*-agent. If the agent dies, opening a new terminal window will spawn one automatically (and add your keys for you), which is shared between all subsequent terminal windows.

Ahh, that's better. A single, respawning *ssh*-agent on demand.

See Also:
- "Quick Logins with ssh Client Keys" **[Hack #66]**
- "'Turbo-mode' ssh Logins" **(#67)**

X over ssh

#70

Run remote X11 applications easily and securely with ssh

Surprisingly few people realize that *ssh* is perfectly capable of forwarding X11 traffic. If X11 forwarding is permitted by the *ssh* server that you're logging into, starting X applications is as simple as:

```
rob@florian:~$ ssh -X catlin
Last login: Thu Sep 5 22:59:25 2002 from florian.rob.nocat
Linux 2.4.18.

rob@catlin:~$ xeyes &
[1] 12478
rob@catlin:~$
```

As long as you're running X on your local machine, this will display xeyes on your desktop. This xeyes is actually running on catlin, the machine we're currently logged into. All X11 traffic is being encrypted and sent down the *ssh* connection that we're logged in under and is displayed locally.

The real work is done by *ssh*, which sets up a local X11 proxy server for you:

```
rob@catlin:~$ echo $DISPLAY
catlin:10.0
```

X11 forwarding is normally disabled by default in openssh. To enable it, add the following line to your *sshd_config*, and restart *sshd*:

```
X11Forwarding yes
```

While xeyes isn't the most useful example of why you would want to do this, here are a couple you might find more interesting:

ethereal
Does packet capturing and visual analysis on a server at your *co/lo*

vnc
Takes command of remote X desktops from your local terminal, as if you were sitting at the console

gkrellm
Shows a nice graphical system status for your server (or even several at a time)

To make X11 traffic forward over *ssh* automatically, try setting this in your *~/.ssh/config*:

```
ForwardX11 yes
```

With this option in effect, you won't need the -X switch any more. Combine this with the *ssh-to* script (as described in "'Turbo-mode' ssh Logins" **(#67)**), and you have a very quick way of firing off secure, remote X11 jobs:

```
rob@florian:~$ catlin ethereal &
```

This will instantly give you an *ethereal* session running on catlin, encrypted over *ssh*. Hanging up on the *ssh* connection (say, with ~.) will kill all running X applications instantly. But if you need to pause them temporarily, suspending your *ssh* session (with ~^Z) and resuming later with *fg* works just fine.

See also:

- Ethereal packet sniffer: *http://www.ethereal.com/*
- VNC (a free X remote desktop client): *http://www.uk.research.att.com/vnc/*
- gkrellm system monitor: *http://www.gkrellm.net/*

Forwarding Ports over ssh
H A C K
#71 Keep network traffic to arbitrary ports secure with ssh port forwarding

In addition to providing remote shell access and command execution, OpenSSH can forward arbitrary TCP ports to the other end of your connection. This can be very handy for protecting email, web, or any other traffic you need to keep private (at least, all the way to the other end of the tunnel).

ssh accomplishes local forwarding by binding to a local port, performing encryption, sending the encrypted data to the remote end of the *ssh* connection, then decrypting it and sending it to the remote host and port you specify. Start an *ssh* tunnel with the -L switch (short for Local):

```
root@laptop:~# ssh -f -N -L110:mailhost:110 -l user mailhost
```

Naturally, substitute *user* with your username, and *mailhost* with your mail server's name or IP address. Note that you will have to be root on laptop for this example, since you'll be binding to a privileged port (110, the POP port). You should also disable any locally running POP daemon (look in */etc/inetd.conf*) or it will get in the way.

Now to encrypt all of your POP traffic, configure your mail client to connect to localhost port 110. It will happily talk to mailhost as if it were connected directly, except that the entire conversation will be encrypted.

The -f forks *ssh* into the background, and -N tells it not to actually run a command on the remote end (just do the forwarding). If your *ssh* server supports it, try the -C switch to turn on compression—this can significantly improve the time it takes to download your email.

You can specify as many -L lines as you like when establishing the connection. To also forward outbound email traffic, try this:

```
root@laptop:~# ssh -f -N -L110:mailhost:110 -L25:mailhost:25 \
  -l user mailhost
```

Set your outbound email host to localhost, and your email traffic will be encrypted as far as mailhost. This generally is only useful if the email is bound for an internal host, or if you can't trust your local network connection (as is the case with most wireless networks). Obviously, once your email leaves mailhost, it will be transmitted in the clear, unless you've encrypted the message with a tool such as *pgp* or *gpg*.

If you're already logged into a remote host and need to forward a port quickly, try this:

- Hit Enter
- Type ~C
- You should be at an ssh> prompt; enter the *-L* line as you would from the command line.

For example:

```
rob@catlin:~$
rob@catlin:~$ ~, then C (it doesn't echo)
ssh> -L8080:localhost:80
Forwarding port.
```

Your current shell will then forward local port 8000 to catlin's port 80, as if you had entered it in the first place.

You can also allow other (remote) clients to connect to your forwarded port, with the *-g* switch. If you're logged in to a remote gateway that serves as a NAT for a private network, then a command like this:

```
rob@gateway:~$ ssh -f -g -N -L8000:localhost:80 10.42.4.6
```

will forward all connections from gateway's port 8000 to internal host 10.42.4.6's port 80. If the gateway has a live Internet address, this will allow anyone from the Net to connect to the web server on 10.42.4.6 as if it were running on port 8000 of the gateway.

One last point worth mentioning: the forwarded host doesn't have to be localhost; it can be any host that the machine you're connecting to can access directly. For example, to forward local port 5150 to a web server somewhere on an internal network, try this:

```
rob@remote:~$ ssh -f -N -L5150:intranet.insider.nocat:80 gateway.nocat.net
```

Assuming that you're running a TLD ("Running Your Own Top-Level Domain" [Hack #80]) of *.nocat*, and that *gateway.nocat.net* also has a connection to the private *.nocat* network, all traffic to 5150 of *remote* will be obligingly forwarded to *intranet.insider.nocat:80*. The address *intranet.insider.nocat* doesn't have to resolve in DNS to *remote*; it isn't looked up until the connection is made to *gateway.nocat.net*, then it's gateway that does the lookup. To securely browse that site from *remote*, try connecting to *http://localhost:5150/*.

Although *ssh* also has functionality for acting as a Socks 4 proxy (with the -*D* switch), it just isn't well suited for routing all network traffic to the other end of a tunnel. Take a look at "Tunneling: IPIP Encapsulation" **[Hack #50]** for a way to use *vtun* in conjunction with *ssh* to forward *everything*. And see the documentation for the -*D* switch; it's a pretty neat feature. (What, did you think we'd do *all* of the work for you? ;)

ssh is an incredibly flexible tool, with much more functionality than I can cover here. See the references below for more fun things you can do with *ssh*.

See also:

- man ssh
- *SSH, The Secure Shell: The Definitive Guide* (O'Reilly)
- "Tunneling: IPIP Encapsulation" **[Hack #50]**
- "Quick Logins with ssh Client Keys" **[Hack #66]**
- "Running Your Own Top-Level Domain" **[Hack #80]**

Scripting
Hacks #72–75

Sometimes, you want to do something more complicated than can be expressed on a single command line. Once you've done something complicated more than two or three times, you'll probably begin to think that there must be a better way to do it (which doesn't involve a whole bunch of typing each time). This is usually when sysadmins begin to evolve into that strange breed of problem solver known as the *programmer*.

This section is *not* a crash course in programming, but rather a demonstration of a couple of pieces of applied programming hackery. I've found that the best way to learn how to program is to learn by doing, and the easiest way to get started is to see how other people have solved similar problems. The examples in this section are useful on their own but are even more useful as a starting point in building your own custom tools. Even if you're an old hand at scripting, take a look at some of these examples for some ideas on how to use some lesser known invocation switches and language features to get more done with less effort.

HACK #72 Get Settled in Quickly with movein.sh
Keep your local environment in sync on all of your servers

When you use a machine for some time, you will inevitably end up customizing it to your liking. As we saw in "At Home in Your Shell Environment" [Hack #10], the shell environment is a tremendously flexible tool that can be fine tuned to your precise specifications.

Usually these little tweaks take weeks (or even years) to perfect and span several files: different environment settings (depending on if it's a login shell or a subshell), editor preferences, email settings, mysql preferences, aliases to be set and options for every occasion, etc. When the environment is precisely programmed, tasks become easier and the system becomes more fun to work with.

Of course, all of this goes out the window when you log into a remote machine. It can be terribly frustrating to fire off your favorite command, only to see bash: xyz: command not found. Or to run *ls* and not see the colors. Or any of a thousand little adjustments that make life on your home machine such a joy, but working on remote machines such a barren, joyless existence.

You can always copy over your settings by hand, as most of them are kept as dotfiles in your home directory (like *.bashrc* and *.vimrc*). But it's difficult to remember them all by hand, and it leads to the classic versioning problem: once you make a change to your local copy, the remote copies all need to be updated again.

Make your life simpler with this very simple shell script.

Listing: movein.sh

```
#!/bin/sh

if [ -z "$1" ]; then
echo "Usage: `basename $0` hostname"
exit
fi

cd ~/.skel
tar zhcf - . | ssh $1 "tar zpvxf -"
```

Call it *movein.sh*, and stick it in your *~/bin* directory. Now create a *~/.skel* directory, and make symlinks to all of the files you'd like to copy to remote servers:

```
rob@caligula:~/.skel$ ls -al
total 12
drwxr-xr-x 6 rob staff 204 Sep 9 20:52 .
drwxr-xr-x 37 rob staff 1258 Sep 9 20:57 ..
lrwxr-xr-x 1 rob staff 11 Sep 9 20:52 .bash_login -> ../.bash_login
lrwxr-xr-x 1 rob staff 11 Sep 9 20:52 .bashrc -> ../.bashrc
lrwxr-xr-x 1 rob staff 11 Sep 9 20:52 .my.cnf -> ../.my.cnf
lrwxr-xr-x 1 rob staff 11 Sep 9 20:52 .pinerc -> ../.pinerc
drwxr-xr-x 3 rob staff 102 Sep 9 20:51 .ssh
lrwxr-xr-x 1 rob staff 9 Sep 9 20:52 .vimrc -> ../.vimrc
lrwxr-xr-x 1 rob staff 6 Sep 9 21:27 bin -> ../bin
```

Note that *~/.skel/.ssh* is a special case: it's a directory, not a symlink. DO NOT SYMLINK YOUR *~/.ssh* TO *~/.skel*! The last thing you need is to copy your private *ssh* key all over the place; that's what the *ssh*-agent is for (see "Using ssh-Agent Effectively" [Hack #68]). Instead, make a directory called *~/.skel/.ssh* and make a symlink like this:

```
rob@caligula:~/.skel$ cd .ssh
rob@caligula:~/.skel/.ssh$ ls -al
total 4
```

```
drwxr-xr-x 3 rob staff 102 Sep 9 20:51 .
drwxr-xr-x 6 rob staff 204 Sep 9 20:52 ..
lrwxr-xr-x 1 rob staff 26 Sep 9 20:51 authorized_keys2 ->
    ../../.ssh/id_dsa.pub
```

This is a link called *authorized_keys2*, and it points to your live public key. You *are* using public key *ssh* connections, right? If not, consult "Quick Logins with ssh Client Keys" **[Hack #66]**.

Now when this script runs, it will copy the contents of *~/.skel* to the host you specify on the command line, straight into your home directory. The *h* flag to tar means "copy these symlinks as if they were files, not symlinks," so you end up with a copy of the contents of each link on the remote end. If you make changes to your local copy, just run the script again, and it will overwrite everything on the remote end.

Only include the *.ssh* directory as mentioned above if you'd like to be able to log into the remote host automatically, without a password. As long as your local machine's keys are kept secure, there is no inherent security risk in leaving extra *authorized_keys2* files lying around. That's what public key cyptography is all about.

See also:

- "Quick Logins with ssh Client Keys" **[Hack #66]**
- "Using ssh-Agent Effectively" **[Hack #68]**
- "At Home in Your Shell Environment" **[Hack #10]**
- *SSH: The Secure Shell, The Definitive Guide* (O'Reilly)

Global Search and Replace with Perl
#73 Manipulate files and streams with arbitrary Perl substitutions, without a script

There are a couple of switches that make Perl a very useful command-line editing tool. Learn these switches, and you too can learn how to mumble magic Perl one-liners to confound your friends (and frighten your project manager).

The first is *-e*. Give Perl a *-e* followed by a line of code, and it will run it as if it were an ordinary Perl script:

```
rob@catlin:~$ perl -e 'print "Hi, Ma!\n"'
Hi, Ma!
```

Note that a trailing ; isn't needed on one-liners. It's generally a good idea to wrap your line in single quotes to prevent the shell from attempting to interpret special characters (like the ! and \ above).

The next switch is a little more complicated, it but becomes second nature once you start using it: *-p*. From perldoc perlrun:

> **-p** causes Perl to assume the following loop around your program, which makes it iterate over filename arguments somewhat like **sed**:
>
> ```
> LINE:
> while (<>) {
> ... # your program goes here
> } continue {
> print or die "-p destination: $!\n";
> }
> ```

The line in question ($_) is automatically printed on every iteration of the loop. If you combine *-p* and *-e*, you get a one-liner that iterates over every file on the command line or on the text fed to it on STDIN. For example, here's a complicated *cat* command:

```
rob@catlin:~$ perl -pe 1 /etc/hosts
#
# hosts This file describes a number of hostname-to-address
# mappings for the TCP/IP subsystem.
#

# For loopbacking.
127.0.0.1 localhost
```

The *1* is just a return code (as if you entered 1; in a Perl script, which is equivalent to return 1;). Since the lines are printed automatically, we don't really need the program we specify with *-e* to do anything.

Where it gets interesting is in providing a bit of code to manipulate the current line before it gets printed. For example, suppose you wanted to append the local machine name to the localhost line:

```
rob@catlin:~$ perl -pe 's/localhost/localhost $ENV{HOSTNAME}/' /etc/hosts
#
# hosts This file describes a number of hostname-to-address
# mappings for the TCP/IP subsystem.
#

# For loopbacking.
127.0.0.1 localhost catlin.nocat.net
```

or maybe you'd like to manipulate your *inetd* settings:

```
rob@caligula:~$ perl -pe 's/^(\s+)?(telnet|shell|login|exec)/# $2/' \
    /etc/inetd.conf
```

That will print the contents of */etc/inetd.conf* to STDOUT, commenting out any uncommented *telnet*, *shell*, *login*, or *exec* lines along the way. Naturally, we could redirect that back out to a file, but if we just want to edit a file in place, there's a better way: the *-i* switch.

-i lets you edit files in place. So, to comment out all of the above lines in */etc/inetd.conf*, you might try:

```
root@catlin:~# perl -pi -e 's/^(\s+)?(telnet|shell|login|exec)/# $2/' /etc/
inetd.conf
```

or better yet:

```
root@catlin:~# perl -pi.orig -e 's/^(\s+)?(telnet|shell|login|exec)/# $2/' /
etc/inetd.conf
```

The second example will backup */etc/inetd.conf* to */etc/inetd.conf.orig* before changing the original. Don't forget to HUP *inetd* to make your changes take.

It's just as easy to edit multiple files in place at the same time. You can specify any number of files (or wildcards) on the command line:

```
rob@catlin:~$ perl -pi.bak -e 's/bgcolor=#ffffff/bgcolor=#000000/i' *.html
```

This will change the background color of all html pages in the current directory from white to black. Don't forget that trailing i to make the match case insensitive (to match bgcolor=#FFFFFF or even BGColor=#FfFffF).

What if you're in the middle of working on a CVS project, and need to change the CVS server that you'd like to commit to? It's easy, if you pipe the output of a *find* through an *xargs* running a *perl -pi -e*:

```
schuyler@ganesh:~/nocat$ find -name Root | xargs perl -pi -e 's/cvs.
oldserver.com/cvs.newserver.org/g'
```

Then reset your $CVSROOT and do your CVS check in as normal, and your project will automagically end up checked into *cvs.newserver.org*.

Using Perl from the command line can help you do some powerful transformations on the fly. Study your regular expressions, and use it wisely, and it can save piles of hand edits.

See also:

- *Programming Perl* (O'Reilly)
- perldoc perlrun
- "At Home in Your Shell Environment" [Hack #10]
- "CVS: Making Changes to a Module" [Hack #30]

HACK #74 Mincing Your Data into Arbitrary Chunks (in bash)

Use bash arithmetic and dd to chop large binary files into reasonable chunks

Here's an example of how to use environment variables and arithmetic evaluation in *bash* to chop any file into arbitrary sized chunks.

Listing: mince

```
#!/bin/bash

if [ -z "$2" -o ! -r "$1" ]; then
echo "Usage: mince [file] [chunk size]"
exit 255
fi

SIZE=`ls -l $1 | awk '{print $5}'`

if [ $2 -gt $SIZE ]; then
echo "Your chunk size must be smaller than the file size!"
exit 254
fi

CHUNK=$2
TOTAL=0
PASS=0
while [ $TOTAL -lt $SIZE ]; do
PASS=$((PASS + 1))
echo "Creating $1.$PASS..."
dd conv=noerror if=$1 of=$1.$PASS bs=$CHUNK skip=$((PASS - 1)) count=1 2> /
dev/null
TOTAL=$((TOTAL + CHUNK))
done

echo "Created $PASS chunks out of $1."
```

Note that we take advantage of conv=noerror, since the last chunk is almost guaranteed to run beyond the end of your file. Using this option makes *dd* blithely continue to write bits until we run out of source file, at which point it exits (but doesn't throw an error, and more importantly, doesn't refuse to write the last chunk).

This could be handy for slicing large files into floppy-sized (zip disk, cd-r, dvd, Usenet) chunks prior to archiving. As it uses *dd*'s skip feature, it will work on any sized file, regardless of the amount of available RAM (provided that you supply a reasonable chunk size). Since the block size (bs) is set to whatever you have selected as your chunk size, it runs quite quickly, especially with chunks larger than a couple of kilobytes.

It saves your chunks as multiple files (ending in a . followed by the chunk number) in the current directory. Running *ls FILENAME.** will show you your chunks in numerical order. But what if you have more than nine of them?

```
ls FILENAME.* | sort -n -t . +2
```

How do you reassemble them?

```
cat `ls FILENAME.* | sort -n -t . +2` > FILENAME.complete
```

Don't believe me?

```
diff FILENAME FILENAME.complete
```

(This of course assumes that your filename has only one . in it. If you have a ridiculously.long.filename.with.multiple.dots, consult man sort(1).)

Colorized Log Analysis in Your Terminal
View your log files in an xterm window in full, living color

If you find yourself slowly going cross-eyed while looking at line after line of system logs, then you should consider using tools to help you organize your logs. While a properly configured syslog (as shown in "Steering syslog" **[Hack #54]**) goes a long way toward logfile sanity, it can still be a bit overwhelming to sift through a multi-megabyte */var/log/messages* looking for patterns.

Just as a colorized *ls* can help identify types of files at a glance, a colorized *grep* is a handy tool for making patterns leap out of a sea of grey lines. There are a number of X applications that will do this for you, but why not make it easy to view your colorized logs from the command line?

Save this as *~/bin/rcg* (short for Regex Colored Glasses):

```perl
#!/usr/bin/perl -w
use strict;
use Term::ANSIColor qw(:constants);

my %target = ( );

while (my $arg = shift) {
my $clr = shift;

if(($arg =~ /^-/) | (!$clr)) {
print "Usage: rcg [regex] [color] [regex] [color] ...\n";
exit;
}

#
# Ugly, lazy, pathetic hack here
#
$target{$arg} = eval($clr);
}

my $rst = RESET;

while(<>) {
foreach my $x (keys(%target)) {
s/($x)/$target{$x}$1$rst/g;
}
print;
}
```

rcg is a simple filter that uses Term::ANSIColor to colorize arbitrary regexs, specified on the commandline. It is intended to help visually slog through log files.

You must pass *rcg* an even number of command line parameters. The odd terms specify the regex, the even terms specify the color.

Suppose you wanted anything with the word *sendmail* in your messages log to show up magenta, instead of grey:

```
$ rcg sendmail MAGENTA < /var/log/messages | less -r
```

The less -r is optional but handy (as it displays the intended colors in *less*, instead of the ESC characters.)

You can use any arbitrary regex as an odd term:

```
$ rcg '\d+\.\d+\.\d+\.\d+' GREEN < /var/log/maillog
```

Or chain colors together:

```
$ tail -50 /var/log/messages | rcg WARNING 'BOLD . YELLOW . ON_RED'
```

You can specify any number of regex/color code pairs on a single command-line. This is where teeny shell scripts or aliases would come in handy (one for messages, one for firewall logs, one for Apache).

See the Term::ANSIColor docs for the full list of colors and combinations.

Some other useful strings:

\w+=\S+
> Variables, such as TERM=xyz

\d+\.\d+\.\d+\.\d+
> Probably an IP address

^(J|F|M|A|S|O|N|D)\w\w (\d|)\d
> Might be a date

\b\d\d:\d\d:\d\d\b
> Possibly the time

.*last message repeated.*
> Makes this "BOLD . WHITE"

Use your imagination, but be warned: color params are just eval( )'d. Theoretically, many valid Perl expressions can be substituted for regexes or colors; exploiting this, uh, *feature* is left as an exercise to the reader. You probably shouldn't be running arbitrary *rcg* lines as root, unless you wrote them yourself. Also note that colorization is applied in arbitrary order, so it's not possible to guarantee the behavior of overlapping regexes.

Information Servers
Hacks #76–100

Linux is a powerful platform for building information servers. But the information systems themselves are rarely a part of Linux. Usually, Linux is simply a "life support system" for more complicated, dedicated information services.

In this final section, we'll look at three major applications. They all run quite well on Linux and have become the backbone of Internet information services. BIND (by the Internet Software Consortium) is by far the most common DNS information server on the planet, serving the Domain Name to IP address information that keeps the Internet running. For more generic information needs, MySQL is a very lightweight, fast, and scalable SQL database that drives many enterprise network applications. Finally, when it comes to serving information to users, Apache is by far the most popular web server on the planet. Apache is run on more servers than all of the rest of the known web servers *combined* and for good reason: it is mature, stable, fast, and full of useful and interesting features.

If you're looking for more information about running any of these packages, consult the online documentation for each. These applications are running the current incarnation of the Internet, and have been widely and extensively documented. In addition, O'Reilly has a number of good books on all three applications, such as *DNS and Bind*, *MySQL Reference Manual*, and *Apache: The Definitive Guide* to name a few. *MySQL* by Paul DuBois (New Riders) is also an excellent guide to running MySQL.

In the following hacks, we'll see some non-obvious techniques for getting these servers to deliver information the way you want them. We will take a look at some methods for making them scale to large installations, while keeping maintenance of even very complex sites to a minimum.

Running BIND in a chroot Jail

#76 Keep your named isolated from the rest of the system with the judicious use of chroot

The vast majority of the Internet relies on BIND for its name resolution needs. While tremendous effort has gone toward shoring up potential security holes in BIND, you can never be absolutely certain that any code is completely free of possible exploits. To minimize the possible damage done by remote root exploits (due to buffer overflows, bugs, or misconfiguration), many sites choose to run their *named* service in a chroot jail. This helps ensure that even if the *named* process is compromised, the attacker's job won't be finished yet. While a chroot jail isn't necessarily impenetrable, it poses a very difficult challenge for a would-be system cracker.

These steps outline the minimum effort required to get BIND 9 running in a chroot jail. DNS security is a large and complex issue, and should be taken very seriously. Consult the resources at the end of this hack for more information.

To begin with, we'll want to run *named* as some user other than root. Create a named user and group that will only be used for running the *named* process:

```
root@gemini:~# groupadd -g 53 named
root@gemini:~# useradd -u 53 -g named -c "chroot BIND user" \
  -d /var/named/jail -m named
```

We'll instruct *named* to *chroot* to */var/named/jail* at startup. We will need to create enough of a skeleton file structure under this directory to allow *named* to start normally. Create the */var* structure, and copy your DNS data into it:

```
root@gemini:~# cd ~named
root@gemini:/var/named/jail# mkdir -p var/{run,named}
root@gemini:/var/named/jail# cp -Rav /var/named/data var/named/
```

If you act as a slave for any zones, then the *named* process will need write access to a directory (to keep track of updated slave data). Create a directory specifically for slave data, independent of your regular data files:

```
root@gemini:/var/named/jail# mkdir var/named/slave
root@gemini:/var/named/jail# chown named.named var/named/slave
```

Next, create the *dev/* and *etc/* directories, and copy the critical system files and devices to them:

```
root@gemini:/var/named/jail# mkdir {dev,etc}
root@gemini:/var/named/jail# cp -av /dev/{null,random} dev/
root@gemini:/var/named/jail# cp -av \
  /etc/{localtime,named.conf,rndc.key} etc/
```

Clean up the ownership and permissions of these directories:

```
root@gemini:/var/named/jail# chown root.root .
root@gemini:/var/named/jail# chmod 0755 .
root@gemini:/var/named/jail# chown named.named var/named/data/
root@gemini:/var/named/jail# chmod 0700 var/named/data/
root@gemini:/var/named/jail# chown named.named var/run/
```

If you're using syslog for your DNS logs, you'll need to add a switch like this to your syslogd startup rc. It will tell syslog to listen on that socket as well (which is needed since the system's */dev/log* won't be reachable from inside the jail):

```
syslogd -m 0 -a /var/named/jail/dev/log
```

If you're using filesystem logs, you won't need to change your syslogd configuration. Just be sure that the log files are writable by the named user, and that your log directory exists under */var/named/jail/*.

Finally, fire up *named*, passing the username, chroot directory, and initial configuration file on the command line:

```
root@gemini:~# /usr/sbin/named -u named -t /var/named/jail \
   -c /etc/named.conf
```

If your *named* doesn't start cleanly, take a look at the system's */var/log/syslog* or */var/log/messages*, and track down the source of the trouble. It can be tricky to be sure that your permissions are all what they need to be. Here's a sample recursive *ls* output from a machine with a running *chroot*'d BIND:

```
root@gemini:/var/named/jail# ls -lR
.:
total 12
drwxr-xr-x 2 root root 4096 Sep 20 12:45 dev/
drwxr-xr-x 2 root root 4096 Sep 20 13:08 etc/
drwxr-xr-x 5 root root 4096 Sep 20 13:04 var/

./dev:
total 0
crw-rw-rw- 1 root root 1, 3 Jul 17 1994 null
crw-r--r-- 1 root root 1, 8 Dec 11 1995 random

./etc:
total 16
-rw-r--r-- 1 root root 1017 Sep 20 12:46 localtime
-r--r--r-- 1 root root 1381 Sep 20 13:08 named.conf
-rw------- 1 root root 77 Sep 11 04:22 rndc.key

./var:
total 12
drwxr-xr-x 4 root root 4096 Sep 20 13:01 named/
drwxr-xr-x 2 named named 4096 Sep 20 13:15 run/

./var/named:
total 8
```

```
drwx------ 3 named named 4096 Sep 20 13:03 data/
drwxr-xr-x 2 named named 4096 Sep 20 12:43 slave/

./var/named/data:
total 42
-rw-r--r-- 1 root root  381 Apr 30 16:32 localhost.rev
-rw-r--r-- 1 root root 2769 Sep 20 13:03 named.ca
-r--r--r-- 1 root root 1412 Sep 17 16:44 nocat.net

./var/named/slave:
total 0

./var/run:
total 4
-rw-r--r-- 1 named named 6 Sep 20 13:15 named.pid
```

A *chroot*'d environment can help keep daemons sequestered away from the rest of a running system, but they're not a magic bullet for instant system security. This hack should get you started, but be sure to read up on the complexities of using and running BIND.

See also:

- *http://www.losurs.org/docs/howto/Chroot-BIND.html*
- *DNS Bind,* Fourth edition (O'Reilly)

HACK #77 Views in BIND 9

Change the results that your DNS server returns depending on where the requests are coming from

Until recently, presenting one view of a zone to one community of hosts and another view to others has entailed running multiple sets of name servers or multiple name server processes on a single host in a tricky configuration. Nobody ever said being two-faced is easy.

BIND 9 introduced a new feature called *views* that makes delivering different versions of a zone and even different name server configurations easy.

Basic Syntax

The key to configuring views is the new BIND 9 configuration statement, view. view takes a view name as an argument and has one required substatement, match-clients. The view name is simply a convenient mnemonic for identifying the view; I usually use names such as "internal" and "external" or "Internet." If you use a name that conflicts with a reserved word in *named.conf*, be sure to quote it. I quote all of my view names, because I can't remember which words are reserved.

The match-clients substatement takes an address match list as an argument. Only quarriers whose IP addresses match this address match list will see the configuration specified in the enclosing view. If a querier's IP address matches multiple view statement's match-clients substatements, the first view statement is the one that applies.

Here's an example of a simple view statement:

```
view "global" {
match-clients { any; };
};
```

This view statement doesn't do anything useful, because it applies to all queries (in the absence of other view statements) and it doesn't include any substatements besides match-clients, which would change the configuration of this view from the default configuration.

If you don't specify a particular substatement within a view, the view inherits the global setting for that substatement. So, for example, if you don't turn recursion off within a view, that view would inherit the recursion setting from your options statement (specified by the recursion substatement), or if you don't have one, would inherit the global default, which is recursion yes.

Here's an example of turning recursion off within a view:

```
view "external" {
match-clients { any; };
recursion no;
};
```

Here's a complete *named.conf* file that includes the previous view statement:

```
/*
 * BIND 9 name server allowing recursive queries from
 * localhost, disallowing from anywhere else
 */

options {
directory "/var/named";
};

view "localhost" {
match-clients { localhost; };
recursion yes; /* this is the default */
};

view "external" {
match-clients { any; };
recursion no;
};
```

This name server allows recursive queries only if they come from the local host. (The localhost access control list [ACL] is predefined to be all of the IP

addresses of the host that runs the name server, plus the loopback address.)
Queries from all other addresses are treated as non-recursive.

Here's a similar configuration, this one of a name server that allows recursive queries from our internal network but not from the Internet:

```
/*
 * Same name server serving an internal network and the
 * Internet
 */

options {
directory "/var/named";
};

view "internal" {
match-clients { localnets; };
recursion yes; /* this is the default */
};

view "external" {
match-clients { any; };
recursion no;
};
```

This configuration takes advantage of the built-in ACL localnets, which is predefined as all of the networks to which our name server is directly connected.

Defining Zones in Views

In order to present a version of a zone to only some queriers, you need to define the zone within a view. You simply use a zone statement as a view substatement. Otherwise, its syntax is the same as if it were a top-level statement. Note that if you define even one zone within a view, all of your zones need to be defined inside views.

Here's an example:

```
/*
 * A name server showing different zone data to different
 * networks
 */

options {
directory "/var/named";
};

view "internal" {
match-clients { localnets; };
recursion yes; /* this is the default */

zone "oreilly.com" {
type master;
```

```
file "db.oreilly.com.internal";
allow-transfer { any; };
};
};

view "external" {
match-clients { any; };
recursion no;

zone "oreilly.com" {
type master;
file "db.oreilly.com.external";
allow-transfer { none; };
};
};
```

Note that the zone oreilly.com is defined in both the internal and the external view, but the zone data file for oreilly.com is db.oreilly.com.internal in the internal view and db.oreilly.com.external in the external view. Presumably, the contents of the zone data files are different.

If you prefer to use different subdirectories for the internal and external zone data, you can do that, too. For example, the file substatement for oreilly.com in the internal view could be file "internal/db.oreilly.com"; and the external view could use file "external/db.oreilly.com";.

This way, you can keep all of your internal zone data files in the /var/named/internal directory and your external zone data files in the /var/named/external directory.

Views in Slave Name Servers

One minor wrinkle in views is the configuration of slave name servers. Many people configure a primary master name server with multiple views, then want to configure a slave with the same views. Unfortunately, when the slave tries to transfer the zones (or the two versions of the same zone) from the primary master name server, it only sees one version of the zone, the one defined in the view the slave's IP address can see.

The solution to this problem is to configure an IP address alias on the slave name server, giving it two IP addresses from which to initiate zone transfers. Then configure the primary master to present one view to one of the slave's IP addresses and the other view to the slave's other IP address. Finally, force the slave to initiate zone transfers from the appropriate IP address within each view.

Here's an example. Our slave has two IP addresses, 192.168.0.2 and 192.168.0.254. Our primary master has just one, 192.168.0.1. First, here's the slave's *named.conf* file:

```
options {
directory "/var/named";
};

view "internal" {
match-clients { localnets; };
recursion yes;

zone "oreilly.com" {
type slave;
masters { 192.168.0.1; };
transfer-source 192.168.0.2;
file "internal/bak.oreilly.com ";
allow-transfer { any; };
};
};

view "external" {
match-clients { any; };
recursion no;

zone "oreilly.com" {
type slave;
masters { 192.168.0.1; };
transfer-source 192.168.0.254;
file "external/bak.oreilly.com ";
allow-transfer { none; };
};
};
```

Notice that the slave is configured to initiate transfers of oreilly.com within the internal view from the IP address 192.168.0.2 and within the external view from 192.168.0.254.

Now, here's the primary master's *named.conf* file:

```
options {
directory "/var/named";
};

view "internal" {
match-clients { !192.168.0.254; localnets; };
recursion yes;

zone "oreilly.com" {
type master;
file "internal/db.oreilly.com ";
allow-transfer { any; };
};
};

view "external" {
match-clients { any; };
recursion no;
```

```
zone "oreilly.com" {
type master;
file "external/db.oreilly.com ";
allow-transfer { 192.168.0.254; };
};
};
```

Notice that the internal view's match-clients substatement explicitly places 192.168.0.254 into the external view by negating it in the address match list. Any time the slave initiates a zone transfer from that IP address, it'll get the version of oreilly.com described by the zone data file */var/named/external/db. oreilly.com*.

HACK #78 Setting Up Caching DNS with Authority for Local Domains

Get BIND running quickly with a forwarding, caching server

Running BIND can be very tricky business if you have a particularly complex network topology. Multiple DMZs, public versus private IP addresses, and delegated subdomains can make DNS administration a full time job for a large site. If you're looking for a way to alleviate some of the complexity, see "Views in BIND 9" **[Hack #77]**. Or if you're feeling particularly adventurous, try wildcard domain matching and delegation, as described in "Ultrahosting: Mass Web Site Hosting with Wildcards, Proxy, and Rewrite" **[Hack #100]**.

But in the majority of small to medium installations, BIND is really only needed for two things: to act as the authoritative source for a domain or two and provide forwarding to another DNS server for all other requests.

Here is a simple (but complete) *named.conf* that does exactly that:

```
options {
directory "/var/named";
pid-file "/var/run/named.pid";
statistics-file "/var/named/named.stats";
};

logging {
channel default_out {
file "/var/log/named.log";
};

category default { default_out; };
category config { default_out; };
category xfer-in { default_out; };
category xfer-out { default_out; };
category lame-servers { null; };
};
```

```
zone "0.0.127.in-addr.arpa" in {
type master;
file "data/localhost.rev";
};

zone "." {
type hint;
file "rootservers.cache";
};

// Authoritative domains go here

zone "nocat.net" {
type master;
file "data/nocat.net";
};
```

This makes us authoritative for the domain nocat.net, with its data stored in the file */var/named/data/nocat.net*. Requests made for domains other than nocat.net (or for the loopback network 127.0.0.0) are automatically forwarded along according to the root servers contained in *rootservers.cache*. A suitable rootserver cache should have shipped with BIND, but if you can't find it, try something like this:

```
# dig @a.root-servers.net > rootservers.cache
```

If your network doesn't have unrestricted access to the Internet (e.g., you are behind a restrictive firewall), then forwarding to authoritative servers may not work. If that's the case, try an explicit forwarding rule in place of the hint entry above:

```
zone "." {
type forward;
forward only;
forwarders { 192.168.1.1; };
}
```

Naturally, replace 192.168.1.1 with the IP address of a valid name server for your network. This will direct all DNS traffic to your network's DNS server, which presumably has permission to do domain lookups through the firewall.

See also:

- "Views in BIND 9" [Hack #77]
- "Ultrahosting: Mass Web Site Hosting with Wildcards, Proxy, and Rewrite" [Hack #100]
- *DNS & BIND*, 4th Edition (O'Reilly)

#79 Distributing Server Load with Round-Robin DNS

Direct traffic to multiple servers simultaneously with round-robin DNS

If you serve a particularly popular site, you will eventually find the wall at which your server simply can't serve any more requests. In the web server world, this is called the *Slashdot effect*, and it isn't a pretty site (er, sight). While adding RAM, upgrading processors, and using faster drives and buses will help in the short term, you may eventually find that a single machine can't possibly perform the work that needs to be done.

One way to overcome the limits of the monolithic server is to distribute the load across many machines. By adding a second (or third) server to the available pool of machines, you can not only increase performance but also add to the stability of the network. If you have a hot spare (or three) running all of the time, then if one develops trouble, the others can take over for it without any downtime.

Perhaps the easiest way to distribute the load of public traffic is to have the public do the work of distributing the load for you. Through the magic of round-robin DNS, inbound requests to a single host name can be directed to come from any number of IP addresses.

In BIND 9, this is as easy as adding multiple A records for a single host. For example, suppose we use this in the zone file for oreillynet.com:

```
www 60 IN A 208.201.239.36
www 60 IN A 208.201.239.37
```

Now, when a hosts looks up www.oreillynet.com in DNS, about half of the time they will see:

```
rob@caligula:~$ host www.oreillynet.com
www.oreillynet.com has address 208.201.239.36
www.oreillynet.com has address 208.201.239.37
```

and the rest of the time, they get:

```
rob@caligula:~$ host www.oreillynet.com
www.oreillynet.com has address 208.201.239.37
www.oreillynet.com has address 208.201.239.36
```

As most applications only use the first address returned by DNS, this works rather nicely. Approximately half of the requests will go to each address, and therefore the load of two servers should be roughly half of that of a single server. We set the TTL low (to 60 seconds) to prevent any intervening caching DNS servers from hanging onto one sort order for too long, which will hopefully help keep the number of requests to each host more or less equal.

It is only useful to spread out the load if all of the servers are in agreement about what they're serving. If your data gets out of sync, then browsers might get one version of a web page on the first hit and another when they hit reload. If you're looking for a way to keep that from happening, take a look at "Keeping Parts of Filesystems in sync with rsync" [Hack #41].

Also, keep in mind that doing actual IP takeover (in case one host is unable to perform its duties) is tricky business. If one server dies, you can't change DNS and wait for it to propagate to the entire Internet. You'll need something that takes over for the down server immediately. Take a look at one method of how to do this in "Cheap IP Takeover" [Hack #63].

See also:

- "Keeping Parts of Filesystems in sync with rsync" [Hack #41]
- "Cheap IP Takeover" [Hack #63]

HACK #80   Running Your Own Top-Level Domain
Set up your own TLD in BIND for ease of navigation

If you admin a network that uses private addressing, you've almost certainly encountered the disassociated schizophrenia of trying to maintain zone files that properly reflect internal and external IP addresses. With the introduction of views in "Views in BIND 9" [Hack #77], supporting multiple address ranges in a single domain has been significantly streamlined.

While using views is one way to attack the problem, consider the ease of setting up your own top-level domain. Normally, zone entries in *named.conf* look something like this:

```
zone "oreillynet.com" {
type master;
file "data/oreillynet.com";
};
```

This is an entry appropriate for an authoritative DNS server for the oreillynet. com subdomain. The actual top level domains (i.e., .com, .net, .org, .int, etc.) are only delegated to the mysterious 13 known as the root DNS servers. Even though your servers won't be consulted by the rest of the Internet, it can be handy to set up your very own TLD that works only on your local network.

For example, suppose you have a group of machines that use the private 192.168.1.0/24 network. These machines aren't directly reachable from the Internet, and you don't really want to advertise their DNS information to would-be network crackers. Try a non-standard TLD:

```
zone "bp" {
type master;
file "data/bp";
allow-transfer { 192.168.1/24; };
allow-query { 192.168.1/24; };
};
```

(The bp is short for BackPlane, and more to the point, is just plain short.)
With the above added to your zone file, set up a master record for bp just as
you would any other domain:

```
$TTL 86400
@ IN SOA ns.bp. root.homer.bp. (
2002090100 ; Serial
10800 ; Refresh after 3 hours
3600 ; Retry after 1 hour
604800 ; Expire (1 week)
60 ; Negative expiry time
)

IN NS ns.bp.

ns IN A 192.168.1.1

homer IN A 192.168.1.10
bart IN A 192.168.1.11
lisa IN A 192.168.1.12
```

Reload named, and you should be able to simply ping homer.bp. If you'd
like other name servers to maintain slave copies of your TLD, just add them
as usual:

```
zone "bp" {
type slave;
file "db.bp";
masters { 192.168.1.1; };
};
```

In this way, you can extend your new TLD across your entire private network architecture. If you're running tunnels over the Internet (as in "Tunneling: IPIP Encapsulation" [Hack #50]) to connect remote offices or friends,
support for your TLD could theoretically grow to be as large as you like.

HACK #81 Monitoring MySQL Health with mtop
Display MySQL threads in real time in a format similar to top

Much like its *top* counterpart, the *mtop* utility gives real time, running statistics of your mysql server all in a terminal window. On a busy database
server, this can give you very precise details about what queries are running
(and taking up all of your resources).

When running *mtop*, you'll need to pass at least the following two switches on the command line:

```
mysql --dbuser=monitor --password=n0telling
```

Naturally, substituting your own database username and password. If you're running *mtop* from some host other than your database server, also specify the --host={mysql_host} switch. Once it's running, you'll be presented with a top-like screen that refreshes every few seconds:

```
load average: 0.72, 0.47, 0.26 mysqld 3.23.51 up 33 day(s), 4:48 hrs
2 threads: 2 running, 0 cached. Queries/slow: 71.5K/0 Cache Hit: 99.99%
Opened tables: 42 RRN: 4.0M TLW: 0 SFJ: 0 SMP: 0

ID USER HOST DB TIME COMMAND STATE INFO
26049 root localhost test Query show full processlist
26412 root localhost nocat 1 Query Writing to n select * from Member where
User like '%rob%'
---
```

Here we see the attached users, the hosts they are connecting from, the queries they're running (and on which databases), as well as how long each thread has been executing (in seconds). The numbers on the left are the thread ID of each running query, not the mysql PID. If a particular query is in danger of becoming a slow query, the line will turn magenta. If the query then becomes a slow query, the color changes to yellow. If the thread is still running after twice MySQL's long_query_time value has passed, the line becomes red. This makes it easy to tell at a glance if some queries are taking a particularly long time to execute.

Just as with *top*, hitting ? while *mtop* is running shows all available keystrokes:

```
mtop ver 0.6.2/2002905, Copyright (c) 2002, Marc Prewitt/Chelsea Networks

A top users display for mysql

These single-character commands are available:

q - quit
? - help; show this text
f - flush status
k - kill processes; send a kill to a list of ids
s - change the number of seconds to delay between updates
m - toggle manual refresh mode on/off
d - filter display with regular expression (user/host/db/command/state/info)
h - display process for only one host
u - display process for only one user
i - toggle all/non-Sleeping process display
o - reverse the sort order
e - explain a process; show query optimizer info
t - show mysqld stats (show status/mysqladmin ext)
```

```
v - show mysqld variables (show variables/mysqladmin vars)
z - zoom in on a process, show sql statement detail
r - show replication status for master/slaves
```

Probably the two most commonly used features are *explain* (e) and *kill* (k). Hitting e will prompt you for a thread ID. Type in the number of the query you're interested in, and it will show you details about what mysql is actually doing when running the query:

```
Id: 27134 User: root Host: localhost Db: nocat Time: 0
Command: Query State: cleaning up

select *
FROM Member
WHERE User like '%rob%'

table |type |possible_keys |key | ken_len|ref | rows|
Member |ALL | | | | | 9652|where used
```

Likewise, the k key will allow you to kill a thread by supplying its thread ID. This is tremendously handy for killing long-running (or process intensive, poorly optimized) queries, without having to run *mysqladmin* multiple times from the command line.

]One suggested method for skipping the need for specifying the user and password on the command line is to create a *mysqltop* user with restricted privileges. From perldoc mtop:

> The most convenient way to setup your system to use *mtop* is to create a database user called mysqltop which has no password. For security purposes, this user should have all privileges set to N except *Process_priv*, which must be set to Y.

To grant these privileges, execute the following from the MySQL command prompt:

```
mysql> grant select on test.* to mysqltop;
mysql> grant select on test.* to mysqltop@localhost;
mysql> update user set process_priv='y' where user='mysqltop';
mysql> flush privileges;
```

With *mtop* installed and in your PATH, you can save yourself a lot of typing (and guesswork) compared to hunting down misbehaving threads with *mysqladmin* alone.

See also:

- The *mtop* package is available at *http://mtop.sourceforge.net/* (which requires Perl 5)
- Curses.pm (available through CPAN)

Setting Up Replication in MySQL

#82 Keep live copies of your database running to increase performance and provide redundancy

As of Version 3.23.33, database replication is implemented in MySQL. It is accomplished by maintaining a binary log of each database action on one machine (the *master*), and keeping it in sync with each of the replicated copies on other machines (the *slaves*). As of MySQL 3.23, replication is only one-way (that is, you may make changes to the database on master that get propagated to each slave, but changes to the slaves are not sent back to the master). If you need bidirectional replication, take a look at the bleeding edge code in MySQL 4.

The most common reason for setting up replication is to distribute the load of handling database requests across multiple machines. This will not only help with performance, but will add a bit of redundancy should one of your database servers fail. Your application must be smart enough to know that write requests *must* be handed off to the master or else your replicated copies will get out of sync with the master. This is nobody's idea of a fun time, so make sure that every place in your code that needs to write to the database *only* does so to the master copy.

Here are nine easy steps to getting replication running in MySQL 3.23.33 (or later). Before starting, make sure that all of your machines are running the same version of MySQL (preferably, the latest stable version).

1. Decide which database server will be the master, and which will be the slave(s). Generally, the master is your most capable machine. If you have a particularly popular site that needs to handle many database requests, you should strongly consider a multiprocessor machine with plenty of RAM and a hardware raid. If your database server is underpowered, then your entire dynamic application will suffer as other servers block while waiting for the database to be updated, no matter how many machines you distribute the load to.

2. Create a replication user on the master. This is a MySQL user just like any other, only with FILE permission for each database that you wish to replicate:

   ```
   mysql> grant FILE on webdb.* to replicant@'%.mynetwork.edu' identified by
   'seCret';
   ```

3. Enable the binlog on the master, and pick which databases will be replicated. Include something like this in the [mysqld] section of the */etc/my.cnf* on the master:

   ```
   log-bin
   server-id=1
   ```

Also include binlog-do-db lines for each database you'd like to make available via replication.:

```
binlog-do-db=webdb
```

Now bring down MySQL and immediately bring it back up again to make your changes live:

```
root@db:/usr/local/mysql# mysqladmin shutdown; ./bin/safe_mysqld&
```

4. Bring down the database on the master, and make an archive of the *data/* directory. No, recent mysqldumps are not sufficient for this job; you will need an actual copy of the *data/* directory. This may take a few seconds to several minutes, depending on how much data you have in your databases:

```
root@db:/usr/local/mysql# mysqladmin shutdown; tar cvf ~/data.tar data/
```

Your database server will be unavailable during the entire time that the copy is running, so be sure to run this at an off-peak time. With any luck, you'll only have to do this once.

5. Bring the database back up on the master. If it looks like your *tar* ran okay, turn MySQL back on:

```
root@db:/usr/local/mysql# ./bin/safe_mysqld&
```

6. Copy the archive to each of the slaves, and make sure MySQL isn't running on them. Try something like this on each slave:

```
root@slave:~# mysqladmin shutdown; scp db:data.tar .
```

7. Pick a unique ID for each of the slaves, and enable replication. Include the following in the [mysqld] section of the */etc/my.cnf* on each of the slaves:

```
master-host=db.mynetwork.edu
master-user=replicant
master-password=seCret
server-id=10
```

Note that the server-id *must* be unique for each slave. Choose any integer that hasn't already been used for a slave (or the master).

If this slave will only be serving as a slave to the master-host (and won't be serving any read/write databases of its own) then you can get a bit of a performance boost by including these options as well:

```
low-priority-updates
skip-bdb
delay-key-write-for-all-tables
```

This will eliminate the overhead of some of the code that is only used when writing to the database. If you're acting as a slave, you'll never actually write to a database, and so won't need MySQL to be ready to handle it.

8. Extract the data archive on each slave. This should do it:

    root@slave:/usr/local/mysql# `mv data data.old; tar vxf ~/data.tar`

    For good measure, make sure that the new *data/* directory and its contents are owned by the mysql user and group:

    root@slave:/usr/local/mysql# `chown -R mysql.mysql data/`

    If you don't need anything from the original *data/* directory on the slaves, feel free to *rm -rf* them (rather than backing them up to *data.old/*).

9. Start MySQL on each slave, and watch the error log for problems. Finally, fire up MySQL on each slave:

    root@slave:/usr/local/mysql# `./bin/safe_mysqld&`

    and watch the database log for errors:

    root@slave:/usr/local/mysql# `tail -f data/slave.err`

    (Naturally, substituting your machine's real name for slave.) If you see a message to the effect of Starting replication at position XYZ, then congratulations: you're replicating! Try making an update to the master, and then do a query on a slave to see if the change propagates. Updates typically happen almost instantaneously. If there are any problems with replication, they will be reported in the mysql log on the slave that encountered the problem.

Usually, problems with replication tend to be permission problems (check your GRANT syntax in step 2) or else your data set is out of sync on the slaves (repeat steps 4, 5, 6, 8, and 9, *very* carefully.) Proceed slowly, and always consult the mysql error logs on each machine.

If you intend to add more slaves at a later date, then keep a copy of your *data.tar* handy. You can use it at any time to create a new slave (it will sync up with the master over the network, replaying the binlog that has been generated since the *data.tar* archive was created).

Simply enabling replication and maintaining a replicated database installation are very different propositions. As long as your application is smart enough to only make updates to the master, and if your hardware is reliable, then you generally won't run into difficulty. But should your slave copies ever get out of sync for any reason, then you'll need to be armed with much more information than I can present in this hack. Consult the excellent resources below before attempting to run a replicated installation of any complexity.

See also:

- *MySQL Reference Manual* (O'Reilly)
- MySQL online documentation, *http://www.mysql.com/doc/en/Replication.html*

Restoring a Single Table from a Large MySQL Dump

#83

Here is a method for restoring a single mysql table from a huge mysqldump

Like a good admin, you faithfully dump your *mysql* tables every night, and save them to the filesystem in compressed form (presumably to be picked up by a backup script later). You probably have something like this running in cron on your database server (or one of its replicated slaves):

```
for x in `mysql -Bse show databases`; do
mysqldump $x | gzip -9 > /var/spool/mysqldump/$x.`date +%Y%m%d`.gz
done
```

This will cover you if anything catastrophic happens to your live database. But if your database grows to an appreciable size, doing partial restores can be difficult. On a database with several million rows, your dumps suddenly become massive piles of data that need to be sifted through. How can you easily restore a single table out of a several hundred megabyte compressed dump?

Here's a simple method using Perl. Create a script called *extract-table*, with this in it:

```
#!/usr/bin/perl -wn
BEGIN { $table = shift @ARGV }
print if /^create table $table\b/io .. /^create table (?!$table)\b/io;
```

To extract the User table from the dump of a database called *randomdb*, try something like this:

```
# zcat /var/spool/mysqldump/randomdb.20020901.gz | extract-table Users > ~/
Users.dump
```

Now you can restore your Users table with a simple:

```
# mysql randomdb -e "drop table Users"
# mysql randomdb < ~/Users.dump
```

MySQL Server Tuning

#84

Try these practical steps to help make your MySQL server run as efficiently as it can

Many Linux administrators find themselves suddenly the "DBA in residence" when there is nobody else willing (or able) to take on the job. Many people specialize in tuning and maintaining databases for a living and don't touch sysadmin responsibilities at all, and yet more than one Linux administrator I've known has been required to take on DBA responsibilities with little training (and certainly no increase in pay). While this hack won't turn you into a DBA expert, it will hopefully show you some practical steps that have helped improve performance in real-world installations.

Here are five steps you can take to optimize your MySQL installation, roughly in increasing order of difficulty (and effectiveness).

1. Run `mysqlcheck -o database`. This will optimize your tables, reclaiming lost space by "defragging" your database. This is especially useful if you have recently changed the structure of your database, or have deleted a large amount of data from it.

2. Renice *mysqld*. If you are running a dedicated MySQL server, you can tell the scheduler to run mysql at a much higher priority than other tasks. The *mysql* manual recommends adding a line like this to your *safe_mysqld* script:

```
renice -20 $$
```

However, I have also found it necessary to find the following hunk of code:

```
NOHUP_NICENESS="nohup"
if test -w /
then
NOHUP_NICENESS=`nohup nice 2>&1`
if test $? -eq 0 && test x"$NOHUP_NICENESS" != x0 && nice --1 echo foo > /
dev/null 2>&1
then
NOHUP_NICENESS="nice --$NOHUP_NICENESS nohup"
else
NOHUP_NICENESS="nohup"
fi
fi
```

and replace it with simply:

```
NOHUP_NICENESS="nohup nice --20"
```

Now *safe_mysqld* and all of the mysqld processes will run at the greatest possible priority. It does this at the expense of all other processes, so if you are trying to run other services along with *mysql* on the same machine, you may want to pick a higher number (somewhere in the -10 to -5 range is probably a bit more conservative).

3. Create indices. If you have long running queries, one very good optimization you can make is to add appropriate indices. If you see a long running query when running *mtop* (as discussed in "Monitoring MySQL Health with mtop" [Hack #81]), then consider creating a relevant index:

```
mysql> create index name on Member (Name(10));
```

Indexing is a trade-off of disk space for performance, and in this age of inexpensive storage, there's no excuse for neglecting your indices. Having too many indices usually doesn't hurt, but doing a linear search (or a unique insert) on a large table that doesn't have an associated index can make your server crawl.

4. Check your server variables. The default server variables are designed to provide safe, sensible settings for modestly equipped machines. If you have a large amount of RAM (512MB or more) then you can see tremendous benefits by increasing the size of the default buffers and caches.

Here are some variables that we run on a production database server (a dual Pentium 4/1.0GHz with 2GB RAM and lots of fast disk space). Put them in the [mysqld] section of your /etc/my.cnf:

```
set-variable = key_buffer=384M
set-variable = max_allowed_packet=1M
set-variable = table_cache=512
set-variable = sort_buffer=2M
set-variable = record_buffer=2M
set-variable = myisam_sort_buffer_size=64M
set-variable = tmp_table_size=8M

set-variable = max_connections=768
```

Note that many of these are straight out of the *my-huge.cnf* sample included with the mysql distribution (we haven't had to change them, since they work fine for our installation.) Since we run Apache::DBI on our web servers, we also run with a *wait_timeout* of a few minutes:

```
set-variable = wait_timeout=120
```

This helps prevent idle DBI threads from hanging out and taking up all available *max_connections*.

5. Patch glibc and threads. When you have exhausted the abilities of the default installation of glibc, consider patching it (see "Optimizing glibc, linuxthreads, and the Kernel for a Super MySQL Server" **[Hack #86]**) to allow for smaller threads and more open files. This is normally not an issue except for very large, very busy MySQL installations.

As with many topics in this book, database tuning and administration is a much more complicated topic than can be covered in a few short pages. Consult the resources below for more authoritative discussion on the subject.

See also:

- *MySQL Reference Manual* (O'Reilly)
- *MySQL* (New Riders)
- *http://www.mysql.com/doc/en/Linux.html*
- *http://www.mysql.com/doc/en/SHOW_VARIABLES.html*

HACK #85 Using proftpd with a mysql Authentication Source

Eliminate the need for user accounts for ftp users with proftpd and mysql

The *proftpd* ftp daemon is a powerful ftp daemon with a configuration syntax much like Apache. It has a whole slew of options not available in most ftp daemons, including ratios, virtual hosting, and a modularized design that allows people to write their own modules.

One such module is *mod_sql*, which allows *proftpd* to use a SQL database as its back end authentication source. Currently, *mod_sql* supports MySQL and PostgreSQL. This can be a good way to help lock down access to your server, as inbound users will authenticate against the database (and therefore not require an actual shell account on the server). In this hack, we'll get proftpd authenticating against a MySQL database.

First, download and build the source to *proftpd* and *mod_sql*:

```
~$ bzcat proftpd-1.2.6.tar.bz2 | tar xf -
~/proftpd-1.2.6/contrib$ tar zvxf ../../mod_sql-4.08.tar.gz
~/proftpd-1.2.6/contrib$ cd ..
~/proftpd-1.2.6$ ./configure --with-modules=mod_sql:mod_sql_mysql \
--with-includes=/usr/local/mysql/include/ \
--with-libraries=/usr/local/mysql/lib/
```

(Naturally, substitute the path to your mysql install, if it isn't in */usr/local/mysql/*.) Now, build the code and install it:

```
rob@catlin:~/proftpd-1.2.6$ make && sudo make install
```

Next, create a database for *proftpd* to use (assuming that you already have mysql up and running):

```
$ mysqladmin create proftpd
```

then permit read-only access to it from *proftpd*:

```
$ mysql -e "grant select on proftpd.* to proftpd@localhost \
    identified by 'secret';"
```

Create two tables in the database, with this schema:

```
CREATE TABLE users (
userid varchar(30) NOT NULL default '',
password varchar(30) NOT NULL default '',
uid int(11) default NULL,
gid int(11) default NULL,
homedir varchar(255) default NULL,
shell varchar(255) default NULL,
UNIQUE KEY uid (uid),
UNIQUE KEY userid (userid)
) TYPE=MyISAM;
```

```
CREATE TABLE groups (
groupname varchar(30) NOT NULL default '',
gid int(11) NOT NULL default '0',
members varchar(255) default NULL
) TYPE=MyISAM;
```

One quick way to create the tables is to save the above to a file called *proftpd.schema* and run a command like `mysql proftpd < proftpd.schema`.

Now we need to tell proftpd to use this database for authentication. Add the following lines to */usr/local/etc/proftpd.conf*:

```
SQLConnectInfo proftpd proftpd secret
SQLAuthTypes crypt backend
SQLMinUserGID 111
SQLMinUserUID 111
```

The `SQLConnectInfo` line takes the form database user password. You could also specify a database on another host (even on another port) with something like:

```
SQLConnectInfo proftpd@dbhost:5678 somebody somepassword
```

The `SQLAuthTypes` line lets you create users with passwords stored in the standard Unix crypt format, or *mysql*'s PASSWORD() function. Be warned that if you're using *mod_sql*'s logging facilities, that the password may be exposed in plain text, so keep those logs private.

The `SQLAuthTypes` line as specified won't allow blank passwords; if you need that functionality, also include the empty keyword. The `SQLMinUserGID` and `SQLMinUserUID` specify the minimum group and user id that *proftpd* will permit on login. It's a good idea to make this greater than zero (to prohibit root logins) but should be as low as you need to allow proper permissions in the filesystem. On this system, we have a user and group called www, with both its uid and gid set to 111. As we'll want web developers to be able to log in with these permissions, we'll need to set the minimum values to 111.

Finally, we're ready to create users in the database. This will create the user jimbo, with effective user rights as www/www, and dump him in the */usr/local/apache/htdocs/* directory at login:

```
mysql -e "insert into users values ('jimbo',PASSWORD('sHHH'),'111', \
    '111', '/usr/local/apache/htdocs','/bin/bash');" proftpd
```

The password for jimbo is encrypted with *mysql*'s PASSWORD() function before being stored. The /bin/bash line is passed to *proftpd* to pass *proftpd*'s RequireValidShell directive. It has no bearing on granting actual shell access to the user jimbo.

At this point, you should be able to fire up *proftpd* and log in as user jimbo, with a password of sHHH. If you are having trouble getting connected, try running *proftpd* in the foreground with debugging on, like this:

```
# proftpd -n -d 5
```

Watch the messages as you attempt to connect, and you should be able to track down the source of difficulty. In my experience, it's almost always due to a failure to set something properly in *proftpd.conf*, usually regarding permissions.

The *mod_sql* module can do far more than I've shown here; it can connect to existing mysql databases with arbitrary table names, log all activity to the database, modify its user lookups with an arbitrary WHERE clause, and much more.

See also:

- The mod_sql home is at *http://www.lastditcheffort.org/~aah/proftpd/mod_sql/*
- The proftpd home is at *http://www.proftpd.org/*

HACK #86 Optimizing glibc, linuxthreads, and the Kernel for a Super MySQL Server

Make sure that your database system's OS is running as efficiently as possible with these tweaks

If you have a very busy MySQL server (serving, say, 800+ queries/second and hundreds of simultaneous clients), you may begin to run into limitations of the operating system that prevent *mysql* from operating as efficiently as it could. In extreme cases (on systems with a misbehaving threads library), *mysql* has been observed to suddenly take up all available CPU cycles, artificially driving the load to 100+ once a critical resource threshold has been reached.

By building a dedicated *mysql* server, and adjusting some default values in glibc, linuxthreads, and the Linux kernel, it is possible to make a single database machine serve thousands of simultaneous requests. Naturally, you'll need hardware capable of supporting the load, but with these modifications, the OS and MYSQL build will probably not be the limiting performance factor.

WARNING: the following hack makes changes to critical, sensitive areas of your server. Don't go monkeying with your libc and kernel source lightly, and even then only if you have a complete, verified, offline (and preferably off-site) backup of your entire system. This procedure should only be followed on dedicated MySQL server machines, and then only when you are certain that everything else is in order (especially your *etc/my.cnf* variables). You have been warned!

Step 1: Build glib. Download the glibc source code from *http://www.gnu.org/software/libc/libc.html*. The latest version as of this writing is glibc 2.2.5. Also pick up a copy of linuxthreads to go along with whichever glibc you download.

Expand the glibc archive, and install the linuxthreads module (as per the instructions in the glibc distribution). Next, follow the hacks suggested at *http://www.mysql.com/doc/en/Linux.html*, including:

- *sysdeps/unix/sysv/linux/bits/local_lim.h* set PTHREAD_THREADS_MAX to 4096
- *linuxthreads/internals.h* set STACK_SIZE to 256 KB

Now, when running `configure`, include this switch: `--prefix=/usr/local/glibc-2.2.5`. This will build glibc into its own directory, rather than replace the system's existing glibc. This is critical when running `make install`, as attempting to overwrite a running system's glibc will typically result in library soup! A broken libc is difficult to fix without statically built system tools and a boot disk, and I don't recommend attempting it unless you have time on your hands (and a full backup of the machine you just broke). Building glibc to an alternate directory (like */usr/local/glibc-2.2.5*) neatly sidesteps the problems of upgrading the system's libc.

Now build glibc and install it. If all went well, you should have a shiny new glibc installed to */usr/local/glibc-2.2.5/*.

Step 2: The Kernel. Make the following changes to your kernel source tree:

- *include/linux/limits.h* set NR_OPEN to 4096
- *include/linux/fs.h* set INR_OPEN to 4096

Now rebuild your kernel (and modules), install the new kernel, and reboot.

Step 3: Build a New MySQL. Download and unpack the MySQL source tree. When you run `configure`, include the `--use-other-libc=/usr/local/glibc-2.2.5` switch. This will link mysql against your new glibc instead of the system's glibc. Now build and install MySQL as normal.

Step 4: Expand the Maximum Filehandles at Boot. Add the following line to your */etc/rc.d/rc.local* (or other part of the boot sequence, before *safe_mysqld* runs):

```
echo 65536 > /proc/sys/fs/file-max
```

Now reboot (or run the above command by hand), and fire up *safe_mysqld*. In benchmarks we have run in-house, the maximum number of available connections was increased from several hundred to 4090, with no observed CPU spike. We run dedicated database servers configured with these settings in production, with absolutely no performance or stability issues.

If you have a significant amount of database traffic, you should consider distributing the load across multiple machines discussed in "Setting Up Replication in MySQL" [Hack #82].

Apache Toolbox

#87   Use this great installation script to automatically download, configure, compile, and install Apache (and friends)

Bryan Andrew's Apache Toolbox is a Swiss army knife of a script, providing a customisable, menu-driven interface to downloading and compiling Apache, *mod_perl*, MySQL, PHP—and more! The Apache Toolbox has out-of-the-box support for:

Apache
> Our favorite web server

SSL
> Secure Sockets Layer for secure web server interactions

PHP, mod_perl, and mod_fastcgi
> For speedy scripting language support

MySQL
> The ubiquitous lightning fast database server

OpenLDAP, mod_auth_ldap, mod_auth_radius, mod_auth_pop3, mod_auth_sys and mod_accessref
> Various means of authentication and authorization

WebDAV and mod_layout
> For simple, yet powerful Web design functionality

mod_dynvhost, mod_throttle, mod_gzip, and mod_bandwidth
> For efficient hosting and server control

And more! Apache Toolbox is customisable and has support (it's just a shell script after all) for anything else you'd care to plug in.

Apache Toolbox comes in two different flavours: just the script, which will download the various component sources as needed, or the full package, including the script and all required sources. The toolbox even catches RPM conflicts should they arise.

The Apache Toolbox itself is simply a shell script that runs from the command line. It must be run as root (as it'll remind you) to install all the various bits into their appropriate locations. The first step is a menu-driven GUIsh interface to selecting the various packages you wish to install:

```
--------------------------------------------------------------------
Apache Toolbox 1.5.59
Support: http://www.apachetoolbox.com
--------------------------------------------------------------------
[+] apache) Apache submenu...
[-] php) PHP submenu (v4.2.2)...
[-] rpm) Build an RPM with your choices?
[-] page2) Apache Modules PAGE 2 ...
--------------------------------------------------------------------
[-] 1) GD 2.0.1 [-] 2) -SQL DB Menus-
[-] 4) Mod Python 2.7.8 [-] 5) Mod_SSL+OpenSSL
[-] 6) -Mod Throttle 312 [-] 7) -WebDAV 1.0.3-1.3.6
[-] 8) -Mod FastCGI [-] 9) -Mod AuthNDS 0.5
[-] 10) -Frontpage 2002 [-] 11) -Mod GZIP 1.3.19.1a
[-] 12) -Mod DynaVHost [-] 13) -Mod Roaming
[-] 14) -Mod AccessRef 1.0.1 [-] 15) -Mod AuthSYS
[-] 16) -Mod Bandwidth [-] 17) -Mod Perl 1.27
[-] 18) -Mod Auth LDAP [-] 19) -Apache Jakarta
[-] 20) -Mod Auth Radius [-] 21) -Mod Auth POP3
[-] 22) -Mod Layout 3.2 [-] 23) -Mod DTCL
q) Quit 99) Descriptions
go) Compile selections...
--------------------------------------------------------------------
```

Not sure what all these goodies are? Type 99<enter> for complete descriptions. After putting together your grocery list of preferred features, type go and the toolbox springs into action. First stop: RPM conflict checks:

```
---------------------------------------------------------
-------------- Scanning for RPM's --------------------
---------------------------------------------------------
Testing for PHP RPM... not found.
Testing for PHP IMAP RPM... not found.
Testing for GD RPM... not found.
Testing for GD Devel RPM... not found.
Testing for Apache RPM... not found.
...
Testing for OpenLDAP RPM... not found.
Testing for OpenLDAP Devel RPM... not found.
[+] Wget found!
---------------------------------------------------------
```

The toolbox confirms Apache install path (*/usr/local/apache*), allowing you to change the final destination per your preference, then continues on its way.

Any time a source (*tar.gz* archive) isn't found, the toolbox script prompts you for permission to download it:

```
[+] Setting up Apache source...
[-] apache_1.3.26.tar.gz detection failed
Do you wish to download it now? [y/n] y

--21:35:40--
--ftp://mirrors.partnersforever.net:21/pub/apache/dist/
apache_1.3.26.tar.gz => `apache_1.3.26.tar.gz'
Connecting to mirrors.partnersforever.net:21... connected!
Logging in as anonymous ... Logged in!
==> TYPE I ... done. ==> CWD pub/apache/dist ... done.
==> PORT ... done. ==> RETR apache_1.3.26.tar.gz ... done.
Length: 2,303,147 (unauthoritative)

OK -> .......... .......... .......... .......... [ 2%]
50K -> .......... .......... .......... .......... [ 5%]
...
```

The toolbox then silently hums away configuring, integrating, preheating, and so on:

```
[+] Uncompressed Apache source...
[+] Getting apache pre-configured
[+] Apache pre-configured
[+] Apache httpd.conf-dist updated for SSI support
[+] Getting GD lib's with PNG and zlib support ready...
...
```

After a short while, the toolbox gives you the chance to edit the Apache configuration script, if you're just that bold. If all's well you should end up with a rather familiar site if you've ever configured Apache before:

```
Configuring for Apache, Version 1.3.26
+ using installation path layout: Apache (config.layout)
+ activated php4 module (modules/php4/libphp4.a)
+ Warning: You have enabled the suEXEC feature. Be aware
+ that you need root privileges to complete the final
+ installation step.
Creating Makefile
Creating Configuration.apaci in src
Creating Makefile in src
+ configured for Linux platform
...
Creating Makefile in src/modules/standard
Creating Makefile in src/modules/php4
[+] Done Configuring Apache source

------------------------------------------------------------
If there where _no_ errors run "cd apache_1.3.26;make" now.
Start debugging and have a blast...
Run "make install" in the apache source
directory to install apache 1.3.26
------------------------------------------------------------
```

Mosey on over to the Apache directory, as specified, make, make test, and make install!

See Also:

- See the original article at *http://www.onlamp.com/pub/a/apache/2000/11/17/wrangler.html*
- Apache Toolbox
- *Linux Apache MySQL PHP (LAMP) Guide* (Linux Help.Net)
- *HTTP Wrangler* columns (O'Reilly Network)

Display the Full Filename in Indexes
Stop truncating the filenames in your auto-indexed directories

Have you ever noticed that Apache will truncate filenames in directory listings? It's terribly frustrating to go to a web page full of fun archives, only to see something like:

```
Index of /~rob/stuff/kernel

Name Last modified Size Description

Parent Directory 03-Sep-2002 00:33 -
patched-linux-2.4.12..> 11-Oct-2001 00:59 22.0M
patched-linux-2.4.12..> 11-Oct-2001 00:59 1k
patched-linux-2.4.12..> 11-Oct-2001 00:59 27.1M
patched-linux-2.4.12..> 11-Oct-2001 00:59 1k
patched-linux-2.4.13..> 23-Oct-2001 22:28 22.0M
patched-linux-2.4.13..> 23-Oct-2001 22:28 1k
patched-linux-2.4.13..> 23-Oct-2001 22:28 27.2M
patched-linux-2.4.13..> 23-Oct-2001 22:28 1k
patched-linux-2.4.14..> 05-Nov-2001 15:30 22.1M
patched-linux-2.4.14..> 05-Nov-2001 15:30 1k
patched-linux-2.4.14..> 05-Nov-2001 15:30 27.4M
patched-linux-2.4.14..> 05-Nov-2001 15:30 1k
patched-linux-2.4.15..> 22-Nov-2001 22:18 22.6M
patched-linux-2.4.15..> 22-Nov-2001 22:18 1k
patched-linux-2.4.15..> 22-Nov-2001 22:18 28.0M
patched-linux-2.4.15..> 22-Nov-2001 22:18 1k
```

How can you tell which files are which without hovering over every link? Fix it by setting your IndexOptions line in the *httpd.conf* to include a NameWidth option:

```
IndexOptions FancyIndexing NameWidth=*
```

By default, Apache only ships with FancyIndexing on. Now issue an *apachectl restart*, and reload that page to see the full filename:

```
Index of /~rob/stuff/kernel

Parent Directory 03-Sep-2002 00:33 - Description
patched-linux-2.4.12.tar.bz2 11-Oct-2001 00:59 22.0M
patched-linux-2.4.12.tar.bz2.sign 11-Oct-2001 00:59 1k
patched-linux-2.4.12.tar.gz 11-Oct-2001 00:59 27.1M
patched-linux-2.4.12.tar.gz.sign 11-Oct-2001 00:59 1k
patched-linux-2.4.13.tar.bz2 23-Oct-2001 22:28 22.0M
patched-linux-2.4.13.tar.bz2.sign 23-Oct-2001 22:28 1k
patched-linux-2.4.13.tar.gz 23-Oct-2001 22:28 27.2M
patched-linux-2.4.13.tar.gz.sign 23-Oct-2001 22:28 1k
patched-linux-2.4.14.tar.bz2 05-Nov-2001 15:30 22.1M
patched-linux-2.4.14.tar.bz2.sign 05-Nov-2001 15:30 1k
patched-linux-2.4.14.tar.gz 05-Nov-2001 15:30 27.4M
patched-linux-2.4.14.tar.gz.sign 05-Nov-2001 15:30 1k
patched-linux-2.4.15.tar.bz2 22-Nov-2001 22:18 22.6M
patched-linux-2.4.15.tar.bz2.sign 22-Nov-2001 22:18 1k
patched-linux-2.4.15.tar.gz 22-Nov-2001 22:18 28.0M
patched-linux-2.4.15.tar.gz.sign 22-Nov-2001 22:18 1k
```

Much better. Install this by default on all of your Apache installations, and your users will thank you.

HACK
#89　Quick Configuration Changes with IfDefine
Make changes to your running Apache configuration without editing httpd. conf

Apache allows you to modify its configuration quickly and easily with the IfDefine and IfModule directives. IfDefine allows you to designate blocks of configuration to only be active when a command line flag has been passed, like so:

```
# /usr/local/apache/bin/httpd -DSSL
```

The above is a common example, defining (-D) a flag called SSL. This will enable parts of the configuration that look like:

```
<IfDefine SSL>
# anything in here will be enabled if -DSSL
# has been passed on the command line.
</IfDefine>
```

Likewise, the IfModule directive checks to see if a module is currently loaded (i.e., uncommented) in the Apache configuration file. If *mod_userdir.c* is loaded, for example, then the following configuration will be enabled. If it's not, it will be silently ignored.

```
<IfModule mod_userdir.c>
UserDir public_html
</IfModule>
```

As Apache has grown, the *httpd.conf* file has become steadily more modularized as shown above, allowing you to tweak the various modules that load without fear of breaking your installation due to missing dependencies.

With the above examples in mind, you can easily change how Apache operates by passing simple command lines. Let's assume that every Friday you release a newsletter to ten thousand people. You know from experience that the weekends are when your web server gets hit the heaviest. Here's a snippet from a Apache configuration file using IfDefines:

```
<IfDefine !WEEKEND>
MinSpareServers 1
MaxSpareServers 5
StartServers 1
MaxClients 150
</IfDefine>

<IfDefine WEEKEND>
MinSpareServers 5
MaxSpareServers 15
StartServers 5
MaxClients 300
</IfDefine>
```

With the above configuration, if you start up your server normally:

```
# /usr/local/apache/bin/httpd
```

then you'll use the default Apache settings for the number of servers to start and maintain during normal running operation. However, before you leave work on Friday, you can simply stop the daemon and restart it with:

```
# /usr/sbin/httpd -DWEEKEND
```

Upon restart, you'll have a configuration that's better tuned for the weekend traffic.

Here's an example of one way to use IfModule:

```
<IfModule libperl.so>
PerlModule Apache::Registry
<Location /usr/local/httpd/cgi-bin>
SetHandler perl-script
PerlHandler Apache::Registry
Options +ExecCGI
</Location>
</IfModule>
```

In this case, *mod_perl* is activated for all of our (hopefully well-written) CGI scripts automatically, whenever the *mod_perl* module is loaded. This could also be useful during the scenario described above—by turning on *mod_perl*, our scripts will respond faster during the heavier traffic. If we don't need the overhead of *mod_perl* during the weekdays (or to make debugging cgi problems easier), we can simply comment *mod_perl*'s LoadModule and AddModule lines, and we'll be back to normal.

You can use the ideas presented above to create developer specific configurations, usable with a -DEVELOPER command, or even a -DVIRTUAL_HOSTS flag, which can be removed when your web hosting clients haven't paid:

```
<IfDefine VIRTUAL_HOSTS>
# all your various <VirtualHosts> blocks would
# go in here. Without the command line flag of
# -DVIRTUAL_HOSTS (to signify that your clients
# have paid you, for instance), then all virtual
# hosts would be disabled.
</IfDefine>

<IfDefine EVELOPER>
# notice our trickery with "EVELOPER"
# to make the command line more readable.
# when -DEVELOPER has been passed, we load
# various modules that aren't used during production.
LoadModule proxy_module libexec/httpd/libproxy.so
LoadModule expires_module libexec/httpd/mod_expires.so
LoadModule usertrack_module libexec/httpd/mod_usertrack.so
AddModule mod_proxy.c
AddModule mod_expires.c
AddModule mod_usertrack.c
</IfDefine>
```

If your site uses *apachectl* to bring Apache up and down, you can edit *apachectl* to include your favorite defines (it's just a shell script.) Find this line in *apachectl*:

```
HTTPD=/usr/local/apache/bin/httpd
```

and change it to something like this:

```
HTTPD="/usr/local/apache/bin/httpd -DSSL -DEVELOPER -DVIRTUAL_HOSTS"
```

Now when you run apachectl start, your -D defines will be properly passed to httpd.

Simplistic Ad Referral Tracking

#90 Create simple user tracking in print ads using the QUERY_STRING

You're planning on advertising in a number of magazines, web sites, and newspapers, and you realize that you'd like to gauge how much traffic is coming in from each advertisement—it'll help you better spend your money in the future. Unfortunately, you have no time to implement something complicated, so you're looking for a low-tech solution, as well as something that will make it easy to analyze the results.

Apache happily logs all environment variables passed to the pages it serves to the outside world. Thus, the hack is simple: pass an advertisement-based QUERY_STRING to the main page of your site. The QUERY_STRING will be ignored if you don't specifically act on it (with SSI, PHP, CGI, etc.), but Apache will still log the information to it's *access_log*.

For example, say you're advertising in the New York Times. Instead of saying "Come visit us at *http://www.GatesMcFaddenCo.com*," change the advertisement to specifically match the readership:

```
http://www.GatesMcFaddenCo.com/?nyt
```

In the above example, anytime someone types in that address, Apache will serve the main page normally but silently log that a QUERY_STRING of "nyt" has been passed. Using a log analyzer (like analog, or the simple one below), you can then find out how many people visited your site from seeing your ad in the New York Times.

Since you're using QUERY_STRINGs, you can also act upon them with Server Side Includes, PHP, or any other server-side language. For instance, the example HTML page below would show different greetings based on the web site address that the user typed in.

```
<html>
<head>
<title>Apache Hack #12396 - Simplistic Ad Referrel Tracker</title>
</head>
<body>
<!--#if expr="\"$QUERY_STRING\" = \"nyt\"" -->
<h1>Welcome New York Times Reader!</h1>
<!--#elif expr="\"$QUERY_STRING\" = \"xml\"" -->
<h1>Welcome XML.com Reader!</h1>
<!--#else -->
<h1>Welcome To Our Site!</h1>
<!--#endif -->
</body>
</html>
```

The above will show special greetings if the user types in a QUERY_STRING that corresponds to advertisements at XML.com or at the New York Times. If the user didn't type in either, then a generic welcome is shown. Some sites have been known to change more than just the greeting, customizing the color, logos, and internal ads served.

Be careful when you're choosing your QUERY_STRING—if it's too long, hard to remember, or suitably threatening, then the user may mistype the address (creating bad statistics) or else not type the QUERY_STRING at all. In a worst case scenario, they may not even make the attempt to visit. These are all bad choices:

```
# this one is simply too long.
http://www.gamegrene.com/?newyorktimes-04-21

# this one would be hard to remember or type.
http://www.gamegrene.com/?04xlmfo3d

# and this may worry people.
http://www.gamegrene.com/?track=nyt
```

If you are advertising online, encoding query strings in anchor tags works just fine (and can be as long as you like, as it's all just one click as far as the user knows). To analyze your stats upon request, try the following Perl script.

Listing: referral-report.pl

```perl
#!/usr/bin/perl -w
use strict; my %ads;

# define each of your QUERY_STRINGS,
# and the matching "real name" here.
# this script will only look for
# QUERY_STRINGS that are letters and
# numbers only (no dashes, etc.)
$ads{"xml"} = "XML.com";
$ads{"nyt"} = "New York Times";
$ads{"ora"} = "O'Reilly and Associates";

# your Apache access log location.
my $logfile = "/var/log/httpd/access_log";

# define some counters.
my %ads_count; my $total;

# open the logfile.
open(LOG, "<$logfile") or die $!;

# and loop through each line.
while (<LOG>) {

# skip over lines we're not interested in.
next unless /GET/; next unless /\?(\w+)\s/;

# save the query_string.
my $query_string = $1;

# move on if not defined, else increment.
next unless exists $ads{$query_string};
$total++; $ads_count{$query_string}++;

}
```

```
# and print out the data.
print "There were a total of $total ad referrals.\n";
foreach ( sort keys %ads_count ) {
print "$ads{$_} had $ads_count{$_} ad referrals.\n";
}


# close logfile and
# exit the program.
close(LOG); exit;
```

The results of this script would look like:

```
There were a total of 17 ad referrals.
XML.com had 6 ad referrals.
New York Times had 7 ad referrals.
O'Reilly and Associates had 4 ad referrals.
```

Being simplistic, this code does not track multiple hits from the same IP address, nor does it create percentages based on the total amount of referrals received. Both should be easy for any Perl hacker to implement.

HACK #91 Mimicking FTP Servers with Apache
Set up multiple levels of anonymous access in Apache

You want to set up a portion of your web site to act like an FTP server—some users should have accounts for downloading, while others should have anonymous downloading access. Still others should be allowed to download one type of file but not another. You don't trust the intelligence of your clientele to handle installing and using an FTP program, so you'd like to make things work within a normal browsing environment.

Using an oft-ignored Apache module included by default, you can allow authenticated anonymous access to certain parts of your site, as well as falling back on normal authentication methods with *mod_auth*. This becomes handy if you've got a large amount of documents that you don't want indexed by search engines, or you want to create the effect of multiple levels of user power, such as anonymous, privileged, and leech. You want to do it all through a browser and all without additional programming.

The first step is to enable the *anon_auth_module*, which is normally commented out within the Apache configuration file. To do so, look for the following lines (which may be slightly different in your installation) and remove the #:

```
#LoadModule anon_auth_module libexec/httpd/mod_auth_anon.so
#AddModule mod_auth_anon.c
```

With the above uncommented and Apache restarted, you can now start adding relevant directives to *httpd.conf*, or an *.htaccess* file located in the directory you want protected. Below, we'll assume you're using an *.htaccess* file. Plop the following into your *.htaccess* and save to the directory you want to protect:

```
AuthName "anonymous/your email address"
AuthType Basic
Require valid-user

Anonymous orko bender
Anonymous_Authoritative on
```

You should recognize the first three directives, as they're used when you normally protect a directory with *mod_auth*. The Anonymous directive controls what usernames should be considered an anonymous user—in this case, we've got orko and bender, but we could just have easily chosen mundania such as anonymous, anon, or guest.

The Anonymous_Authoritative controls whether we want to pass unauthorized usernames and passwords off to another authentication scheme for processing. If we say on, then anonymity is king, either the visitor logs in with orko or bender or they're not allowed access.

On the other hand, if we say off, then we can include the full functionality of *mod_auth*—authentication via passwords, groups, and so forth. Take a look at the configuration below. If the user does not log in with heenie or retrogirl, then the username is passed off to the AuthUserFile, where it's also checked against for those accounts. If they don't exist in that file either, then the user is denied:

```
AuthName "anonymous/your email address"
AuthUserFile /Library/WebServer/.htpasswd
AuthType Basic
Require valid-user

Anonymous heenie retrogirl
Anonymous_Authoritative off
```

As is typical, you can be as simplistic or as complicated as you need. The following configuration will allow any user to get a directory listing (allowing them to see what you have available). Any user listed in the AuthUserFile can get access to all *.jpg* files, as well as any anonymous user logging in with the mrs_decepticon or spiderj usernames, assuming they enter a valid email address (one with a "@" and "." character—Apache doesn't check that the hostname exists). Finally, only the eustace user can download *.mp3* files:

```
AuthType basic
AuthName "anonymous/your email address"
AuthUserFile /Library/WebServer/.htpasswd

Anonymous mrs_decepticon spiderj
Anonymous_Authoritative off
Anonymous_VerifyEmail on
```

```
<Files *.jpg>
Require valid-user
</Files>

<Files *.mp3>
Require user eustace
<Files>
```

You can, of course, get even more convoluted, restricting by IP address or hostname, environment variables, and so forth. Just make sure you comment your craziness—it's very easy to get confused about who has access to what.

Unfortunately, you can't duplicate the other side of FTP and that's uploading. Neither can any of the modules that are shipped with Apache by default. To do so, you'd have to use one of the many CGI scripts that accept file uploads, or else craft your own.

HACK #92 Rotate and compress Apache Server Logs

Use this tiny Perl script to compress all of your Apache logs automatically, even when you add more to your site

Here's a handy script that will rotate and gzip your Apache logs for you automatically. It reads your *httpd.conf*, descends all Included configuration files, and makes a note of each unique Log file. It then renames each to a file with a datestamp, restarts Apache, then gzip compresses the datestamped log files. As a bonus, it *chgrp*s the compressed logs to whatever group you have set in $gid, and sets permissions up for that group to be able to read or write to them. This makes it simple for other (non-root) processes to come along later and post-process the compressed logs.

Run this nightly (or weekly, depending on your traffic) in *cron* to collect a regular repository of compressed logs, and keep your live log files down to a manageable size.

Listing: logflume.pl

```
#!/usr/bin/perl -w
#
# logflume.pl
#
# Roll over and compress Apache log files, following Includes within the
# httpd.conf (and all other configuration files).
#
#
use strict;
$|++;
```

```
my $server_root = "/usr/local/apache";
my $conf = "$server_root/conf/httpd.conf";
my $gid = "wwwadmin";

my (%logs, %included, @files, @gzip);

my $date = `date +%Y%m%d`; chomp $date;

push @files, $conf;

for $conf (@files) {
open(CONF, "<$conf") || die "Cannot open config file $conf: $!\n";

while (<CONF>) {
chomp;
next if /^(\s+)?#/;

if (/(Transfer|Custom|Error)Log\s+(\S+)(\S+)/i) {
$logs{$2}++;

} elsif (/^(ResourceConfig|Include)\s+(\S+)/i) {
if(!$included{$2}) {
push @files, $2;
$included{$2}++;
}
}
}

close CONF;
}

for my $logfile (sort keys %logs) {
$logfile = "$server_root/$logfile" unless ($logfile =~ m|^/|);
rename($logfile, "$logfile.$date");
push(@gzip, "$logfile.$date");
}

system("$server_root/bin/apachectl restart");

for my $logfile (@gzip) {
system("gzip $logfile");
system("chgrp $gid $logfile.gz");
system("chmod 664 $logfile.gz");
}
```

Generating an SSL cert and Certificate Signing Request

HACK #93

Make an SSL key, CSR, and cert for use with Apache

In order to use Apache with *mod_ssl* or *Apache-ssl*, you'll need a certificate signed by a trusted Certificate Authority. In this example, we'll assume that you're generating a cert to be used at *https://propaganda.discordia.eris/*. To generate a key with OpenSSL:

```
hagbard@fnord:~/certs$ openssl genrsa 512/1024 \
> propaganda.discordia.eris.key
warning, not much extra random data, consider using the -rand option
Generating RSA private key, 512 bit long modulus
..+++++++++++++
...+++++++++++++
e is 65537 (0x10001)
```

This just makes the private key, not the cert. If you'd like to protect this key with a passphrase, use the *-des3* option on the command line:

```
hagbard@fnord:~/certs$ openssl genrsa -des3 512/1024 \
> propaganda.discordia.eris.key
warning, not much extra random data, consider using the -rand option
Generating RSA private key, 512 bit long modulus
.......++++++++++++
.....++++++++++++
e is 65537 (0x10001)
Enter PEM pass phrase:
Verifying password - Enter PEM pass phrase:
```

But be warned: you'll need to enter this phrase every time you restart Apache, which can be inconvenient when performing regular maintenance (such as rotating http logs). Weigh the inconvenience against the potential damage done if some miscreant should acquire this key. If you lose the passphrase, it is essentially unrecoverable, so keep it safe!

Next you'll need to generate the Certificate Signing Request, to submit to a trusted CA (such as Thawte/VeriSign) for signing. Type in everything appearing in boldface, substituting your own information where appropriate:

```
hagbard@fnord:~/certs$ openssl req -new -key propaganda.discordia.eris.key \
> propaganda.discordia.eris.csr


Using configuration from /usr/local/ssl/openssl.cnf
You are about to be asked to enter information that will be incorporated
into your certificate request.
What you are about to enter is what is called a Distinguished Name or a DN.
There are quite a few fields but you can leave some blank
For some fields there will be a default value,
If you enter '.', the field will be left blank.

Country Name (2 letter code) [AU]:US
State or Province Name (full name) [Some-State]:Texas
Locality Name (eg, city) []:Mad Dog
Organization Name (eg, company) [Internet Widgits Pty Ltd]:Discordia, Inc.
Organizational Unit Name (eg, section) []:Operations
Common Name (eg, YOUR name) []:propaganda.discordia.eris
Email Address []:norton@discordia.eris
```

```
Please enter the following 'extra' attributes
to be sent with your certificate request
A challenge password []:
An optional company name []:
```

Finally, you're ready to create the cert itself. If you're going to use a well-known CA, then you'll need to send the *.csr* file to them for signing. In the meantime, you can self-sign your cert and use it while you're waiting for the CSR to be processed:

```
hagbard@fnord:~/certs$ openssl req -x509 \
  -key propaganda.discordia.eris.key \
  -in propaganda.discordia.eris.csr \
  > propaganda.discordia.eris.crt

Using configuration from /usr/local/ssl/openssl.cnf
hagbard@fnord:~/certs$
```

If you intend to build your own Certificate Authority, then *use your own CA key* to sign your cert.

See also:

- "Creating Your Own CA" **[Hack #94]**
- The OpenSSL home at *http://www.openssl.org/*

HACK #94 Creating Your Own CA

Become your own Certificate Authority, and sign your own (or others') SSL certs

Well-known Certificate Authorities (such as Thawte/VeriSign) exist to serve as an authoritative, trusted third-party for authentication. They are in the business of signing SSL certificates that are used on sites deal with sensitive information (such as account numbers or passwords). If a site's SSL certificate is signed by a trusted authority, then presumably it is possible to verify the identity of a server supplying that cert's credentials. In order to receive a certificate "blessed" by a well known CA, you have to prove to them beyond a shadow of doubt that not only are you who you claim to be, but that you have the right to use the certificate in the way you intend. For example, I may be able to prove to a CA that I am really Rob Flickenger, but they probably won't issue me a signed cert for Microsoft Corporation, as I have no rights to use that name. Yes, they probably wouldn't do that. Not again.

OpenSSL is perfectly capable of generating everything you need to run your own Certificate Authority. The *CA.pl* utility makes the process very simple.

In these examples, you'll need to type anything in boldface, and enter passwords wherever appropriate (that don't echo to the screen.) To establish your new Certificate Authority:

```
hagbard@fnord:~/certs$ /usr/local/ssl/misc/CA.pl -newca
CA certificate filename (or enter to create)

Making CA certificate ...
Using configuration from /usr/local/ssl/openssl.cnf
Generating a 1024 bit RSA private key
...............++++++
....................................++++++
writing new private key to './demoCA/private/cakey.pem'
Enter PEM pass phrase:
Verifying password - Enter PEM pass phrase:
-----
You are about to be asked to enter information that will be incorporated
into your certificate request.
What you are about to enter is what is called a Distinguished Name or a DN.
There are quite a few fields but you can leave some blank
For some fields there will be a default value,
If you enter '.', the field will be left blank.
-----
Country Name (2 letter code) [AU]:US
State or Province Name (full name) [Some-State]:California
Locality Name (eg, city) []:Sebastopol
Organization Name (eg, company) [Internet Widgits Pty Ltd]:Illuminatus
Enterprises, Ltd
Organizational Unit Name (eg, section) []:Administration
Common Name (eg, YOUR name) []:Hagbard Celine
Email Address []:hagbardceline1723@yahoo.com
```

Congratulations. You're the proud owner of your very own Certificate Authority. Take a look around:

```
hagbard@fnord:~/certs$ ls
demoCA/
hagbard@fnord:~/certs$ cd demoCA/
hagbard@fnord:~/certs/demoCA$ ls -l
total 24
-rw-r--r-- 1 rob users 1407 Sep 8 14:12 cacert.pem
drwxr-xr-x 2 rob users 4096 Sep 8 14:12 certs/
drwxr-xr-x 2 rob users 4096 Sep 8 14:12 crl/
-rw-r--r-- 1 rob users 0 Sep 8 14:12 index.txt
drwxr-xr-x 2 rob users 4096 Sep 8 14:12 newcerts/
drwxr-xr-x 2 rob users 4096 Sep 8 14:12 private/
-rw-r--r-- 1 rob users 3 Sep 8 14:12 serial
```

The public key for your new Certificate Authority is contained in cacert.pem, and the private key is in private/cakey.pem. You can now use this private key to sign other SSL certs.

To use your CA's authority to sign SSL certs, you'll need to make a new cert that a web server (such as Apache) can use. First, generate a private key and certificate request, as shown in "Generating an SSL cert and Certificate Signing Request" [Hack #93]. Now you can sign the new request with your own CA's key:

```
hagbard@fnord:~/certs$ openssl ca -policy policy_anything \
  -out propaganda.discordia.eris.crt \
  -infiles propaganda.discordia.eris.csr
Using configuration from /usr/local/ssl/openssl.cnf
Enter PEM pass phrase:
Check that the request matches the signature
Signature ok
The Subjects Distinguished Name is as follows
countryName :PRINTABLE:'US'
stateOrProvinceName :PRINTABLE:'Texas'
localityName :PRINTABLE:'Mad Dog'
organizationName :PRINTABLE:'Discordia, Inc.'
organizationalUnitName:PRINTABLE:'Operations'
commonName :PRINTABLE:'propaganda.discordia.eris'
emailAddress :IA5STRING:'hail@discordia.eris'
Certificate is to be certified until Sep 8 22:49:26 2003 GMT (365 days)
Sign the certificate? [y/n]:y

1 out of 1 certificate requests certified, commit? [y/n]y
Write out database with 1 new entries
Data Base Updated
```

Now to use the *.crt* and *.key* with Apache + mod_ssl (or *Apache-ssl*), install them as you normally would (perhaps with lines like these):

```
SSLCertificateFile /usr/local/apache/conf/ssl.crt/propaganda.discordia.eris.
crt
SSLCertificateKeyFile /usr/local/apache/conf/ssl.key/propaganda.discordia.
eris.key
```

This is all lots of fun, but what happens when a client actually connects to *https://propaganda.discordia.eris/*? Won't the browser throw an error about not recognizing the Certificate Authority that signed the SSL cert? Naturally. Unless, of course, you've installed your CA's public key to the client browser ahead of time. See the next hack if you'd like to do that.

See also:

- man CA.pl
- The OpenSSL home at *http://www.openssl.org/*
- *http://www.cert.org/advisories/CA-2001-04.html*

Disclaimer: no, I honestly had *nothing* to do with the Microsoft Corporation cert snafu. But it does illustrate one of the fundamental facts of life online: it's difficult to know *who* to trust.

Distributing Your CA to Client Browsers
#95
Installing your shiny new CA cert to client browsers is just a click away

There are two possible formats that browsers will accept for new certificate authority certs: *pem* and *der*. Early versions of Netscape expected *pem* format, but recent versions will accept either. Internet Explorer is just the opposite (early IE would only accept *der* format, but recent versions will take both). Other browsers will generally accept either format. You can generate a *der* from your existing *pem* with a single openssl command:

```
hagbard@fnord:~/certs$ openssl x509 -in demoCA/cacert.pem \
   -outform DER -out cacert.der
```

Also, add the following line to your *conf/mime.types* file in your Apache installation:

```
application/x-x509-ca-cert der pem crt
```

Now restart Apache for the change to take effect. You should now be able to place both the *cacert.der* and *demoCA/cacert.pem* files anywhere on your web server, and have clients install the new cert by simply clicking on either link.

You will get a dialog box in your browser when downloading the new certificate authority, asking if you'd like to continue. Accept the certificate, and that's all there is to it. Now SSL certs that are signed by your CA will be accepted without warning the user, as in Figure 8-1.

> You have been asked to trust a new Certificate Authority (CA).
>
> Do you want to trust "Snake Oil CA" for the following purposes?
> - ☑ Trust this CA to identify web sites.
> - ☐ Trust this CA to identify email users.
> - ☐ Trust this CA to identify software developers.
>
> Before trusting this CA for any purpose, you should examine its certificate and its policy and procedures (if available).
>
> [View] Examine CA certificate
>
> [OK] [Cancel] [Help]

Figure 8-1. Click OK to accept the new Certificate Authority or View to read the fine print

Keep in mind that Certificate Authorities aren't to be taken lightly. If you accept a new CA in your browser, you had better trust it completely—a mischievous CA manager could sign all sorts of certs that you should never trust, but your browser would never complain (since you claimed to trust the CA when you imported it). Be very careful about who you extend your trust to when using SSL enabled browsers. It's worth looking around in the CA cache that ships with your browser to see exactly who you trust by default.

For example, did you know that AOL/Time Warner has its own CA? How about GTE? Or VISA? CA certs for all of these entities (and many others) ship with Netscape 7.0 for Linux and are all trusted authorities for web sites, email, and application add-ons by default. Keep this in mind when browsing to SSL-enabled sites: if any one of the default authorities have signed online content, then your browser will trust it without requiring operator acknowledgment, as in Figure 8-2.

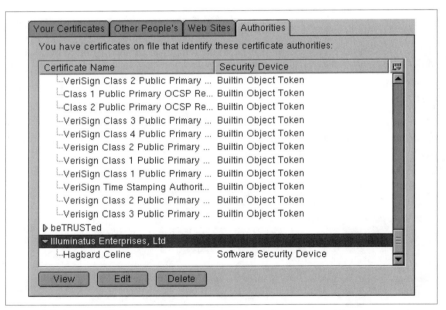

Figure 8-2. It's a good idea to review exactly who your browser considers trustworthy.

If you value your browser's security (and, by extension, the security of your client machine), then make it a point to review your trusted CA relationships.

See also:

- The OpenSSL FAQ at *http://www.openssl.org/support/faq.cgi*
- "Generating an SSL cert and Certificate Signing Request" **[Hack #93]**
- "Creating Your Own CA" **[Hack #94]**

Serving multiple sites with the same DocumentRoot
#96

Through creative use of mod_rewrite, several sites can share a DocumentRoot and yet still appear to be independent sites

Occasionally, it is useful for a couple of sites to share the same DocumentRoot but have unique front pages. Perhaps you want to share a graphics or javascript directory, but for some reason can't be bothered to set up an appropriate Alias entry. Or maybe you need to be able to share most of a directory structure, but don't want to FollowSymLinks. Whatever your reason for needing a common DocumentRoot, *mod_rewrite* will provide a solution.

Let's assume that you are running a site called *www.fruit.yum*, and would like to serve information about apples and oranges. You've already had much success with *http://www.fruit.yum/apples* and *http://www.fruit.yum/oranges*, but you are suddenly able to obtain the much coveted *apple.yum* and *orange.yum* domain names. You'd like to keep the existing *www.fruit.yum* directory structure for users who browse to directories under your new domain names (for example, to *http://www.apple.yum/order* or *http://www.orange.yum/faq*), but would like to deliver a custom page to users who simply browse to the front page (e.g., *http://www.apple.yum/*).

This is no problem with mod_rewrite. Let's assume that you already have a VirtualHost entry for *www.fruit.yum* like this:

```
<VirtualHost *>
ServerName www.fruit.yum

ServerAdmin webmaster@fruit.yum

DocumentRoot /home/www/htdocs
CustomLog /home/www/logs/access_log combined
ErrorLog /home/www/logs/error_log
</VirtualHost>
```

Add a couple of new VirtualHost entries for your new domains but with some additional RewriteRule lines:

```
<VirtualHost *>
ServerName www.apples.yum

ServerAdmin webmaster@fruit.yum

DocumentRoot /home/www/htdocs
CustomLog /home/www/logs/access_log combined
ErrorLog /home/www/logs/error_log

RewriteEngine On
```

```
RewriteRule ^/$ /home/www/htdocs/apples/index.html
RewriteRule ^/index.html$ /home/www/htdocs/apples/index.html
</VirtualHost>

<VirtualHost *>
ServerName www.oranges.yum

ServerAdmin webmaster@fruit.yum

DocumentRoot /home/www/htdocs
CustomLog /home/www/logs/access_log combined
ErrorLog /home/www/logs/error_log

RewriteEngine On

RewriteRule ^/$ /home/www/htdocs/oranges/index.html
RewriteRule ^/index.html$ /home/www/htdocs/oranges/index.html
</VirtualHost>
```

As these are handled as internal rewrites, the URL line will not change on
the client's browser. As far as they are concerned, browsing to *http://www.
oranges.yum/* appears to display an independent site. Browsing directly to
http://www.fruit.yum/oranges/ is functionally equivalent, as long as relative
links (or appropriate Alias lines) are used in all of your html. If you'd like a
more general solution that will work for as many www.*.yum addresses as
you care to register, you might try something like this:

```
<VirtualHost *>
ServerName www.fruit.yum
ServerAlias www.*.yum

ServerAdmin webmaster@fruit.yum

DocumentRoot /home/www/htdocs
CustomLog /home/www/logs/access_log combined
ErrorLog /home/www/logs/error_log


RewriteCond %{HTTP_HOST} www.(.*).yum
RewriteCond %{HTTP_HOST} !www.fruit.yum
RewriteRule (.*) $1 [E=SITE:%1]

RewriteCond %{REQUEST_URI} ^/index.html$
RewriteCond /home/www/htdocs/%{ENV:SITE}/index.html -f
RewriteRule .* /home/www/htdocs/%{ENV:SITE}/index.html

RewriteCond %{REQUEST_URI} ^/$
RewriteCond /home/www/htdocs/%{ENV:SITE}/index.html -f
RewriteRule .* /home/www/htdocs/%{ENV:SITE}/index.html
</VirtualHost>
```

This will strip off the middle part of the requested domain name (the bit between www. and .yum) and check to see if an *index.html* exists in the directory of that name under the DocumentRoot for the site. If so, and if the request was for / or *index.html*, then it performs an internal rewrite to it.

Working with *mod_rewrite* can be confusing. One tool that helps greatly with debugging rewrite problems is the RewriteLog functionality. If you're stuck on figuring out a RewriteRule, try a couple of lines like this in your VirtualHost entry:

```
RewriteLog /tmp/rewrite.log
RewriteLogLevel 9
```

This will turn on full debugging to the log you specify. It is handy to watch it with a `tail -f /tmp/rewrite.log` or `less -f /tmp/rewrite.log` as you request various URLs in a browser. Don't run with this enabled for very long on a production server, as all rewrite actions will be logged (and consequently make your Apache run slower).

HACK #97 Delivering Content Based on the Query String Using mod_rewrite

Control content delivery based on a URL's query string without a CGI script

It can be useful to use the query string of a URL line (that is, anything after the first ?) to direct what content Apache will serve. While the query string is normally used by CGI applications to read and write program variables, *mod_rewrite* can use it without the need for an external script.

For example, suppose you have a publication system that splits large articles into multiple pages. The content is normally delivered by a script the takes the page= query string and delivers the requested page number. If you can save a local copy of each page to the filesystem, then you can use a RewriteRule to deliver the cached copy, and bypass the overhead of running the script on every hit.

Let's suppose we're trying to serve the second page of an article at *http://mysite.com/news/article.html?page=2*. Install the following rules:

```
RewriteCond %{QUERY_STRING} page=([0123456789]+)
RewriteCond /home/www/htdocs/%{REQUEST_URI}.%1 -f
RewriteRule .* /home/www/htdocs/%{REQUEST_URI}.%1 [L]
```

If */home/www/htdocs/news/article.html.2* exists, then it will be served as an internal redirect and exit before the publication script is run. If the file doesn't exist, then processing will fall through the last rule, and will be picked up by the normal publication delivery method (presumably by running a script specified by a ScriptAlias called */news*). This will work for any number of pages that end in an integer.

Likewise, the absence of a query string might be meaningful. Suppose your content delivery script will manipulate content depending on a variety of variables, but if no variables are specified, it returns predictable contend (say, the default view of the first page of an article.) This is another case where a judicious RewriteRule can save you the unnecessary computing overhead of dynamic rendering:

```
RewriteCond %{QUERY_STRING} =""
RewriteCond /home/www/static/%{REQUEST_URI} -f
RewriteRule .* /home/www/static/%{REQUEST_URI} [L]
```

Here we assume that if a query string exists, then it must necessarily involve dynamic content. Otherwise, check first to see if a local copy of the requested content exists (under *home/www/static/*) and if so, serve it. If the local copy doesn't exist, then processing falls through to the next set of directives (which most likely runs the dynamic content generator). As long as an external process manages the expiration of old content from the cache (via *cron* or a dedicated daemon that watches for content changes), then this caching will be completely seamless from the user's point of view. To expire old content, simply delete the cached version, and future hits will be generated dynamically.

You can direct Apache to take any action you like based on the query string. The power of *mod_rewrite* is really limited only by your imagination (and the strength of your regex-fu).

See also:

- "Distributing Load with Apache RewriteMap" **[Hack #99]**
- "Ultrahosting: Mass Web Site Hosting with Wildcards, Proxy, and Rewrite" **[Hack #100]**
- Apache's mod_rewrite guide can be found at *http://httpd.apache.org/docs/mod/mod_rewrite.html*

Using mod_proxy on Apache for Speed
#98 Offload complex dynamic requests to another apache (or another machine entirely)

A tremendous amount of effort has gone into optimizing Apache to make it rip files from the filesystem and throw them at incoming http requests as quickly as possible. Unfortunately, sites that solely serve content that sits in files within the filesystem are not typically very popular sites. The huge demand for interactive content has given birth to many projects that are specifically designed to give the end user a highly customizable, dynamic browsing experience.

Unfortunately, as the interactivity of a web site increases, performance typically goes out the window. Interactive content demands a programming language, and interpreting arbitrary code is very expensive (compared to serving static files). One classic "worst case" example is a Perl CGI that makes database requests and sends email by spawning an external *sendmail*. Compared to the time it takes to serve a static file, a single CGI request of that sort takes an eternity (and many requests therefore take many eternities, bringing your entire server to a crawl).

Apache modules such as *mod_perl* and *mod_php* (along with a large helping of programming sanity) can significantly alleviate the pain of spawning external processes on every hit. But even with interpreters built into Apache itself, the rate of serving dynamic requests rarely approaches that of a static web server. One reason for this is that most hits suffer the performance penalty of supporting embedded languages, regardless of whether the request is dynamic or not.

Consider the case of a large *mod_perl* installation. After having run for a few minutes, an individual httpd process may consume 40 or 50MB of RAM as Perl modules are cached into memory, for speedy execution. Now imagine that a request for a single-pixel transparent gif is made (as this is one trick commonly used by web designers to make arbitrary-sized blank spaces on a web page, exact to the pixel). In the absolute worst case, suppose that all available httpd processes are busy, so Apache decides to spawn another. The server must now invoke the behemoth of *mod_perl*, creating a child that takes up 50MB of RAM and a huge amount of processing time, just to serve a single static file of only a few bytes. Clearly, if we could only invoke the shaggy shoggoth of *mod_perl* when absolutely necessary, we could reap huge benefits every time someone requested a graphic (or other file that is guaranteed to require no dynamic processing).

You might consider running two installations of Apache: one with every module, bell, whistle, and vibra-slap that your dynamic content management system requires, and another that is as stripped-down and simple as you can possibly make it. If all requests come into the lightweight Apache, then we can serve static content as normal, and proxy dynamic requests to the dynamic content servers.

Suppose you're running the slimmed-down Apache on standard port 80, and the application server on port 8088. Using the following rewrite rule, you can proxy requests for anything but graphics and archives to the application server. Put this at the bottom of the VirtualHost entry for your site (on the server running on port 80):

```
RewriteEngine On

RewriteCond %{REQUEST_URI} !.*\.(jpg|gif|pdf|png|zip|tgz|gz)$
RewriteRule ^/(.*) http://%{HTTP_HOST}:8088/$1 [P]
```

That [P] at the end of the RewriteRule line means proxy. This will cause the lightweight Apache to make a connection to the dynamic server running on 8088 and make the request as if the client itself had made it. When it receives the reply, it passes it along to the client as if it had served the request itself. As far as the client is concerned, there is only one web server: the really fast one running on port 80. And as long as the site definitions for this site in both apache installations point to the same DocumentRoot, this method will work just fine.

If your application uses cookies, you should also add a ProxyPassReverse line just above the rewrite rules with something like this:

```
ProxyPassReverse / http://%{HTTP_HOST}:8088/
```

This tells Apache to translate http headers when proxying, so that cookies get propagated from the application server to the client as they should.

If you have the hardware for it, you could help distribute the load by using one machine for the proxy server and another for the application server. In that case, try rules like this:

```
ProxyPassReverse / http://your.application.server.here/

RewriteEngine On

RewriteCond %{REQUEST_URI} !.*\.(jpg|gif|pdf|png|zip|tgz|gz)$
RewriteRule ^/(.*) http://your.application.server.here/$1 [P]
```

Of course, with multiple physical servers, you'll have to keep your filesystems in sync (see "Keeping Parts of Filesystems in sync with rsync" [Hack #41]), or else people will see conflicting pages every time your site gets updated. If even two servers aren't capable of serving all of your dynamic content, take a look at "Distributing Load with Apache RewriteMap" [Hack #99] for one method of spreading load across as many application servers as you like.

HACK #99   Distributing Load with Apache RewriteMap

Scale to any number of web application servers with RewriteMap

As we saw in the previous hack, it is possible to transparently serve content from any arbitrary web server using *mod_proxy* and *mod_rewrite*. Rather than using an external redirect [R], the proxy target [P] makes the content appear to come from the server from which the client originally requested content, without changing the URL line in the client browser. As we saw earlier, one application of this technique is to spread the load of serving pages across two machines, making it possible to serve many more hits than a single machine can handle.

But what if you need to serve even more traffic, to the point that a single application server is no longer sufficient? We need a mechanism that will allow the proxy servers to choose from an available pool of application servers, preferably in a way that we can direct more hits at more capable servers. The RewriteMap directive gives us this functionality.

Here's an example of how to specify a RewriteMap:

```
RewriteMap server rnd:/usr/local/apache/conf/servers.map
```

The RewriteMap line just defines a map called server, physically bound to the *servers.map* file in the *conf/* directory. The rnd: makes this a randomized plain text map.

The format of the *servers.map* file is very straightforward:

```
web www1|www2|www3|www4|www5
```

The left-hand side is an arbitrary variable name that we can use just about anywhere in our configuration file, as in this RewriteRule:

```
RewriteRule ^/(.*) http://${server:web}.oreillynet.com/$1 [P]
```

The right-hand side of the lines of the *servers.map* file consists of strings to be returned in random order, separated by pipes. In the case of the RewriteRule above, a random value (one of www1, www2, www3, www4, or www5) will be chosen from the servers.map and will replace the ${server: web} variable. This results in a proxy rule to *http://www4.oreillynet.com/* (or any of the other www* servers) with the original URI appended to it.

The only trouble with a truly random map is that all of the servers specified in it will receive approximately the same amount of traffic over time. If www1 is a quad 2.4GHz Xeon with 8GB RAM, and www2 is a 486SX/33 with 4MB RAM, you'll probably want to direct more traffic at www1 than at www2. To do this, simply specify the more capable servers multiple times in the servers.map:

```
web www1|www1|www1|www1|www2|www3|www3|www4|www5|www5
```

In this example, www1 will receive 4 out of 10 hits, www2 will receive 1 out of 10, www3 will receive 2, www4 will get 1, and www5 will pick up the remaining 2. You can fine tune this in real time by watching *top* (or even *tl*, as discussed in "Constant Load Average Display in the Titlebar" **[Hack #59]**) on every application server while manipulating the servers.map. The mtime of the file is checked on every hit, and Apache will automatically reload the map whenever it changes, without needing a restart. This means that an intelligent systems monitoring tool can watch all of www* and rotate them out of the map in real time whenever it finds a web server that's having trouble. If carefully planned, this can mean web services with zero downtime, routing around problem servers, all without ever having to restart Apache.

Working with multiple application servers can be tricky business. Obviously, you'll need to keep your filesystems in sync, using NFS or possibly *rsync*, as discussed in "Constant Load Average Display in the Titlebar" **[Hack #59]**. But even the best planned server schemes can sometimes go awry. What happens if you notice an Internal Server Error that goes away if you click Reload? One of the application servers has developed a problem, and there's no way to tell which one is having trouble (without consulting the error log on every machine). Here's a handy rewrite rule that will let you select which application server to steer a particular request:

```
RewriteCond %{QUERY_STRING} appserver=(.*)
RewriteRule ^/(.*) http://%1.oreillynet.com/$1 [P,L]
```

Now you can select a particular application server by adding a query string to the URL in your browser, like this:

```
http://www.oreillynet.com/some/path/?appserver=www3
```

This will help you quickly track down the server with the problem. Combined with front-end proxy servers, round robin DNS, and replicated databases, this makes a very straightforward configuration that will scale to very large installations.

See Also:

- Apache mod_rewrite documentation at *http://httpd.apache.org/docs/mod/mod_rewrite.html*
- Proxy Server Hack
- "Using rsync over ssh" **[Hack #38]**
- "Distributing Server Load with Round-Robin DNS" **[Hack #79]**
- "Setting Up Replication in MySQL" **[Hack #82]**

HACK 100 Ultrahosting: Mass Web Site Hosting with Wildcards, Proxy, and Rewrite

Support thousands of internal web servers without lifting a finger

Suppose you have a large private network hiding from the Internet behind a NAT router. Your network layout looks something like Figure 8-3.

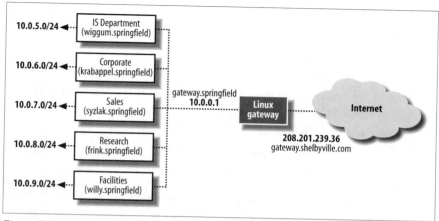

Figure 8-3. Typical corporate lans use private addressing internally and at least one Internet gateway providing Network Address Translation

You want to be able to allow anyone on your private network to set up their own web server. But like all good network administrators, you are smart and lazy and don't want to fiddle with updating forwarding rules on your firewall every time someone needs to make a change. Through the careful use of named virtual hosts, *mod_proxy*, and *mod_rewrite*, you can reduce the administrative overhead of your entire network to simple DNS updates. Then there is little keeping you from delegating *that* responsibility to the departments that wanted the web servers in the first place.

To start, you'll need Apache running on your gateway machine, with *mod_rewrite* and *mod_proxy* installed. You'll also need a DNS server running your own top-level internal domain (as discussed in "Running Your Own Top-Level Domain" **[Hack #80]**). We'll assume that you own the Internet domain *shelbyville.com*, and have the internal TLD of *.springfield* already set up, serving your internal machines.

Add the following to the Apache configuration on your gateway machine:

```
Port 80

BindAddress *
NameVirtualHost *

<VirtualHost *>
ServerName mux.shelbyville.com
ServerAlias *.shelbyville.com

RewriteEngine On
RewriteCond %{HTTP_HOST} (.*).shelbyville.com
RewriteRule ^/(.*) http://%1.springfield/$1 [P]
</VirtualHost>
```

Briefly, this configuration translates to:

- Listen on any available IP address, on port 80
- Accept http requests for any host ending in *.shelbyville.com*
- Strip *shelbyville.com* from the http host that was requested
- Make a connection (via Proxy) to what's left of the hostname with *.spring-field* appended to it
- Post the original URI and return the results to the client

This works because hosts are specified by name in the http header under the http 1.1 specification and aren't tied to a particular IP address. Apache will look up the contents of %1 (everything before *.shelbyville.com*) via the system resolver and attempt to connect to it. Since the gateway is using a DNS server that serves your *.springfield* TLD, it will proxy to the proper internal host.

For example, suppose that the original request was for *http://jimbo.shelbyville. com/index.html*. After the RewriteCond line, the %1 variable simply contains jimbo. It then attempts to proxy to %1 (aka jimbo) with *.springfield* appended to it. The result? A proxy request to the internal web server *jimbo.springfield*, with the original URI passed along as if the gateway weren't even there.

This is the simplest configuration, but it will break internal servers that require cookies. To support cookies on servers residing on the internal network, try something like this:

```
<VirtualHost *>
ServerName mux.shelbyville.com
ServerAlias *.shelbyville.com

RewriteEngine On

RewriteCond %{HTTP_HOST} (.*).shelbyville.com
RewriteRule (.*) $1 [E=WHERETO:%1.springfield]

ProxyPassReverse / http://%{ENV:WHERETO}/

RewriteRule ^/(.*) http://%{ENV:WHERETO}/$1 [P]
</VirtualHost>
```

This uses a "fake-out" RewriteRule that is only called to invoke the side effect of setting the %{WHERETO} environment variable. This gets set to the original requested http host with *.shelbyville.com* stripped off, but with *.springfield* appended. We need to do that to be able to feed the amended hostname to ProxyPassReverse.

By manipulating the DNS configuration for *.shelbyville.com* and *.springfield*, you can bring internal web servers up and down at will, without ever touching the Apache configuration on the gateway. Of course, to make the job even easier, you could use wildcard DNS for *.shelbyville.com*:

```
*.shelbyville.com IN A 12.34.56.78
```

(Naturally, substituting the external IP address of the gateway for 12.34.56. 78). Now, requests for *anything.shelbyville.com* will be fed to the gateway and proxied, without ever changing the zone file again. That just leaves internal DNS maintenance (for *.springfield*). The simplest way to dispense with that responsibility is to divide it into multiple subdomains and defer to other internal DNS servers. For example, you could put something like this in your *named.conf*:

```
zone "wiggum.springfield" {
type slave;
file "wiggum.db";
masters { 10.42.5.6; };
};

zone "krabappel.springfield" {
type slave;
file "krabappel.db";
masters { 10.42.6.43; };
};

zone "syzlak.springfield" {
type slave;
file "syzlak.db";
masters { 10.42.7.2; };
};
```

and so on. Now each department can have their own master DNS server and can add new hosts (and therefore new, Internet-ready web servers) without even dropping you an email. They can get to their new servers from the Internet by browsing to an address like *http://ralph.wiggum.shelbyville.com/*, which translates to *http://ralph.wiggum.springfield/* internally and is ultimately looked up from the DNS server for the division that is responsible for the wiggum subdomain. As far as the Internet users are concerned, the information came directly from the gateway machine, and aren't even aware that *.springfield* even exists.

Now, just what will you do with all of the time that this saves you?

Index

` (backtick), 14, 20
^D, 21
. (dot) and CVS tags, 56
/ (forward slash), 66
| (pipes), efficiency of, 15
? (question mark) and top, 119
; (semicolon) and Perl one-liners, 151
~ expansion facility, 21

Numbers

1024th cylinder limit, kernel install, 73

A

access
  ACL (access control list), local
    host, 161
  hosts, assigning trust-levels to, 89
  lost root password, 6
ad referral tracking, 188–191
advanced routing tools, 98
anon_auth_module, 191
Apache, 157, 182–211
  ad referral tracking, 188–191
  anon_auth module, enabling, 191
  Apache Toolbox script, 182–185
    installation, 183–185
    supported applications, 182
  apachectl, 188
  certificate generation and signing
    requests, 194–196
  certificates, distribution to client
    browsers, 199–200

  configuration files, automatic
    updates across a network, 28
  ftp servers, mimicking, 191–193
    controlling access, 191
  httpd.conf, 187
    configuring display of full
      filenames, 185
  IfDefine, configuration changes
    using, 186–188
  IfModule directive, 186, 187
  mass web site hosting, 208–211
  mod_proxy, speeding content
    delivery using, 204–206
  mod_rewrite, 201–204
  multiple installations, increasing
    efficiency using, 205
  RewriteMap, load distribution
    using, 206–208
  server logs, rotation and
    compression, 193
  serving cookies, 206
  sites with a shared
    DocumentRoot, 201–203
  ssl keys and certificates, using, 198
  URL query strings, content delivery
    using, 203
archiving with pax, 67–72
  restoring, 68
  and renaming, 69
at, disabling, 23
automount, 4

We'd like to hear your suggestions for improving our indexes. Send email to *index@oreilly.com*.

B

backtick (`), 14, 20
backups, 64–87
  of the boot sector, 72
  CDR/CDRWs, 84–87
  over a network, 65–67
    rsync, 66
    scp command, 65
    tar, using over ssh, 65
  with pax, 67–72
    incremental backups, 71
    restoring compressed archives, 68
  snapshot-style, 79–84
balance-push.sh script, 77
bash
  ~ expansion facility, 21
  clearing history, 22
  files, breaking into chunks, 153
  login shells, csutomizing, 22
  manpage, 20
  shell environment,
    customizing, 20–22
  tab completion, 15
  .bash_logout, 22
  .bashrc, 22
    network configuration, 66
binary files
  chunking, 153–155
  reassembling, 154
BIND, 157, 158–169
  caching DNS with local domain
    authority, setup, 165
  running in a chroot jail (in V.
    9), 158–160
  server load distribution (in V. 9), 167
  views (in V. 9), 160–165
    match-clients substatement, 161
    named.conf, 161
    named.conf, primary master, 164
    named.conf, slave name
      servers, 163
    syntax, 160
    zones, defining, 162
BIOS, 1024th cylinder boot sector
    limit, 73
blacklists, 89–91
boot messages, viewing, 40
boot parameters, 7–9
boot sector, backing up, 72

C

boot time configuration, 2, 3–10
  1024th cylinder limit, 73
  removing superfluous services, 3
  unnecessary drivers,
    eliminating, 40–42

cacert.pem, 197
cakey.pem, 197
CA.pl utility, 197
CDPATH variable, 21
CDR/CDRWs, 84
CD-ROMs, 85–87
Certificate Authorities, 196
  certificates, acquiring from, 194
  creating your own, 196–198
  keys, file locations, 197
  public keys, distributing to
    clients, 199–200
chargen, 5
chattr, 18
chroot jail, 158–160
ci command (RCS), 48
cmdline files, viewing, 33
co command (RCS), 48
CodeRed virus, filtering, 93
command line, 2, 10–46
  complex commands, creating, 12–15
  watch, automating a repeated
    command using, 114
compiles, parallel builds (multiprocessor
    systems), 19
comsat, 5
Concurrent Versioning System (see CVS)
.config file, 41
configuration files, updating with
    make, 27
console= (boot parameter), 8
Control D, 21
cp command
  -a switch, 79
  -l switch, 79
cpio
  pax and, 67
crontab
  automating snapshot-type
    backups, 80
  setuid and, 23

T

tab completion, 15
takeover script, 128
tar, 66
    backups over ssh, 65
    directories, recursive copying, 70
    pax and, 67
tcpdump and network debugging, 100
telnet, 5
terminal windows
    titlebar, customizing, 20
tl script, 120
TLDs (top level domains), 168
TLDs (top-level domains)
    running your own, 168
TLDs (top-level domains), pattern
        matching to, 29
TMOUT variable, 22
top, 119
    ? (question mark), 119
    filtering of results, 119
    sort criteria, specifying, 119
top command, 34
traceroute
    setuid and, 25
transparent Squid proxy, 92
tun, 101
tunneling
    IP tunneling, 97
    NAT, circumvention with vtun over
        ssh, 101–106

U

unmaskirq parameter, hdparm, 45
URL query strings and content
        delivery, 203
users
    closing user accounts, 38–40
using_dma parameter, hdparm, 45
UUCP and setuid/setgid binaries, 25

V

vendor tags (CVS), 53
views (see under BIND)
VirtualHosts, monitoring, 133
virus filters, 93
visudo, 26
vmstat, 35
vtun, 101–110
    NAT, circumvention ssh, 101–106
    ssh, using over, 105
vtund server, launching, 103
vtund.conf, 102–110
    client-side, 103
        automatic generation via Perl
            script, 106–110
    server-side, 102

W

wall
    setgid and, 24
watch, 114
web servers
    diagnosing error conditions
        (example), 12–15
web sites, performance costs of
        interactivity, 205
web traffic, monitoring, 132–138
whitelists, 89–91
whitespace in filenames, handling, 16
write
    setgid and, 24

X

X11 traveling, forwarding over ssh, 145
xargs, 16
    find, used with, 17

Colophon

Our look is the result of reader comments, our own experimentation, and feedback from distribution channels. Distinctive covers complement our distinctive approach to technical topics, breathing personality and life into potentially dry subjects.

The tool on the cover of *Linux Server Hacks* is an ax. An ax is a chopping tool based on one of the six simple machines of physics: the wedge. Though the ax is one of the earliest man-made tools, dating back anywhere from 100,000 to 500,000, its simplicity and efficiency make it indispensable to this day.

Sarah Sherman was the production editor and copyeditor for *Linux Server Hacks*. Colleen Gorman, Mary Brady, and Claire Cloutier provided quality control. John Bickelhaupt wrote the index. Linley Dolby provided production assistance.

Edie Freedman designed the cover of this book. The cover image is an original photograph from the CMCD collection. Emma Colby produced the cover layout with QuarkXPress 4.1 using Adobe's ITC Garamond and Helvetica Neue fonts.

David Futato designed the interior layout. This book was converted to FrameMaker 5.5.6 with a format conversion tool created by Erik Ray, Jason McIntosh, Neil Walls, and Mike Sierra that uses Perl and XML technologies. The text font is Linotype Birka; the heading font is Adobe Helvetica Neue Condensed; and the code font is LucasFont's TheSans Mono Condensed. The illustrations that appear in the book were produced by Robert Romano and Jessamyn Read using Macromedia FreeHand 9 and Adobe Photoshop 6. This colophon was written by Linley Dolby.